The Logic of
American Government

THE LOGIC OF
American Government

Applying the Constitution to
the Contemporary World

Daniel L. Feldman

WILLIAM MORROW AND COMPANY, INC.

New York

Library of Congress Cataloging-in-Publication Data

Feldman, Daniel L.
    The logic of American government: applying the constitution to
the contemporary world / Daniel L. Feldman.
      p.   cm.
    ISBN 0-688-08134-7
    1. United States—Constitutional law. 2. Separation of powers-
-United States. 3. United States—Politics and government.
I. Title.
KF4550.F45   1990
342.73—dc20
[347.302]   89-12991
                                                   CIP

Printed in the United States of America

First Edition

1 2 3 4 5 6 7 8 9 10

BOOK DESIGN BY PAUL CHEVANNES

To Cecilia

Contents

Competing Theories of American Government

Acknowledgments

I used to joke with my Harvard Law School classmates that if they could find me a law firm with a strong department of legal philosophy, I'd be happy to work there. That was because I had the privilege of studying the subject with the late, great scholar in that field, Lon L. Fuller, who inspired and encouraged me, for which I will always be grateful. To my first teacher of constitutional law, and still my friend, Henry Abraham, I am likewise much indebted.

A few elements of this book came to me as I was teaching administrative law to master's degree students in public administration at John Jay College of Criminal Justice in the late 1970s. I am grateful to those students for their lively responsiveness, which helped me formulate my ideas, and to President Gerald Lynch and Professor Eli Silverman, for arranging for me to teach there.

Other key elements crystallized in my mind as I was preparing for, and then as I was presenting, a lecture series at Oxford University in November 1982. For that, I thank Professor J. R. Pole, of St. Catherine's College, who invited me to present my lectures and gave me useful feedback on my ideas. The late Philip Williams, of Nuffield College, was also a wonderful sounding board and a source of inspiration at Oxford.

The College of the Holy Cross invited me, in effect, to present this book as a seminar in the fall of 1987. It probably would never have been written otherwise. My friend and former teacher Caren Dubnoff, and her successor as Political Science Department chair at Holy Cross, Judith Chubb, as well as my students there, have my sincere thanks for that. I taught a similar course in the Department of Politics at New York University in the fall of 1988 while revising the manuscript. For useful influences on those revisions, I thank my NYU students, as well as Professor Steve Brams, who arranged for me to teach the course while he was acting chair of NYU's Politics Department, and Professor Farhad Kazemi, who provided encouragement as present chair of that department. My students at NYU's Graduate School of Public Administration from 1985 to 1988 contributed as well. I thank them, and my friend and former dean there, now at the Kennedy School at Harvard, Alan Altshuler, for that opportunity.

The National Defense University at Fort McNair, Washington, D.C., allowed me to attend a two-day intensive seminar on national security issues in November 1987 that included most of the leading national security practitioners and scholars in the United States. This was an immensely important contribution to my discussion of the Iran-Contra affair in Chapter V, although of course the National Defense University is not responsible for the views I express. Naturally, none of the other institutions or individuals I mention need take any blame either.

Chapters I through IV, in earlier incarnations, were a paper presented in panels at the New York State Political Science Association and at the American Political Science Association, and I thank them for having offered me those opportunities to air my views and receive valuable responses to them. There are small amounts of material in those chapters and in Chapter IX, also, that appeared in a 1977–1978 article I wrote for the *Fordham Urban Law Journal*, and I thank them accordingly. An earlier version of Chapter V appeared in the *International Journal of Intelligence and Counter-Intelligence*, and I thank them for the reuse of that material. The Organized Crime Control Act discussion in Chapter VII had precursors in articles I wrote for *Criminal Justice Ethics* and for *The New York Law Journal*. I thank all those journals for the editorial advice they provided.

In particular, I thank Professor David Schaefer of the College of the Holy Cross; Martin J. Newhouse of the Boston law firm Ropes & Gray; Sigmund Ginsberg, vice-president of Barnard College, and Robert Sullivan of John Jay College for advice on early fragments of the manuscript; Professor John Rohr of Virginia Polytechnic Institute and State University, Professor Louis Lusky of Columbia Law School, Professor David Rosenbloom of the Maxwell School of Syracuse University, Professor Tom Konda of the State University of New York at Plattsburgh, Professor Lotte Feinberg of John Jay College, Professor Marguerite Guinta of Long Island University, Professors Stephanie Harrington and Ronald Replogle of New York University, and David Eichenthal of the Prosecutors' Research Council for advice on Chapters I through IV; Professor Richard Valcourt of Hunter College for advice on Chapter V; Professor Tom Stoddard of New York University Law School for advice on Chapter VI; Professor Jim Jacobs of NYU Law School and present and former New York State Assembly staff members Jim Yates, Ellen Everett, and Mindy Bockstein for advice on Chapter VII; Professor Martin Edelman of the State University of New York at Albany, Professor Henry Abraham of the University of Virginia, and Professor Stanley Brubaker of Colgate College for advice on Chapter VIII; Professor Rosenbloom for advice on Chapter IX; Professor J. R. Pole of St. Catherine's College, Oxford University, for advice on Chapter X; and Professor Abraham again (for suggestions dating back almost twenty years now!) for advice on Chapter XI.

I owe special, enormous debts to Louis Fisher of the Congressional Research Service and to Professor John Rohr of Virginia Polytechnic Institute and State University for reading the entire manuscript in its intermediate draft stages, and for their characteristically generous and insightful suggestions. If I have done my work well, their intellectual influence will be apparent to those familiar with the important contributions they have made to scholarship in our many areas of joint scholarly concern.

When I enrolled in Norman Adler's American politics class at Columbia University in 1968, I doubt that he realized he was undertaking a commitment of several decades' duration. He has been my teacher in political theory and practice since then. His critique of my manuscript, typically, required the most radical revisions. As always, I owe him. Big.

Lynn Solotaroff, Adrienne Knoll, and Enid Stubin, nonspecialists in any academic discipline involved in this book but expert editors indeed, helped try to assure that some other nonspecialists may read it by insisting that I try harder. If anyone outside my immediate family reads it, these three deserve credit. Kathy Remick, Randy Ladenheim-Gil, and Christie Neill contributed their considerable editorial efforts as well, to beneficial effect.

The men and women of the New York State legislature, members and staff, my working colleagues since 1981 (since 1977, counting my years on staff), have provided me with insights into government and a collective wealth of experience that is rich beyond measure. Even more important, their warmth and friendship have sustained me well, and, I'm sure, will continue to do so.

Finally, my faithful secretary, Faith Feierman, was kind enough to undertake the unenviable task of transforming my original handwritten manuscript, whose appearance was once said to reflect inspiration from the abstract impressionist Jackson Pollock, into something accessible to the rest of the world.

Introduction

Who should study the logic of American government? Answer: those who govern. Ideally that means the entire citizenry of the United States because, among other things, the logic of our government calls for a citizenry that makes public-policy decisions through the representatives it elects rather than merely abdicating power to those representatives.

It would be nice if every citizen were to read this book, but that seems somewhat too optimistic. Still, I wrote it for the average citizen, reluctantly understanding that most citizens do not yet choose to participate in governing, and that the most likely readership consists of those with a professional, preprofessional, scholarly, or academic interest in government: judges, legislators, other "public servants," professors, and students.[1]

Even that more likely audience lacks a firm grip on the constitutional values that structure the logic of American government. David Stockman, the first budget director in the Reagan administration, for example, unwittingly revealed that he lacked a sense of the constitutional balance of values when he tried to substitute a succession of rigid ideologies.[2] The Iran-Contra affair supplied at least two well-publicized additional examples of public servants with similar deficiencies.[3] Stockman, Oliver North, and John Poindexter are all perceived as right-wing ideologues. But other ideologies could just as well provide unfortunate substitutes for a constitutional balance of values in the minds and hearts of American public servants.

The logic of American government consists of a number of critical tensions among certain basic values. Those values coexist in a dynamic balance, essentially stable but constantly undergoing marginal change. The success of the American experiment has enabled our attention to stray from the balance of values, but that balance still provides the best guide to the running of a constitution, as well as the framing of one.[4] Too little attention to those values has resulted in an educational vacuum, into which have been drawn far flimsier intellectual structures, with far less worth for the government official or for the ordinary citizen seeking to understand and fulfill the responsibility to command the government.

Neither public opinion, private conscience, nor any of a number of ideologies of the right or the left provide a good substitute for the balance of constitutional values that the best of our history displays.

I said we "ought" to internalize those values: We face a familiar problem in attempting to categorize the forthcoming discussion as descriptive or normative. Is this the logic of what is, or of what ought to be? The answer is: both. The American constitutional experience includes many things. Some of them exemplify what we ought to be, what is best in our tradition. In proposing a guide for American public policymakers, I want to give them something they can use. If it is thoroughly grounded in legitimate American tradition, they will be able to incorporate it into their work and persuade others to accept it. Of course, there are bad American traditions, like violations of constitutional rights, that they should not emulate or continue.

Interpreters of the American constitutional tradition customarily claim that history supports their version. There are plausible interpretations across a fairly wide range. It would be presumptuous of me to claim that I am presenting *the* balance of values that the American constitutional tradition dictates. Rather, I present the best historical arguments available to support the particular balance that I prefer. I offer it as normative: I am preaching.

Most important is my overall paradigm: that the American constitutional tradition does fundamentally demand some reasonable balance of values. In this regard, I describe a logic that exists, not just one that ought to be. I describe a logic that provides questions, not one that supplies answers.

The overall paradigm, then, is the system of logic within which lie the controversies and conflicts that inhabit American political life. An American philosopher said:

> To speak of certain government and establishment institutions as "the system" is to speak correctly. . . .
>
> But to tear down a factory or to revolt against a government or to avoid repair of a motorcycle because it is a system is to attack effects rather than causes; and as long as the attack is upon effects only, no change is possible. The true system, the real system, is our present construction of systematic thought itself. . . . If a revolution destroys a systematic government, but the systematic patterns of thought that produced that government are left intact, then those patterns will repeat themselves in the succeeding government. . . .[5]

Here, of course, I am interested in revitalizing a system, not destroying it. As the Stockman example illustrates, danger threatens our systematic pattern of thought. Apathy and atrophy, rather than attack, constitute the threat. I am presenting an American pattern of thought to remind those who govern the United States—again, ideally, its citizens and you, the reader—of its beauty and usefulness.

What is the nature of the danger from apathy and atrophy? After all, the symbolic power of the Constitution among the American people seems to be holding up very well in this bicentennial era[6] as it has throughout most of American history.[7] Popular descriptions of the place of the Constitution in the American mind are similarly supportive:

> The Constitution has the aura of the sacred about it. It occupies a shrine up in the higher stretches of American reverence. A citizen imagines sunshot clouds, the founders hovering in the air like saints in religious art.[8]

Yet, a September 1987 Gallup poll found that 50 percent of the American public "completely" or "mostly" agreed that "books that contain dangerous ideas should be banned from public school libraries," almost 50 percent agreed that "freedom of speech should not extend to groups like the Communist Party or the Ku Klux Klan," and 61 percent agreed that "the government ought to be able to censor news stories that it feels threaten national security."[9] Older public-opinion surveys showed similar results. This one not surprisingly included the entirely inconsistent response of 74 percent of the same sample agreeing that "the news media should be free to report on any stories they feel are in the national interest."[10] Free speech and the Constitution command a loyalty in the United States that appears to be largely unconnected with any consciousness of their meaning.

John Stuart Mill provided a warning about the danger of that kind of loyalty to an idea—precisely the danger of apathy and atrophy we face. It was a warning about the way established creeds lose their vitality:

[This] is exemplified by the manner in which the majority hold the doctrines of Christianity . . . the maxims and precepts contained in the New Testament. These are considered sacred, and accepted as laws, by all professing Christians. Yet it is scarcely too much to say that not one Christian in a thousand guides or tests his individual conduct by reference to those laws. . . . All Christians believe that the blessed are the poor and humble, and those that are ill-used by the world; that it is easier for a camel to pass through the eye of a needle than for a rich man to enter the kingdom of heaven . . . that they should love their neighbors as themselves; that if one take their cloak, they should give him their coat also; . . . that if they would be perfect they should sell all they have and give it to the poor. They are not insincere when they say they believe these things. They do believe them, as people believe what they have always heard lauded and never discussed. But in the sense of that living belief which regulates conduct, they believe these doctrines just up to the point at which it is usual to act upon them. . . . They have an habitual respect for the sound of them, but no feeling which spreads from the words to the things signified. . . . When conduct is concerned, they look round for Mr. A and B to direct them how far to go in obeying Christ.

Now we may be assured that the case was not thus, but far otherwise, with the early Christians. . . . When their enemies said, "See how these Christians love one another" (a remark not likely to be made by anybody now), they assuredly had a much livelier feeling of the meaning of their creed than they ever had since. . . .[11]

Thus, I want to re-create a consciousness of the meaning and content of the American constitutional tradition, to the point that readers will "believe" its "doctrines" not "just up to the point at which it is usual to act upon them," but to the pcint where such readers will indeed "act upon them." These, of course, are doctrines of aspiration, not doctrines of dogma.[12]

I wrote this book also to help Americans make public policy decisions, in line with the American constitutional tradition. Part I sets forth the outlines of the decisionmaking framework, explaining the five values to be used to measure the worth of policy proposals, and then suggesting four supplementary rules to ensure better long-term optimization of the five values. I then present various conflicts among the five values, with the rules helping decisionmakers to find appropriate resolutions to the conflicts that leave the values in healthy balance.

In Part Two, I apply the model to several public-policy questions: the Iran-Contra affair, the Nazis' effort to demonstrate in Skokie, Illinois, the efforts of public-interest groups to leaflet at privately owned shopping malls, and the enactment of New York's Organized Crime Control Act.

Part Three surveys competing theories of American government upon which I have drawn. Theorists like John Rawls and Ronald Dworkin have advised Americans on making public-policy decisions. Those two emphasize considerations of equality. Robert Bork, the unsuccessful but well-publicized Supreme Court nominee in 1987, stressed the role of representativeness—majority rule—in his approach to American government. I review, and reject, the offerings of these and other theorists for reasons I hope you will find persuasive.

Some of the reasons have to do with the special nature, spirit, and character that our history has given to the United States. Therefore, Part IV starts with a history of the development of key themes and values from colonial times forward. I then offer evidence that those constitutional themes and values really do exercise major influence in the United States, notwithstanding regular strayings from the best in our tradition.

The basic values in balance are liberty, equality, property, security, and efficiency. I show how the "elemental" values of liberty, equality, and property coalesce in various combinations and permutations, transmuting into the "compound" values of representativeness, fairness, and dissent. So I sometimes refer to the mix of values as representativeness, fairness, dissent, security, and efficiency.

This general approach requires that public policy be selected depending on how well it fosters the five preferred values. Along with use of the rules I recommend, suggesting an appropriate balance among the values, this approach will maintain and extend those aspects of the American constitutional tradition that have served our people best. I believe those are the permanent and fundamental aspects of that tradition.

It has been argued, against this presentation, that "the constitution is a filter or laundering device through which we pass raw interests in order to legitimize them" and, therefore, "its values do not have to be remembered." Otherwise, the argument continues, we must accept the thesis that "slavery was a constitutional value, as was the exclusion of women from the polity." Herbert Storing has persuasively argued, at least with respect to slavery, that this "is a gross calumny on the Founders."[13] He quoted Frederick Douglass, a former slave, who was closer to the issue in time and in status, who said ". . . the Constitution . . . was purposely so framed as to give no claim, no sanction to the claim, of property in man. If in its origin slavery had any relation to the government, it was only as the scaffolding to the magnificent structure, to be removed as soon as the building was completed."[14]

The present thesis is that the "magnificent structure" was indeed built on certain foundational values, and if the people of the United States are to fare well, those values do indeed have to be remembered.

PART ONE

The Theoretical Framework

I

A Constitutional Framework for Public Decisionmaking

Public-administration theorists have wandered back and forth among the Hamiltonian, Madisonian, and Jeffersonian schools since the origin of the discipline.[1] It is no wonder, then, that practitioners may feel somewhat at sea from time to time, and may need to derive a sense of their proper role not merely from the boundaries of their individual responsibilities but from "a broader understanding of the bureaucrat's place within a more encompassing set of political institutions and processes."[2] Judges and legislators, too, are practitioners of public administration, and may well share the same needs.

A "unified field theory" of American public administration

could prove helpful to public administrators who grapple with current incarnations of such persistent American dilemmas as the proper degree of political control over bureaucracy,[3] the proper limits on policymaking by courts,[4] and the proper balance between public access to information and executive secrecy.[5]

Buried deep in the Lockean roots of the American constitutional tradition, however, are apparent contradictions between majoritarianism and individual freedom,[6] between utilitarian and natural-rights premises,[7] that have impeded the construction of such a theory. Instead, modern versions of natural-rights theory seem to be winning the day.[8] The present essay argues for a framework balancing five fundamental values, liberty, equality, property, security, and efficiency, in preference to rights-based theories or theories too heavily emphasizing only one or another of the five values. The five-value theoretical framework better resolves and reflects the American constitutional tradition and provides better guidance to practitioners, and more intellectual satisfaction to theorists.

After two hundred years under the United States Constitution, we ought to have a fairly good sense of how the thing works. We have some experience, under its terms, in maintaining a balance among two more or less universal values, security and efficiency, and what John Rohr has identified as our own, more distinctly American "regime" values of liberty, equality, and property.[9]

By efficiency, I mean the use of resources most productive of desirable values (not only our five). A classic of the anthropological literature describes a ceremony during which members of a certain tribe consume and/or destroy huge quantities of their own possessions.[10] If ego reinforcement is a scarce and important commodity as compared with material possessions, and if the ritual produces more ego reinforcement than any other marginal use of material possessions, this ritual is efficient in the tribe's terms. In the context of the United States, I use the word in its ordinary sense of getting the most out of available resources. Hamilton, in the First Federalist

Paper, noted what was already the commonplace tendency to fear, even to exaggerate, the relationship between government efficiency and despotism.[11] Later, Hamilton explained that efficiency is more properly the concern of the executive, while "[i]n the legislature, promptitude of discussion is oftener an evil than a benefit."[12]

By security, I mean the human tendency to preserve a people's society as they know it. National insecurity is often the real basis for things done in the name of security. Nevertheless, the latter is a legitimate value that seems widely, if not universally, shared. Each of the authors of the Federalist Papers made reference to safety and security as a primary objective of the Union.[13]

These universal values, efficiency and security, may be weak in the United States as compared with other nations because until recently, prosperity[14] tended to reduce the role of the former, and geographical isolation[15] tended to reduce somewhat the role of the latter.

Our American values, by contrast, are unusually strong for different historical reasons unique to the United States.[16] The primacy of the Bible, as opposed to human institutions, spurred the great Puritan revolution in England. The Puritans' disposition toward the primacy of a written document carried over, upon their migration to the colonies, to an expanded notion of the rule of law when another written document, the Constitution, made its appearance. The Congregationalists contributed the idea of "covenanting": ordinary people asserting the authority, by the simple fact of their own agreement, to form a church. This was a foundation for the later notion of similarly ordinary people constituting a state.

The Pilgrims' joint-stock corporations, along with the old sea law of passenger associations for self-government on matters not within the captain's concerns, pointed the way toward voter control. The Mayflower Compact encapsulated some of the foregoing in a covenant, a major step toward constitutionalism. The charter of the Massachusetts Bay Company was amended to provide for representation as a convenient way for numerous voters to exercise their power.

The Puritans, the Congregationalists, and other dissenting religious groups, despite the intolerance some of those groups themselves displayed from time to time, imparted a legitimacy to dissent that is deeply rooted in the American constitutional tradition. Some historians argue that the thrust of that freedom to dissent, at least in its absolute form, was intended more narrowly, to be limited to the religious context.[17] Still, the legitimacy of dissent in a nation that won its independence through revolution can scarcely be overlooked.

"Natural law" was a dominant theme in the political philosophy the Framers studied. The natural-law tradition gave depth, content, and meaning to phrases like "life, liberty, and the pursuit of happiness" and "due process of law."[18] The constitutional guarantee of due process means fair play at trial, including, for example, the right to be heard. One English judge in 1723 traced that right to divine law, which from medieval times intertwined with and informed the natural-law tradition. "Even God himself" gave Adam an opportunity to be heard before passing judgment on him: "Adam, where art thou? Hast thou eaten of the tree, whereof I commanded thee that thou shouldst not eat?"[19] Natural law developed over the centuries from ancient times, as philosophers tried to observe human behavior and determine which characteristics were natural and which were not.

The Constitution reflected and crystallized these themes, and assumed the place that in European social theory was held by natural law, as the "higher law" to which government's decisions might be appealed.[20]

The colonial and Revolutionary experience hammered home several lessons to build the concept of liberty as a fundamental American value: Individuals may resist and limit the power of government to compel compliance, even if government holds the support of the majority. Dissent is legitimate. The clash of differing opinions is indeed intrinsic to the normal processes of government.

That each individual asserts part of the power of government, that no one may deprive another of life, liberty, or property other than by the due process of law, were the lessons that built the concept of equality. From the twentieth-century point of view the Constitution incorporated hideous elements of inequality, at least with respect to slavery and limited suffrage. But those elements were, as Frederick Douglass said of slavery, "only as scaffolding to the magnificent structure, to be removed as soon as the building was completed."[21]

Liberty and equality were closely linked with the protection of individual property rights. A people inspired to revolution in substantial part under the slogan "No taxation without representation" clearly had internalized the right to property as a basic value; and attachment to the idea of property grew, if anything, throughout at least the first century of independent nationhood.[22]

These three American values are basic. To understand their relationship—often one of conflict and tension—with universal values, examine the American values when they are bound up with one another in any of three forms: representativeness, fairness, or dissent. The following discussion, so to speak, grinds up the three basic elements, pushes the results through a pasta machine, and identifies the three separate strands that emerge:

If liberty entails self-government, and each individual equally asserts part of the power of government, but can practically do so only through representatives, then liberty and equality in this context translate into representativeness.

If equality requires each person to be subject to the rule of law, and the law must operate with respect to the liberty and property of persons only within certain standard formal rules of procedure, then the three values in this context translate into fairness.

If representativeness is to be meaningful, individuals must have access to information relevant to policy issues, and government's ability to suppress dissent must be very limited. Liberty limits government's power to suppress any expression,

and equality limits government's power to suppress expression
for reasons of bias against particular contents. For purposes of
this discussion, we will include "access to information relevant
to public-policy issues" in the translation here of liberty and
equality into "dissent."

But representativeness and fairness can conflict with efficiency, and dissent can conflict with security. Policymakers
must find some reasonable balance among them. By "plugging
in" the right constants, some formula, using as variables liberty, equality, property, efficiency, and security, can provide a
usable, fairly consistent theory of American public administration. That version of utilitarian theory, "the greatest good for
the greatest number," thus defined, tracks the best of American tradition.

The five-value utilitarian approach has several advantages
over the rights-based approach. First, decisionmakers customarily use it: Cost-benefit analysis is utilitarianism writ small,
and even Ronald Dworkin, who rejects any utilitarian approach, acknowledges that "at least an informal kind of utilitarianism has for some time been accepted in practical
politics. . . ."[23] It grows most naturally out of the American
experience.

Second, it includes more values. Americans have a lot of
goals, including at least the values listed above, and the "utility" or net aggregate benefit of a policy option can be measured
by totaling up its effect on all the goals in question. For a stark
example, Americans just won't approve of the wartime exercise of free speech to reveal troop and battleship movements
that endanger the survival of the United States. A rights-
based approach that has no place for survival values, or security, is incomplete, inadequate, and unacceptable. But any
utilitarian test depends for its results on the choice of values to
be maximized, i.e., how one chooses to define "net aggregate
social utility." American constitutional utilitarianism weights
liberty and our other four values heavily in its calculations. Reports of the "demise of the heretofore dominant utilitarian paradigm"[24] are, as Mark Twain might have said, greatly
exaggerated.

The use of our five values as measures of utility does not necessarily overcome the customary objection to utilitarianism. It allows for intuitively unacceptable unjust decisions, such as exploitation of a minority for the benefit of the majority. That objection can be mitigated, however, by the adoption of certain appropriate rules. Experience shows that in some situations apparent costs of a policy will, in the long run, be more than outweighed by the benefits, even if in any given instance such benefits do not show up in the immediate calculations.

A critic of this rationale suggested that a policymaker could easily have persuaded most American colonists, who were white, that they could get the most liberty, equality, property, security, and efficiency (the greatest good for the greatest number, in their view) by appropriating American Indian land and by enslaving black Africans.[25]

That may have been true. In today's society, though, that kind of utilitarian test works better because it is less likely to produce results harmful to minorities. The level of social, physical, and psychological interdependence and thus mutual vulnerability among Americans is much higher. A sufficiently furious member of an exploited group can easily enough throw a Molotov cocktail into any handy power station. Therefore, the costs to the majority of any exploitative policy are greater and more easily understood than they used to be. Thus, the constitutional understandings that have developed down to our day precluding exploitative policies may match a five-value utilitarian calculation as to their long-term net aggregate social disutility.

In essence, as a nation, we have chosen to adopt constitutional "rules" prohibiting the more outrageous varieties of exploitation. Given our interdependence and mutual vulnerability, maybe we adopted such rules out of the security need for self-protection rather than out of a widespread commitment to fairness. In any case, if one incorporates "fairness" (or its liberty, equality, and property components) as a value to be maximized in the five-value utilitarian calculation (presented, then, as representativeness, fairness, dissent, security, and efficiency), the utilitarian model easily produces constitutional rules barring exploitation of minorities.

Rule utilitarians must be willing to countenance, at least in the short run, some unfairness that the rights-based theorist could reject. But the greater practicality and durability of the utilitarian approach outweighs this weakness.

Another critic noted that rule utilitarianism tends to dissolve into "act" utilitarianism, or the simple, short-term-assessment variant. That is, the rules will be disregarded if the rulemaker sees enough long-term net benefit, so rulemakers should skip the wasteful step of making rules and just figure out all the costs and benefits. If they do so they will no longer be able to assure anyone that obnoxious action A, B, or C is really prohibited.[26] This objection fails, however. Appropriate rules do reverse decisions that utilitarians would otherwise make. Civil libertarians who hate the Nazis would have fought against their proposal to march in Skokie were it not for the long-term consequences of suppressing political speech.[27]

Some opponents of the New York Health Council's 1987 regulations limiting smoking in public accommodations would have loved the results—limiting involuntary exposure to cigarette smoke—but for the council's undermining the principle of representative government by its usurpation of legislative power.[28]

Judge Frank Johnson's rights-based decisions in *Wyatt* v. *Stickney*,[29] the Bryce Hospital cases, required Alabama to bring operations at a state mental hospital up to a level consistent with human decency, arousing support in any person of compassion and conscience. If, however, courts should reject resource-allocation decisions for which the constitutional structure ill equips them, Johnson's decisions were wrong.[30]

The five-value theory has an extra safeguard against exploitation, besides rules prohibiting it, for those who worry that the rules will be broken when long-term calculations appear to show that it is "worth it" to break the rules. Liberty is one of our measures of utility. So is fairness. When calculating benefits of a social policy, those doing the calculating must take into account the impact of the policy on liberty and fairness. If the policy destroys liberty or creates unfairness, it starts off with a huge negative, and is unlikely, by that form of calculation, to show a net benefit. Thus, our model prevents massive or long-term injustice of the sort feared by the traditional critics of utilitarianism.[31]

However, justice and fairness are not the only legitimate values. A rational, comprehensive policy must recognize and pursue additional goals, such as survival and security. A proper balance will guarantee the vigorous pursuit of justice and fairness. Liberty, equality, property, efficiency, and security compete and are allied in various permutations and combinations. The policymaker should seek an appropriate balance among them for each given issue with due respect for each.

Legislatures best express representativeness, since the public most directly and effectively controls legislators, who ideally can be "fired" by the electorate on a regularly scheduled basis. Courts, freest of considerations other than law and fairness, best express fairness, as applied through due process of law, merging our concerns for liberty, equality, and property interests. The clearest expression of liberty is dissent, which threatens the executive branch most directly, since that branch carries out government policies. Dissent should find happier homes in courts and in legislatures.

Agencies are more efficient than legislatures, though less representative. Legislatures can be efficient in circumstances requiring courts to be fair instead. Free expression, and other protections of individual liberty, can run up against concern for security, whether justified or not. Governments, including ours, will tend to want to control information.

Thus, efficiency competes with representativeness, and with fairness. Dissent competes with security, and with government's tendency to exercise control. So our theory will be guided by at least four rules that may reverse what otherwise might be the results of short-term calculation of the impact of particular policy choices:

RULE 1: Agencies must respect legislative intent where it is discernible.

RULE 2: Decisions regarding the allocation of society's resources to groups are to be made by legislatures, not by courts.

RULE 3: No person shall be deprived of the exercise of otherwise available First Amendment rights on the basis of the political point of view expressed in that exercise.

RULE 4: The executive and agencies must provide access to information concerning controversial policies to the widest possible audience consistent with the security of the United States against physical threats. The likelihood of legislative disapproval of such policies shall be a factor to be weighed in favor of access.

The balance of values implicit in the foregoing suggests a number of additional rules beyond the four listed. The fourth footnote to the decision in *U.S.* v. *Carolene Products*[32] indirectly suggests that the Supreme Court might more readily void as unconstitutional such legislation as appears to violate the Bill of Rights or restricts access to the political process, especially as a result of "prejudice against discrete and insular minorities. . . ." The footnote was enormously influential. Its influence on modern constitutional law and theory[33] might well be reflected in some additional rules for our theory, based on the belief that such rules best promote the long-term vitality of liberty, equality, property, efficiency, and security. But the four rules listed above are sufficiently illustrative.

Legislatures for "political" representativeness, executives for "managerial" efficiency, and courts for "legal" fairness[34] are associated with various strains in American public-administration theory.[35] But as Professor David Rosenbloom has pointed out, "all three governmental functions have been collapsed into the administrative branch" in the rulemaking, executive, and adjudicative roles of agencies.[36] A public-administration theory useful to modern practitioners must therefore address public administration in the broadest sense.

Over thirty years ago, Herbert Kaufman identified "emerging conflicts" in public-administration theory among representativeness, neutral competence, and executive leadership[37] and noticed the inadequate efforts of the various branches to "integrate the component elements."[38] While the key tensions in public administration now appear to be to some extent of a different nature, the challenge to produce a unified theory integrating "the component elements" remains essentially the same.

II

Representativeness vs. Efficiency: Legislatures vs. Agencies and Executives

RULE 1: Agencies must respect legislative intent where it is discernible.

That old dead horse of public-administration theory, the politics versus administration dichotomy,[1] somehow still keeps kicking. This is surprising only because the conventional wisdom of the 1960s and 1970s was that the debate was over, and that bureaucratic control over policy is the unavoidable cost of efficiency in an era of very big government.[2] But the public made known its increasing discomfort with "out of control" unelected bureaucrats making decisions affecting the lives of citizens.[3] The advent of the Reagan administration brought an attack on bureaucratic government—and the resurgence of the power of the president—an elected official directly accountable to the voter, that came as a real surprise to scholars.[4]

In our tradition the elected legislature, not the elected executive, more properly defends the public against agency power.[5] The Framers did not intend the president to exemplify the virtue of representativeness.[6] Congress was to make policy on the people's behalf.

The tension between representativeness and efficiency, between democratic accountability and delegation, started at least as far back as 1789. In the same year that the Constitution was adopted, delegating the people's inherent legislative power to Congress, Congress decided that veterans' benefits should be based on service in the Revolutionary War "under such regulations as the President of the United States may direct."[7] Immediately, there were problems: What if the veteran had been hurt tripping over a sack of flour, off duty, not in uniform? It was obviously inefficient for Congress to enact increasingly specific legislation to deal with such matters as they arose. It was also clearly inefficient for judges dealing with many other matters to become experts in the eighteenth-century version of worker's compensation. With the hiring of clerks by the executive branch to answer such questions, bureaucrats began making policy decisions.

Andrew Jackson's 1829 "democratizing" argument that government work is "plain and simple" provided justification for appointments based on political loyalty rather than merit.[8] Fifty-four years later, the Pendleton Act "counterrevolution" was the reverse pendulum swing: The bureaucracy had become too political, too unprofessional, and therefore needed more insulation against "political" control. Legal theory, meanwhile, ignored both revolution and counterrevolution, hewing to the line that bureaucrats were not making policy and politics had nothing to do with it. The general scholarly perception was that a fairly substantial degree of "government by bureaucracy" was inevitable.[9]

Most law is agency law: Agencies promulgate four or five thousand regulations annually, compared with roughly three or four hundred congressional statutes each year.[10] For example, Internal Revenue Service regulations determine far more decisions on individuals' returns, albeit usually smaller decisions, than Internal Revenue Code provisions enacted by Congress. Thousands of times more labor decisions depend on National Labor Relations Board rulings than on the National Labor Relations Act itself, which was enacted by Congress.[11]

Congress had no choice but to establish agencies; it could not deal itself with the enormous range of issues in need of resolution each year. At times, however, agencies make decisions that Congress dislikes. To overturn each such decision by passing legislation is difficult and awkward. Furthermore, if the President supports the agency and vetoes the legislation, Congress might not even be able to muster the two-thirds vote of each house necessary to retrieve the power it had initially granted to the agency by a mere majority vote.

Instead, Congress developed a tool for dealing with those individual agency actions of which it disapproved: the legislative veto. The original legislation creating the agency or giving it power would include a provision allowing the House of Representatives and the Senate, or sometimes only one house of Congress, to overrule an agency regulation or adjudicative decision. The president would have no opportunity to veto this "overruling." While the device emerged at the end of the administration of President Herbert Hoover in 1932, it had its genesis originally in the Overman Act of 1918, designed to give President Woodrow Wilson increased power to reorganize federal agencies. By 1983, over two hundred federal statutes, including the War Powers Act of 1973, enabling Congress to direct the withdrawal of troops sent by a president without a formal congressional declaration of war, and other major statutes, contained such provisions.

The U.S. Court of Claims upheld the legitimacy and constitutionality of the legislative veto in a 1977 decision, noting in response "[t]o the plaintiff's argument that Congress cannot meddle once it has delegated power, it may be observed that legislation is itself a form of supervision. . . ."[12]

The Immigration and Nationality Act was one of the many statutes that included a legislative-veto provision. Section 244(c)(2) of that act provided that either house of Congress could, by resolution, overturn the U.S. attorney general's determination that an alien should be permitted to remain, and if it did so, the alien in question would be deported. When Congress voted to deport Jagdish Chadha, an East Indian on a British passport, he brought suit questioning the constitutionality of the legislative veto. In *INS* v. *Chadha*,[13] Chief Justice Warren Burger, writing for the Court in 1983, held the legislative veto unconstitutional.

The Constitution requires that "[e]very bill which shall have passed the House of Representatives and the Senate shall, before it becomes a Law, be presented to the President of the United States."[14] Burger reasoned that truly legislative acts are those that alter legal rights of persons "outside the legislative branch"; such acts must meet the aforementioned requirements, and the action in the case at hand indeed so "altered legal rights,"[15] and was therefore unconstitutional, since it was not performed according to the requirements.

Justice Byron White, in dissent, argued that the legislative veto, in reality, constituted the reserving of a power from legislation, rendering the initial delegation of power to the agency somewhat less than it otherwise would have been. After all, Congress need not have delegated any power to the agency at all. Thus, the legislative veto fractionates the lawmaking procedure described in the Constitution, but does not violate it. In any case, given the questionable constitutional theory that underlies broad delegations of power to agencies, however practically necessary they may be,[16] congressional efforts to retain policy control would appear to be a commendable exercise in the restoration of fundamental constitutional balance.

The Court's decision threatened to exacerbate the congressional loss of control over agency action that had accelerated since the Brownlow Commission. The expansion of the role of

government has made it less feasible than ever for Congress to
attend to the details. It is unlikely that this trend could be
reversed. The advantage of the legislative veto was that Congress, after enacting necessarily broad legislation, could be
alerted to problematic details subsequently. Through the legislative veto, it could then attend to such details, with no need to
spend time on the vast majority of ordinary, nonproblematic
matters. Given the trend toward increased centralization of
power in the executive, it was unrealistic to expect that Congress could succeed instead in defining, limiting, and restricting executive authority by means of more detailed delegations
on an across-the-board basis.

Furthermore, the Court's decision was weakly grounded in
legal reality. Virtually every agency regulation or adjudication
since 1789 "alters the legal rights of persons" without going
through any legislative branch lawmaking process, much less
the process specified: For example, the Immigration and Natu-
ralization Service itself, by its own decision, may order aliens
to be held in detention facilities. ". . . [T]he persistence of the
Administrative State is ample proof that the theoretical model
of legislative action envisioned by the framers applies only in
the most general sense to the 20th century."[17]

In *Bowsher* v. *Synar*,[18] Chief Justice Burger may have man-
aged to write a worse decision than *Chadha*. The Gramm-
Rudman law of 1985 provided for automatic agency budget cuts
if Congress would otherwise enact a budget more than $10 bil-
lion beyond stated deficit levels, and provided that the comptroller general would play the key role in identifying the excess
deficits. Burger held that since Congress had since 1921 shared
with the president statutory power to remove the comptroller
general (which power Congress had never exercised), and
could override a presidential veto of a congressional removal
with the usual two-thirds vote, it could not delegate such "executive branch" responsibility to an officer thus beholden to the
legislative branch without violating the constitutional principle
of separation of powers.[19]

This is, of course, utter nonsense. The separation of powers doctrine was intended only to prevent abuse by providing that one branch would check the power of another, a process that Gramm-Rudman-Hollings in no way threatened. Hamilton and Madison clearly approved of overlapping powers among the branches.[20]

The Court noted that the Constitution "does not contemplate an active role for Congress in the supervision of officers charged with the execution of the laws it enacts."[21] As Louis Fisher notes:

> Of course the Constitution does not contemplate a number of things, including the active role of the President in supervising the passage of laws or the ability of the President to make law unilaterally by issuing executive orders and proclamations. . . . For two centuries, congressional oversight of executive affairs has been a legitimate constitutional responsibility. . . .[22]

Chadha and *Bowsher* would make it hard for the "representative" branch, Congress, to control the "executive" branches, agencies and the president.

But the pendulum swing toward bureaucratic power may once again have reached its limit. One rather surprising indication of the swing's limit was the one hundred and two legislative vetoes enacted into law *after* the *Chadha* decision in 1983 and before the end of the Ninety-ninth Congress in 1986.[23] President Reagan attempted to stop the flow of legislative-veto provisions reaching his desk for signature subsequent to *Chadha*. But the relationships between congressional committees and agencies that have developed over the years have produced a variety of expedited procedures that are of value to both sides, and insistence on formal procedures can have unpleasant consequences for either side, as Congress apparently made clear to the president.[24]

With Chief Justice William Rehnquist's majority opinion in *Morrison* v. *Olson*,[25] the special prosecutor case, the Court took a giant step back toward reasonable readings of the constitutional balance between Congress and the executive. Alexia

Morrison was appointed by a special three-judge federal appellate court, not by the president or his appointees, to investigate possible abuses by Justice Department officials. The Ethics in Government Act, passed by Congress in 1978, authorized appointments such as hers.

The Justice Department, which she was investigating, however, argued that law enforcement, investigation, and prosecution are executive-branch functions. Article II of the Constitution, in vesting executive power in the president, meant *all* such power, and so, the Justice Department argued and Justice Antonin Scalia agreed in his dissenting opinion, the president must have "complete control over investigations and prosecution of violations of the law."[26]

Practical considerations would give rise to concern about the vigor with which investigators dependent upon the president's entourage for their positions would investigate and prosecute that entourage. The Framers would have felt quite comfortable with such considerations. Rehnquist steered back toward sound government in noting that the Constitution "give[s] Congress significant discretion to determine whether it is 'proper' to vest the appointment of, for example, executive officials in the 'courts of law.'" Attempting to downplay his sharp course away from the direction of *Chadha* and *Bowsher*, claiming that *Morrison* differed because Congress wasn't claiming executive-style power for itself but vesting it in courts, Rehnquist said, "[W]e have never held that the Constitution requires that the three branches of government 'operate with absolute independence.'"[27]

The vision behind the decisions in *Chadha* and *Bowsher*, and behind Justice Scalia's dissent, "was of a Presidency supreme and essentially unchallengeable. It was as if those who framed the Constitution at Philadelphia in 1787 had created a President on the model of King George the Third."[28]

Morrison represented an important reaffirmation of legislative power vis-à-vis the federal executive. At the state level, agencies similarly dominated by their respective chief executives' appointment power had similarly assumed unwarranted power vis-à-vis state legislatures. Finally, in 1987, the highest court in New York State fired a powerful shot across the bow of arrogated agency power.

Sections 225(4) and 225(5)(a) of New York's Public Health Law, read together, authorize the state's Public Health Council, an administrative agency whose members are appointed by the governor, to "deal with any matters affecting the security of life or health or the preservation and improvement of public health in the State of New York. . . ." In 1975, the state Legislature enacted Article 13-E of the Public Health Law regulat ing smoking in some public places. Between 1975 and 1986, legislation to require restaurants and other privately owned facilities to set aside nonsmoking areas failed to pass after lengthy and extensive debate in one house of the Legislature, and was not reported to the floor in the other house.

In 1987, the Public Health Council promulgated regulations essentially equivalent to the unsuccessful legislation. In a decision voiding the council's action, the trial court noted that although the delegation of power to the agency was broad, rules nonetheless "will be struck down when they conflict with State policy as set by the legislature."[29]

However, under the leading case precedents, *Clark* v. *Cuomo*,[30] and *Flanagan* v. *Mount Eden Gen. Hospital*,[31] the Legislature, in failing to enact legislation, was not considered to have "set" state policy. The Appellate Division rejected as "inherently dubious" any such inference from the Legislature's failure to enact legislation,[32] but upheld the decision of the trial court on the grounds that the proposed change in law would affect the lives of millions of New Yorkers, and therefore, "however meritorious in terms of the public health, [is] the function of the Legislature, not an administrative agency."[33]

In light of the massive delegations of power granted to agencies and upheld as constitutional by courts over the past few decades, the Appellate Division's decision appeared to rest on shaky ground. The New York Court of Appeals rested its affirmance on stronger grounds. *Clark* v. *Cuomo* and *Flanagan* each referred to "legislative inaction."[34] The case at hand was not one of legislative inaction. The Legislature had rejected the legislation in question firmly, explicitly, recently, and after lengthy debate, refusing to expand the existing restrictions on smoking contained in Article 13-E of the New York Public Health Law.

The sponsor of the legislation[35] testified before the Legislative Administrative Regulations Review Committee that

> having tried this measure, having tried beyond most reasonable standards that I would normally use to work out a compromise that was acceptable to the Senate Committee chairman and after that to the Senate, that we have gone absolutely nowhere with that, to continue this effort of pursuing a one-house bill when there is so much at stake in public health consequences, I don't think is really worth much more of the time that I have put in. . . .[36]

The present writer noted in his *amicus* brief to the Appellate Division:

> While it is understandable that the sponsor of A.2926b would seek to accomplish his worthy and admirable purpose through non-legislative means when the legislative route seems firmly blocked, in our constitutional system that blockage is definitive and dispositive. Whatever the surface appearance of the case law in this area, the realities of the case at hand present an inescapable constitutional question: can the clear intent of the legislature to reject a policy be overridden by an administrative agent of that legislature? The constitutional answer must be in the negative.[37]

The Court of Appeals reached a roughly similar conclusion. In penetrating the surface of the leading precedents to the real underlying constitutional issue of the nature of representative government, the court sent a message the likes of which had not been seen in many years—that bureaucratic policymaking must remain within reasonable bounds. The Court said:

A number of coalescing circumstances that are present in this case persuade us that the difficult-to-define line between administrative rulemaking and legislative policymaking has been transgressed. . . .[38]

. . . [I]n this case it is appropriate for us to consider the significance of legislative inaction as evidence that the Legislature has so far been unable to reach agreement on the goals and methods that should govern in resolving a society-wide problem.[39]

On the national level, as well as the state level, Congress and the other legislatures have tried to find more effective ways to reassert control over unelected bureaucrats. "Sunset" legislation, for example, means legislation that creates agency power that automatically expires after a given time period. That power is not renewed unless the agency can justify it; but sunset reviews tend to stretch legislative resources too thin to be an effective tool most of the time.[40] Legislative "watchdogs"[41] and legislative casework provide some response to the expansion of executive government.

The 1987 Iran-Contra congressional hearings should have been an outstanding illustration of a legislative effort to reestablish control over a runaway bureaucracy. The National Security Council was an arm of the White House. The president and his staff, too, are the agents of Congress in carrying out the law, including law affecting foreign policy. Unfortunately, the conduct of those hearings may not have duly educated the American polity in this regard.[42]

The question of electoral control of bureaucratic power will remain alive as long as bureaucrats must carry out legislative and presidential intent, whether the locus of leadership remains with the executive or returns at least in part to the legislative branch. (The bureaucratization of legislatures themselves, as staff has proliferated, is also a problem, but at least in theory legislative staff simply reflect the policies of their elected employers, and experience seems to bear out the theory.)[43]

The tension between the need for bureaucratic government on the one hand, and democratic control on the other, creates an ongoing dialectic, but commitment to our particular constitutional values requires more vigilance in defense of democratic control and representativeness than in defense of bureaucratic government and efficiency. Every modern industrial society has tendencies toward the latter. One of our special virtues is the former. The trial judge in *Boreali* v. *Axelrod*, the New York State smoking-rules act, was not entirely overstating the matter when he said, "Defendants' view of the executive power would have us come full circle from the old days of rule by benevolent autocrat to a modern rule of the benign bureaucrat."[44]

III

Fairness vs. Efficiency: Courts vs. Elected Officials and Agency Bureaucrats

RULE 2: Decisions regarding the allocation of society's resources to groups are to be made by legislatures, not by courts.

The second question of decisionmaking locus—courts or the other institutions of American government—can be framed as fairness versus efficiency. In this context, in contrast with the previous section, we will assume that bureaucracy acts as the agent of elected officials. What follows is a suggestion that elected legislatures and executives and agencies operating under their direction should control the distribution of society's material resources in seeking greater equality. Courts serve vital "fairness" functions, but functions that make them generally unsuitable for pursuing distributional equality. Our subsequent rules explicitly reinforce the role of courts in protecting and enhancing the other component of fairness, equality in process. But in the distribution of resources, "[f]airness and efficiency . . . often collide. . . . This . . . is the main reason courts cannot assume the administrative burden directly."[1]

Fairness, like representativeness, flourishes best in prosperity, when a scarcity of resources does not increase pressure for more efficiency. The much-noted overjudicialization of American life[2] reflected the triumph of constitutional values in a country that could, generally speaking, afford them. Justice Felix Frankfurter's warnings about the dangers of judicial intervention were ignored. He had, indeed, overstated them. But Frankfurter held the higher ground in deferring to legislatures with respect to complex questions of reallocating the public's material resources when he "argued that the judicial process does not alert justices to the multifarious considerations which should enter into an intelligent adjustment of competing claims."[3]

To date, there is no clearer statement of the economic inefficiency of due process than Lon Fuller's:

> To act wisely, the economic manager must take into account every circumstance relevant to his decision, and must himself assume the initiative in discovering what circumstances are relevant. His decision must be subject to change or reversal as conditions alter. The judge, on the other hand, acts upon those facts that are in advance deemed relevant under declared principles of decision. His decision does not simply direct resources and energies; it declares rights, and rights to be meaningful must in some measure stand firm through changing circumstances. When, therefore, we attempt to discharge tasks of economic management through adjudicative forms there is a serious mismatch between the procedure to be adopted and the problem to be solved.[4]

A good illustration, also brought to the author's attention many years ago by the late Professor Fuller, was provided by the distribution of the Timken art collection.

When Mrs. William R. Timken died in 1959, she left eighty-seven paintings to be divided between the National Gallery in Washington and the Metropolitan Museum in New York. She did not leave instructions as to how the collection was to be divided.[5] Fortunately, rather than litigating the matter, the directors of the two museums found a way to divide the collection which satisfied them both. They made their respective selections based on several values: aesthetic merit, historical significance, monetary value, and gaps in their existing collections.

It is hard to imagine that the directors could have obtained as good a mix of the values they sought had they litigated the matter. In that event, arguments concerning rights, and perhaps efforts to weaken the opposition by withholding information, would have played some role. To the extent that any such factors influenced the outcome, it would have been less satisfactory than the actual result. If, for example, the museums had insisted on receiving shares of equal financial value, other values would have been sacrificed. Since the financial value of an art collection may be greater than the sum of its parts, depending on the nature of the groupings, even financial value could have been lost in an adversarial battle for exact division. The two museum directors actually divided the paintings into twenty-six sets of paired groups. While the specific paintings to follow are imaginary, just to illustrate, let us say the division might have included four Rembrandts in one group and three Van Goghs in its paired group. Pair by pair, the directors stated their respective preferences. If they each preferred the same half of a pair, they would toss a coin, and the loser would accept the group not preferred. Both directors were satisfied with the overall results.

Had the matter been litigated, the results could have been much less satisfactory. To illustrate simply, assume that the imaginary set used in the example above was by far the most

valuable set in the collection. Assume that the Van Gogh group
is worth $500,000 and the Rembrandt group is worth $1.5 million, but the Rembrandts broken up and sold separately are
worth only $250,000 each, for a total of only $1 million. Assume
that although the two groups were of unequal value, the directors agreed that since neither should be broken up, the loser of
the coin toss would simply accept the Van Gogh group. In that
scenario, the "managerial" solution produces $2 million worth
of art for the two museums, and through the museums for society.

By contrast, each director could argue that a court's assign-
ment to him of the less valuable group constituted a deprivation of property without due process of law, since parties with
equal claims should get equal shares. To meet this "fundamental fairness" argument, a court might have no choice but to
assign one of the Rembrandts to the museum that received the
Van Goghs, leaving that museum with $500,000 worth of Van
Goghs and one $250,000 Rembrandt, and the other museum
with three $250,000 Rembrandts, for a monetarily equal divi-
sion. This "judicial" solution produces $1.5 million worth of art
for the two museums, and through the museums, for society.
The cost to society of using the judicial solution rather than the
managerial solution is $500,000.

Since this is a vastly oversimplified illustration, it fails to
take into account all of the other values, besides monetary
worth, that are jeopardized by the judicial approach.

A decision between $x = 0$ and $x = 10$ has one center, $x = 5$. A
multidimensional decision, such as allocating budget expenditures among many recipients, each with a different cluster of
needs and justifications, or allocating paintings, each with
many different kinds of value, among museums, each with
many different kinds of needs, is "polycentric." The museum
case is an unusually clear illustration of the inadequacy of the
judicial approach to "polycentric"[6] problems because it provides an actual managerial solution in contrast.

The museum case, however, involved private managerial decisions. The efforts of government to provide managerial solu-

tions to polycentric public problems are all too easily upset by persons who wish to impose solutions that are best for them personally. With the expansion of due-process protection, they may succeed in doing so through litigation, as in school-discipline and welfare-fraud investigation cases.

The application of due-process requirements to school-suspension cases has changed the relationship between schools and students. Public, impersonal, formal proceedings have been substituted for private, personal, and informal processes traditionally used to resolve school-discipline cases. Procedural fairness may have been improved at the expense of privacy, morale, and efficiency.

In *Goss* v. *Lopez*,[7] a 1975 decision, Justice Byron White wrote for the Court that public-school students have a "legitimate entitlement to a public education as a property interest which is protected by the Due Process Clause and which may not be taken away for misconduct without adherence to the minimum procedures required by the Clause." Suspension decisions, made informally in the past by a principal or dean of a school, would be replaced by at least a limited hearing process.[8]

Later cases underscore some of the costs involved. Judge Gurfein, writing for the Second Circuit in another school-related matter, pointed to the inappropriately long delay in such actions, noting that "[a] child who was in the first grade when this action was begun is now ready to enter junior high school."[9]

Goss placed on schools a new and heavy burden of providing numerous hearings. In *Whiteside* v. *Kay*,[10] a student brought a suit, relying on *Goss*, alleging that he had been suspended without adequate due process. His school had provided him with three different opportunities to explain his case to three different authorities, with representation by any person of his choice, before the school arrived at the final decision to suspend him. The court held that he had received adequate due process. However, the provision of three hearings is a considerable burden for a school. The *Goss* requirements have been somewhat limited by decisions like *Whiteside*. Arguably, however, the spectacle of a school system effectively "on trial" each time it attempts to suspend a student is not good for school morale.

Privacy values are sacrificed when personal, confidential, and psychological factors are brought into the open so as to meet the due-process requirement of exclusivity of the record. The requirement means that any decision must be based only on matters stated in the official record of a hearing.[11] If personal, confidential, or psychological factors are crucial to a decision, they must be stated publicly on the record or the decisionmaker is forbidden to consider them.

Board of Curators of the Univ. of Missouri v. *Horowitz*[12] illustrates the sacrifice of privacy values to due process in the school context. Horowitz, a medical student, brought suit to challenge her academic expulsion from medical school. Discussions of Ms. Horowitz's personal hygiene, physical appearance, "eccentric" personal conduct, "handwashing and grooming," and relationships with others appeared in Justice Rehnquist's majority opinion, Justice Powell's concurrence, Justice Marshall's partial concurrence, and the *New York Times* report of the decision.[13]

The Court held that *Goss* guaranteed the right to a hearing for misconduct-based punishments, not for academic expulsions like Ms. Horowitz's.[14] However, it is clearly in the former that personal, private, and psychological factors will have to be brought out for the record. Apparently Ms. Horowitz did not shrink from this kind of personal publicity. (It would seem likely that had she found the possibility of personal publicity highly revolting, she would not have brought suit.) Nevertheless, if due-process requirements should become increasingly prevalent in dealing with school-related problems of suspension, expulsion, and the like, the minimum price to be paid is the sacrifice of privacy, which, for most, is a value greatly prized.

A second example illustrates that as other resources become scarce, their sacrifice to the due-process value becomes more painful and harder to justify. New York City's Department of Social Services promulgated a regulation that cut off welfare payments to recipients who fail to report for interviews concerning fraud.[15] The payments in question were provided under the Aid to Families with Dependent Children program of the Social Security Act.[16] The requirements for eligibility are need, dependency, and submission of certain information which establishes these factors.[17] If the recipient agrees to the interview, benefits are continued even if he or she stands mute or admits committing fraud.[18]

In *Rush* v. *Smith*,[19] a welfare recipient brought suit challenging the regulation. The court held that the sole requirement of attendance at the hearing must fall, as an "additional condition of eligibility not required by the Social Security Act."[20] In 1978, the decision was reversed on appeal, but with a key qualification: Her *children* couldn't be deprived of benefits.[21] Since most or all of the money she received was for her children, and it would still come to her, and be controlled by her, in essence she paid no penalty. The payments, received and controlled by Ms. Rush, could not be terminated other than through the proper application of due-process procedures. Her refusal to cooperate in a fraud investigation was not enough to terminate welfare benefits.

At that time, New York had refused to increase its state contribution to welfare for four years,[22] probably because of its fiscal problems, and had therefore failed to provide the affected poor with enough money to keep up with the rapid rate of inflation. Even with improvements in the economy, of course, the state was willing to allocate only limited amounts to assist the poor.

Ms. Rush's right to refuse cooperation in a fraud investigation directed at herself must be weighed against the needs of poor persons in other categories. Protecting the uncooperative fraud suspect's right to welfare benefits means that other potential recipients willing and anxious to establish the truth may be denied benefits. The social cost of this type of decision increases as available resources become more scarce. Further-

more, the "rights" established have proved of little value to
their intended beneficiaries, with a shortage of poverty lawyers available to represent them.[23]

The values thereby jeopardized by an extraordinary commitment to due process include privacy, efficiency, and distributive justice. Earlier, we noted that legislatures are less
efficient than agencies. But courts are less efficient than either,
because the judicial role involves a commitment to fairness, regardless of economic consequences. It is very hard to imagine
the courts efficient enough to process 50 million Social Security
claims, as did the Social Security Administration in the 1980
fiscal year, when 7,814 of those claims were actually taken to
court: "In almost every case, the administrative agency is,
practically speaking, the only forum available; even if judicial
review were freely obtainable, the amounts involved are usually too small or the parties too poor to meet the costs of court
litigation."[24] Sometimes the forms of due process can be
streamlined, reducing economic costs, without sacrificing the
substance.[25] But some painful inequalities should not be addressed in the adjudicative mode, even if elected officials and
their agents, who are properly situated to address such inequalities, refuse to do so.

A prominent example is Alabama Federal District Judge
Frank Johnson's decision in the Bryce Hospital case, *Wyatt* v.
Stickney,[26] in which representatives of mental patients sued
the state for better care. No humane person could fail to re-
joice at Johnson's ruling that the horrifying conditions at the
hospital, clearly attributable to insufficient state funding, be
remedied, necessitating drastically increased levels of state
funding. Once Johnson decided that these patients had judicially enforceable rights to standards of care higher than the
legislature had provided—rights that he could and should spec-
ify—he was bound to make his further decisions based only on
the evidence before him,[27] along with considerations of fairness
and equity with respect to the parties. As a judge he could not
properly—even if he could practically, which of course he could
not—take into account the needs and priorities of the State of

Alabama with respect to the remainder of the items to be addressed in its annual budget. The state estimated that Johnson's orders would cost 60 percent of its expense budget, excluding education, in addition to $75 million in capital costs.[28]

Thus, when Johnson required Alabama to spend millions of dollars more per year on Bryce Hospital than it had allocated in its budget, he did not, could not, and in his judicial capacity should not have known whether the requisite shift of dollars would, say, kill a physically ill patient in some other state hospital, or reduce the state's welfare grant to the point at which some recipient finally starved to death. Judge Johnson simply said, "[A] failure by defendants to comply with this decree cannot be justified by a lack of operating funds."[29] As far as we know, none of the disasters suggested actually happened, but they illustrate the potential difficulties that can ensue when this kind of "polycentric" decisionmaking is performed by courts rather than by legislatures.[30]

While Johnson might have decided that without a higher level of care necessary to qualify as mental treatment, patients involuntarily committed to Bryce who had been found guilty of no crime had a right to liberty, in fact he decided that they had a right to a higher level of care.

This distinction involves subtle and difficult, but important issues. Judge Johnson said, "[T]his Court held that these involuntarily committed patients 'unquestionably have a constitutional right to receive such individual treatment as will give each of them a realistic opportunity to be cured or improve his or her mental condition.'"[31] In the initial holding, he continued, "The purpose of involuntary hospitalization for treatment purposes is *treatment* and not mere custodial care or punishment. This is the only justification, from a constitutional standpoint, that allows civil commitment to mental institutions such as Bryce. . . ."[32]

Johnson was making the uncontroversial claim that deprivation of liberty for treatment purposes, where there was no conviction of a crime, requires treatment. However, Johnson at no point continued with what might suggest itself as a conclusion, i.e., that the inmates must be provided treatment *or be re-leased*. Upon examination, this omission does not appear to have been accidental.

Johnson appears to have been applying an extended version of the "new property" approach of the *Goldberg* v. *Kelly* "entitlements" revolution,[33] under which public benefits, previously regarded as a sort of privilege easily revocable by the state, now are held by the recipient as a sort of protected property right. The inmates, having been diagnosed as belonging to the category of individuals statutorily "entitled" to receive treatment, therefore have a constitutional right to treatment, as a sort of quasi-property right they have therefore acquired.

But this "new property" jurisprudence presents some problems when applied to constitutional cases of this kind.[34] In *Arnett* v. *Kennedy*,[35] Justice Rehnquist accepted the "property" paradigm in ruling on the case of a nonprobationary civil servant who was fired for making negative comments about his co-worker. Kennedy's contract conditioned his tenure on "good conduct," with no standards defining how such "good conduct" should be assessed. Thus, Justice Rehnquist held that the contract set the boundaries of Kennedy's "property," and when Kennedy ventured beyond that boundary, he could be, and was, summarily fired.

When the Court analyzes the limits on one's "new property," it may prove to be very small. It can well be argued, on the basis of *Arnett* and other cases,[36] that individuals get better protection against procedural arbitrariness and unfairness by use of a liberty interest, rather than a property interest, as the constitutional standard in the administrative-due-process context.[37] A welfare recipient arguably should have property rights in the shoes he or she buys with a welfare grant. But should a government jobholder have property rights in that job? We don't want "officious" public servants.

The "liberty interest" stands on much more solid constitutional footing: The Constitution does not indicate that the Framers envisioned constitutional rights to get things, only constitutional rights to be free of unreasonable restraints.

Thus, in the Bryce Hospital case, the "liberty interest" approach would have required a clear and explicit choice to have been presented to the Alabama legislature: Give those patients something constituting meaningful treatment or *let them out.* This approach, of course, is less humane—the patients in question would probably not do well on their own. But the alternative leaves courts making resource-allocation decisions which, under constitutional theory and under the only way representative government can logically proceed, should be made by legislators. Had the Bryce Hospital decree been enforced, a serious constitutional crisis could have emerged. Thus, the Fifth Circuit noted that "[t]he serious constitutional questions presented by federal judicial action ordering the sale of state lands, or altering the state budget, or which may otherwise arise in the problem of financing, in the event the governing authorities fail to move in good faith to ensure what all parties agree are minimal requirements, should not be adjudicated unnecessarily and prematurely."[38]

In fact, the Bryce Hospital situation continued unresolved. As of 1986, Alabama had yet to achieve compliance with Johnson's 1972 decree.[39] One way Alabama tried to meet Johnson's demand for better staff-to-patient ratios and other changes was by releasing about half its patients, notwithstanding Johnson's failure to mention that alternative in his decisions. His decrees, therefore, "may have done more harm than good,"[40] assuming those patients did worse deprived of custodial care than they would have done at Bryce.[41]

The better approach appears to have been that of the Supreme Court in *Dandridge* v. *Williams.*[42] There, some Maryland welfare recipients sued in federal court to challenge that state's welfare regulations, claiming that they deprived them of equal protection of the laws by providing lower grants for them than for some other recipients. The Court rejected their claim, holding that "[t]he Constitution does not empower this Court to second-guess state officials charged with the difficult responsibility of allocating limited public welfare funds among the myriad of potential recipients."

Judicial resource allocation is an important phenomenon. School-finance cases, in which courts decide that the equal-protection clause of the Fourteenth Amendment requires greater equalization of funding available to school districts within a state, pose an even more difficult problem than custodial-institution cases. Deinstitutionalization, or, for prisons, early parole, may be available options in the latter type of case. But increases in income taxes or sales taxes may be the only options in the school-financing cases.[43]

The authors of an article defending this role for the courts nonetheless concede that "[e]xtended impact cases" (like school, hospital, or prison cases) "have the potential for distorting resource allocations in the public sector."[44] But they have more than "potential": The same authors report that court orders have cost over $3.5 billion in custodial-institution construction.[45]

In defense, they quote Ronald Dworkin's statement that "[t]he nerve of a claim of right . . . is that an individual is entitled to protection against the majority even at the cost of the general interest."[46] But members of the majority are individuals too; it would seem inappropriate to violate the rights of all who do not go to court until and unless they do so. The problem was summarized well in a discussion of the impact of prison-rights decisions requiring more prison construction: "[W]hen the judges make *de facto* budget decisions, there *are* losers. They are the beneficiaries of other programs—education, public works, mental health, recreation—who either must forego new benefits, or give up some of their existing benefits, because the courts are forcing the state legislature to appropriate more funds for prisons within an increasingly austere budgetary environment."[47]

When legislatures allocate funds for housing assistance or for public mental-health care, they are not undertaking unlimited obligations. They are making policy, and like Fuller's economic manager, their decisions are "subject to change or reversal as conditions alter."[48] A court-decreed right is, at least in theory, for all time. A legislative budget item may or may not be renewed in next year's budget. If the electorate no longer wishes to subsidize the homeless or the mentally ill, we may hate the result. But legislatures and administrators making budget decisions must be able to adjust those decisions, year to year, as conditions alter. Courts cannot. If courts could, they would logically require unlimited power to compel production. Such power would quite severely restrict liberty. Further, rights-based resource allocations could not be flexible enough to reflect changing social needs. Severe deficiencies, in terms of mismatches between resources and priorities, would result.

This is where rights-based theorists, like Ronald Dworkin, get into difficulties. Dworkin makes a useful distinction between policy and principle: Policies are designed to further specific social goals, while principles are the most important goals themselves.[49] Judicial decisions should be generated by principle,[50] which derives from a showing of a right;[51] while legislative decisions may be generated by principle or policy. But for Dworkin, elements of distributional equality may be included in the domain of principle, thus generating rights enforceable in court. He distinguishes between "rights against the state and rights against fellow citizens" in that the former justify requiring only the government to act while the latter can justify requiring particular citizens to act, such that, for example, "[t]he right to minimum housing, if accepted at all, is accepted as a right against the state."[52] This kind of distinction tends to overlook the fact that fellow citizens must still be required to pay for that "right to minimum housing," and the tax dollars used for it might otherwise be used for equally pressing or more pressing needs. This kind of theory underlies Johnson's decision, but it goes against workable and traditional American constitutional divisions of role between courts and legislatures.

Finally, the kind of substantive due process that Dworkin encourages invites a court that does not share his viewpoint to return to the jurisprudence of *Lochner* v. *New York*,[53] invalidating protective legislation limiting the hours of bakery workers as an unconstitutional interference with freedom of

contract. If the Court can enact into law John Rawls's *A Theory of Justice*, as Dworkin would appear to prefer, it can enact
Herbert Spencer's *Social Statics*, as Justice Holmes com-
mented in his famous dissent in *Lochner*,[54] and as some future
right-wing Court might still prefer. And if courts habitually
substitute their judgment, "on principle," for the judgment of
legislatures, appointments to courts, by elected executive officials, "will be regarded primarily as prizes in ideological
struggles. Consequently, there will be less stability in constitutional law and, more important for the tenor of Dworkin's argument, activism in the name of conservative causes will be as
likely to triumph as activism in the name of the liberal causes
that Dworkin advocates."[55]

By no means should we as a society, or as public administrators, abandon the pursuit of distributional equality. But a
sound theory of public administration encourages us to engage
in that pursuit as a matter of policy, not as a matter of right; as
a matter to be weighed and adjusted by efficient managerial
and legislative decisionmaking against the abilities of the bur-
dened sections of society to bear such burdens, not as a matter
to be dictated by courts without regard to cost and responsibility.

Courts should determine rights, as best they can, and rights
are to protect citizens against the excesses of majoritarianism,
against unfairness in the democratic *process*, not unfairness in
its outcome.[56] Equality in the process justifies decisions like
Brown v. *Board of Education*,[57] for without equal basic education, individuals cannot hope to compete equally in the democratic process. But there the Court was protecting an
individual's right against discrimination, not a group's right to
get something.

The suit in *Brown* was not brought by plaintiffs claiming that
their status as blacks or as hospital patients or as anything else
entitled them to something different from what the general
population received; the suit was brought by plaintiffs deprived—on the wholly irrelevant basis of their race—of what
everyone else received. The *Brown* v. *Board* decision was not

so much "Black children have a right to equal education" but rather "No child shall be denied an equal education on the basis of race."

The courts should continue to be guardians of liberty. They are inefficient redistributors of property by virtue of their role. Society, in times of scarcity, will permit costly inefficiencies for only so long. For purposes of the guardianship of liberty, the credibility of the courts is too important an asset to be risked.

IV

Dissent vs. Security: Proponents of Unpopular Views and Seekers of Sensitive Information vs. Executive Agencies

RULE 3: No person shall be deprived of the exercise of otherwise available First Amendment rights on the basis of the political point of view expressed in that exercise.

RULE 4: The executive and agencies must provide access to sensitive information concerning controversial policies to the widest possible audience consistent with the security of the United States against physical threats. The likelihood of legislative disapproval of such policies shall be a factor to be weighed in favor of access.

The third basic tension in American public administration, the

conflict between majority-based executive government and dissenters' access to information relevant to public debate contributed to the Iran-Contra controversy. A better sense of that
balance would have precluded various earlier Reagan administration policy initiatives limiting access to information[1] as
well as the initiatives culminating in the 1987 congressional
Iran-Contra hearings. The secrecy that shielded the National
Security Agency's actions in Iran and Nicaragua from congressional scrutiny prior to those hearings[2] teaches important
lessons about the tension between representativeness and efficiency, between elected officials and agency bureaucracy. Its
lessons are at least as portentous for the tension between dissent and security, since meaningful dissent is impossible if
potential dissenters, even in Congress, have no access to information critical to the assessment of controversial policy initiatives.[3]

The American constitutional balance between dissent and security may be assessed from a review of our history in this
area. The Alien and Sedition Acts of 1798, prohibiting and pun-
ishing dissent, produced an overwhelmingly negative national
response.[4] The sponsors' party, the Federalists, never again
achieved the national dominance it had maintained until then.
No such statute was again enacted even when the British were
burning Washington, and dissent was rampant, in the War of
1812.[5] While no such statute was enacted during the Civil War
either, Lincoln did assume emergency war powers and suspended the writ of habeas corpus in arresting some seces-
sionists engaged in anti-Union activity:

> Clearly individuals suffered from the arrests and other
> war policies. But it appears that their imprisonments were
> brief, uncruel, and open rather than secret. Political
> criticism flourished everywhere during the War and Re-
> construction years, and competitive two-party politics
> travelled to occupied southern states in the Union armies'
> knapsacks. . . .[6]

Lincoln followed the doctrine of necessity fairly well: Civil liberties were not, in practice, significantly impaired. Generally, dissent was not considered grounds for arrest.[7] Lincoln took care to seek and find an appropriate balance to preserve both the nation and its central value of respect for dissent.

During the Civil War, only one "conspicuous instance of interference with freedom of speech" took place,[8] in *Ex parte Vallandigham*,[9] and Vallandigham himself suffered no grievous consequences. However, Lincoln aroused great controversy with his suspension of the writ of habeas corpus to permit the military arrest and trial of Vallandigham. The Constitution does permit suspension of the writ "when in Cases of Rebellion or Invasion the public Safety may require it."[10] But that constitutional grant of power appears in the Legislative article, Article I, not the Executive article, Article II, so the president does not seem to have the constitutional authority to exercise it. However, in a lengthy letter of June 12, 1863, to Erastus Corning and Others in Albany, New York, attempting to justify the suspension, Lincoln took pains to note that Vallandigham "was not arrested because he was damaging the political prospects of the administration or the personal interests of the commanding general but because he was damaging the army, upon the existence and vigor of which the life of the nation depends."[11]

A noted nineteenth-century constitutional scholar defended Lincoln's position in terms of the doctrine of necessity: "[T]he constitutional liberty of the individual must be sacrificed, so far as the Government finds it necessary for the preservation of life and the security of the State.[12] And Lincoln appears to have applied the doctrine of necessity quite cautiously: generally, "the mere expression of disloyal sentiments was not ordinarily regarded as grounds for military arrest."[13]

However, American history is rife with examples of suppression of dissent and civil liberties: During World War I, there were the Palmer raids on harmless left-wing dissenters; during World War II, the terrible Japanese internment case, *Korematsu* v. *United States*,[14] when loyal Japanese-Americans were confined to camps and the Court, in perhaps the worst decision it ever wrote, held the practice to have been constitutional;[15] and, after World War II, the McCarthy era. Paul L. Murphy's 1979 history, mostly of the World War I period, provides hundreds of examples of deprivations of civil liberties.[16] As a reviewer noted, those who "revel in the misdeeds and hypocrisy of a government founded on the principles of liberty and justice, will devour Murphy's book with relish. . . . However, what Murphy did not say is that in those governmental systems that lack constitutional forms, dissenters in wartime— or peacetime, for that matter—are simply lined up and shot."[17]

The American record is better. The United States government did not want the embarrassing facts revealed in the Pentagon Papers to be presented to the public; it fought to have them suppressed, but lost.[18] The protesters preventively detained by Nixon during the 1971 May Day demonstrations won substantial damages.[19] Averaging over $2,000 for each of several hundred protesters, the damages paid ran well over a million dollars.[20]

Without question, the news reporters who exposed the realities of the war in Vietnam played a major role in ending it. They did their job against opposition and vilification by the national political leadership, but the reporters and the dissenters, not the political leaders, prevailed. The political leadership did not succeed in suppressing the news, or the dissent it engendered.[21]

And although it took a shamefully long time, in 1988 Congress apologized and created a $1.25 billion fund to pay $20,000 in reparations to each of the roughly sixty thousand survivors among the Japanese-Americans who were unjustly and unconstitutionally interned during World War II.[22]

Much in our record can engender pride in our protection of dissent, as we have seen. In the United States, substantial tradition supports the expression of unpopular political ideas. Justice Holmes said:

If there is any principle of the Constitution that more im-

peratively calls for attachment than any other, it is the
principle of free thought—not free thought for those who
agree with us but freedom for the thought that we hate.[23]

But any lingering doubt that the government will attempt to
suppress what it does not want the public to know, the public
interest notwithstanding, should have been dispelled by the recent history of Reagan administration anti-information initiatives. On October 1, 1984, the administration began a
prosecution for espionage against Samuel Loring Morison for
selling for publication photographs of a Soviet aircraft car-
rier.[24] The Soviet Union already had this information; the Reagan administration preferred to withhold it from the American
people. No administration or court in the United States should
have held the Espionage Act applicable to Morison, under our
third and fourth rules, but both did.[25]

On October 15, 1981, the administration proposed to amend
the Freedom of Information Act to reduce access to documents
concerning federal enforcement of "health, safety and environ-
mental laws" to prevent individuals from obtaining their FBI
files, and to make use of the act too expensive for writers and
reporters.[26] In February 1982 the administration began re-
classifying documents previously declassified, on a large scale,
particularly "thickening the wall of secrecy surrounding the
Administration's wasteful, fraud-ridden military buildup."[27]

On March 11, 1983, National Security Decision Directive 84
required government preclearance for the publications of
128,000 government employees with access to "sensitive com-
partmentalized information" for the rest of their lives, although
the State Department noted that there had been no damaging
information conveyed "through the writings of government employees during the preceding five years. . . ."[28] On January 3,
1984, the Justice Department obtained a "court order barring a
publisher from printing a legal opinion of a Colorado judge because the department [thought] it [was] 'slanderous' to three of
its lawyers."[29]

Of this list, "only" the prosecution for espionage and the reclassification were "successful." The actual litany by Walter Karp, who compiled this information, is much longer, and several other anti-information policies were implemented as well. The unsuccessful efforts took their toll: "When a concerted assault on the habits of freedom ceases to shock us there will be no further need to assault them, for they will have been uprooted once and for all."[30]

Majorities, to which the elected branches of government are particularly responsive, will from time to time urge and support suppression of ideas that frighten them.[31] Agencies are less responsive to majorities than elected officials, but more so than courts. When the majority wants to express bigotry or paranoia by depriving minorities of rights to free expression, fair trial, or equal participation in the political process, courts, then, can provide the best defense, as highlighted by our Rule 3. But the courts, especially in recent years, have failed to protect constitutional rights against claims of national-security interest by the executive branch.[32]

By no means, however, should courts be the only agency of government sensitive to the need for the exposure of policy to scrutiny and dissent. If the White House balks, Congress should protect at least its own role, if not that of the public, in securing the freest possible flow of information, by checking executive government's tendency toward secrecy and over-classification. The "presumption that public debate is a dangerous and inappropriate process" is contrary to the fundamental premises of American constitutionalism.[33]

When any government administration prescreens frightening ideas, or withholds information relevant to controversial issues, it seriously threatens American constitutional democracy. Information that threatens security may legitimately be classified, but Lincoln's example should guide our concerns about the balance between protection of dissent and security interests. In the face of dangers comparable to those the Union faced during his tenure, a military crisis directly, immediately, and physically threatening the survival of the nation, restrictions on information and dissent analogous to his may be imposed. It may be argued that in a nuclear age, comparable danger always threatens. The more frequent and dangerous threat is to the continuation of open, informed public debate. Such debate is the most valuable component of our constitutional tradition.

PART TWO

Applications

Although the various values we have discussed—liberty, equality, property, security, efficiency; or, in different combinations and permutations, representativeness, fairness, dissent, security, and efficiency—can be weighed and traded off against each other, no clear formula can describe the weightings and trades. Illustration and example provide the simplest way to present their respective weights. Charles Lindblom, in his great classic article, said it best: "Somewhat paradoxically, the only practical way to disclose one's relevant marginal values even to oneself is to describe the policy one chooses to achieve them."[1] The case studies that follow are an effort to do just that.

V

The Iran-Contra Affair

The Iran-Contra affair highlighted several of the most difficult value conflicts in the American constitutional system: representativeness versus efficiency, security versus the free flow of information, and even fairness, in a sense, versus security and efficiency.

Fairness vs. Security:
Morality in Covert Operations

To start with the last, Americans have characteristically exhibited distaste for covert operations, "sneaky stuff."[1] The rule of law and due process, on the domestic scene, manifest our attachment to liberty, equality, and property rights; but Americans have never been entirely comfortable in limiting their scope to the water's edge, as our enthusiasm for "morality" in international affairs has demonstrated.[2] Only an American like Woodrow Wilson, with typically American faith in the rule of law and the power of written documents, would have urged upon the world the Treaty of Versailles in the terms he used: ". . . this treaty . . . sets at liberty people all over Europe and Asia. . . . The heart of humanity beats in this document."[3] Our subsequent, more successful efforts to establish the United Nations and its charter likewise characterized a nation with extraordinary confidence in the applicability of the rules of fair play to international relations.

However, representatives of other nations have noted with annoyance that we never notably sacrificed our national interests in this enthusiastic pursuit of morality in all aspects of public life, including the conduct of our foreign policy. Thus, throughout the 1950s, Americans seemed content to "look the other way" while the CIA, on a "long leash," conducted a wide range of covert operations, including attempted assassinations and the overthrow of governments in Iran, Guatemala, and other nations.[4] But in the early 1970s, public skepticism about government increased. The press became much more aggressive in investigating government activities, including the conduct of covert operations. Forced to acknowledge openly the existence of such operations, Americans had to confront their ambivalence about "fairness" and morality.[5]

In 1974, in response to this change in national attitudes, Congress required a written "presidential finding" of national-security importance and a "timely" report to the "appropriate committee of the Congress" for each covert operation.[6] It wasn't that presidents hadn't cleared and appropriate members of Congress been briefed on covert operations before; they had, but "off the record," so presidents could deny knowledge and personal authorization for particular assignments. The key congressional committee chairs who had been briefed in the past had also tended to prefer less, rather than more, information, and had preferred to give the CIA great leeway.[7]

The new requirement, known as the Hughes-Ryan Amendment, clearly did not solve the central dilemma of covert activities, i.e., their intrinsic inconsistency with the "rule of law" implied by traditional American values. In 1978 Congress therefore considered a further measure, a legislative charter for the CIA, prohibiting a range of especially unappetizing covert operations other than during wars,[8] such as political assassination, biological warfare, and torture. Other operations, such as terror, creation of food or water shortages, and the "violent overthrow of democratic governments," could be undertaken only under a presidential determination of the existence of a "grave and immediate threat." Finally, no covert operation could be undertaken without a presidential finding that it was essential to national security, that its benefits outweighed its risks, and that there were no feasible alternatives.

Congress did not approve this charter. There was no clear indication that the people of the United States truly wanted to foreclose the policy option of arranging for the assassination of a foreign leader analogous to "Hitler in 1935," or "Idi Amin in 1978." "A country whose citizens do not want to decide whether to authorize assassinations, or to decide which ones are right, cannot have a statutory CIA charter that does anything more than empower the president to make decisions."[9]

Presidents Gerald Ford, Jimmy Carter, and Ronald Reagan did choose to issue executive orders specifically banning assassinations.[10] But any such order is revocable by the president who issues it, or by a subsequent president. It would, of course, have been possible for Congress to have enacted statutory prohibitions against assassination and the other operations in question, and then for American operatives to be instructed to ignore such prohibitions should the need arise. Our unwillingness even to record such prohibitions in statute may indicate either that outside the territorial boundaries of the United States our commitment to "fairness" is sufficiently weaker or the perceived security interests are sufficiently stronger. Thus, if the overseas use of, say, biological warfare and torture are "unfair," but could conceivably be crucial to

American national security interests, then even "on the record" security wins out over fairness in this instance.

Representativeness vs. Efficiency:
Executive vs. Legislative Control of
Foreign Policy

Executive efficiency and congressional representativeness may or may not conflict in this foreign-policy context. Former CIA Director William Colby's assessment of the executive-congressional relationship, long before the Iran-Contra affair, was well supported by that experience: "Exposure to specified Members of Congress . . . will give our American intelligence greater, rather than less, strength in the long run and avoid the . . . sensational hindsighting . . . of the last several years.[11]

Nonetheless, the argument framed as stated, between executive efficiency and congressional representativeness, goes back a long way into American history. The Constitution gives Congress the power to declare war, to "raise and support Armies" through its appropriation power, the "power of the purse," and to call forth the militia to repel invasions,[12] but the president is commander in chief.[13] In Federalist Paper No. 64, John Jay explained that the president must control treaty-making and manage foreign intelligence because the requisite level of secrecy can be provided only under such unified control. Hamilton argued for a strong executive and placing the foreign-affairs power largely in presidential hands. Locke, Blackstone, and Montesquieu supported that position, but they "had kings, and believed in them"; when Hamilton took their position, "Madison lashed out at him for attempting to import into the Constitution British monarchical prerogatives."[14]

Even Hamilton, however, emphasized the contrast between the British monarch and the American executive in matters of war and foreign policy. The king can declare war and raise fleets and armies; the president merely directs the armed forces, while Congress declares war and raises armies. The king appoints ambassadors and makes treaties and alliances on his own; the president shares those powers with the Senate. Hamilton appears to have "believed that the Senate would propose foreign policy; the President would execute it."[15]

In short, "[t]he Framers intended the Senate to be the principal architect of foreign policy."[16]

Perhaps the worst abuse that monarchs inflicted on their subjects was to cause them to fight in wars that were of no use, value, or interest to them. The economic costs, to say nothing of the costs in terms of lives lost and lives ruined, were tremendous.[17] The argument for representativeness as an important value in foreign relations would seem, at least in part, to stem from a desire to avoid that abuse. "Above all, the president was not to have the king's power to go to war; that power was given to Congress."[18] While Professor Louis Henkin rejects the view that the Framers gave Congress the power to declare war simply "to make going to war difficult and to assure public awareness and support for the war,"[19] it remains plausible that they kept such power out of the hands of the executive to avoid abuse: "The doctrine of the separation of powers was adopted by the Convention of 1787, not to promote efficiency but to preclude the exercise of arbitrary power . . . to save the people from autocracy."[20] Louis Fisher argues strongly that although separation of powers safeguards against abuse, it was also intended by the Framers to promote efficiency, and in fact does so.[21]

In the nineteenth century, the president "had no authority . . . to order aggressive hostilities to be undertaken,"[22] although presidents did so, nonetheless.[23] Congress appears to have been the far more enthusiastic source of support for the 1897 war against Spain than President McKinley; President Cleveland had indicated earlier that he would block mobilization for such a war if Congress initiated it.[24]

War-making power has shifted to the president in the twentieth century. A large permanent standing army seems normal to twentieth-century Americans. It would not have seemed so to Americans of the nineteenth century. The location of U.S. military bases around the world, the general expansion of American military power, and the advent of the nuclear age all increased the president's war-making powers and decreased the leverage Congress can exercise at any given time through the appropriations power. There has been no declaration of war, which only Congress can issue, in any of the armed hostilities in which the United States has been involved since World War II.[25] Congress did attempt to cut off funds for the war in Laos and Cambodia in 1973, failed to override Nixon's veto, and compromised on a forty-five-day extension.[26]

In reaction to that experience, Congress enacted the War Powers Resolution of 1973 to attempt to limit the president's unilateral ability to involve American forces in hostilities by requiring consultation with Congress and by providing for an automatic cutoff of funding in the absence of congressional approval after a sixty-to-ninety-day period. This was an effort to assure reasonably unified national support for American military involvements and restore some of the traditional power of Congress to control the war-making power. While "sound in constitutional principle," it remains controversial, probably because its provisions are somewhat unclear as well as, in some instances, in need of "rethinking."[27]

The Hughes-Ryan Amendment of 1974, noted earlier, which requires intelligence chiefs to report covert operations to the relevant committees of Congress, had a somewhat similar goal. In 1980, responding to Carter administration concerns that too many members of Congress received notice under its provisions, Congress further amended Section 501 of the National Security Act of 1947.[28] These amendments provided that in "extraordinary circumstances," presumably when leakage posed unusually significant dangers, the intelligence chiefs could limit notice to only the ranking members of each house of Congress, and of each house's intelligence committee, for a total of eight members. The 1980 act also increased pressure for prior notice of covert and intelligence activities by referring to "any significant anticipated intelligence activity."[29] Still, the act continued to be read by some legislators, and by the White House, as permitting the intelligence chiefs ("the Director of Central Intelligence and the heads of all departments, agencies, and other entities of the United States engaged in intelligence activities") to withhold such information if necessary to prevent "unauthorized disclosure of classified information" or if their other "applicable authorities and duties" so required.[30]

It was generally expected that covert operations were to be conducted by the CIA. Therefore, the "intelligence chief" involved would be the director of the CIA[31] or, of course, the president.[32] President Reagan's Executive Order 12333 of December 4, 1981, made this understanding explicit: Section 1.8(e) provides that "[n]o agency except the CIA [other than under a declaration of war or period covered by the War Powers Resolution] may conduct any special activity [defined elsewhere as a covert operation] unless the President determines that another agency is more likely to achieve a particular objective."[33] National Security Decision Directive 159, issued by President Reagan, precluded any overseas covert operation without a written finding of authorization by the president.[34]

During this time, the United States government was becoming increasingly concerned about the Sandinista regime in Nicaragua, which had substantially increased its international ties with Communist nations in 1980 and 1981. In January 1981, shortly before leaving office, "President Carter suspended aid to the Nicaraguan regime. . . . [T]he Reagan administration continued this policy,"[35] but went considerably further. In 1982, the press began to report CIA activity in support of the resistance to the Nicaraguan government. In response, Congress passed the first Boland Amendment to the Defense Appropriations Bill for fiscal 1983, limiting aid to the Contras to containing the Sandinista forces in Nicaragua, but prohibiting the use of such aid for overthrowing the Nicaraguan government. The press continued to report CIA assistance to Contra efforts within Nicaragua, apparently in violation of the Boland Amendment, and in 1984, the press disclosed CIA involvement in mining a Nicaraguan harbor. In October 1984, the second

Boland Amendment was signed into law, this time prohibiting any expenditure of U.S. funds for support of the Contras by any "agencies involved in intelligence activities."[36]

American public opinion did not favor support for the Contras. In September 1983, 60 percent opposed such aid, with 24 percent in favor;[37] by January 1987, 60 percent still opposed the policy, with 28 percent in favor and 12 percent were either undecided or had no opinion on the issue.[38]

Increasingly through the first half of the 1980s, the Reagan administration attempted to make public opinion less relevant, in that aid to the Contras became not merely a covert operation, but a covert policy, secret from Congress and secret from the American public. With the Boland Amendments apparently forcing the CIA out of the picture, President Reagan "directed the NSC [National Security Council] staff to keep the Contras together 'body and soul,'" according to testimony by former Assistant for National Security Affairs Robert McFarlane and Colonel Oliver North.[39] This meant that the NSC, formerly responsible for the assessment and formation of national security policy, would now become "operational," i.e., would become involved in implementing that policy, specifically through covert assistance to the Contras. The 1987 congressional report details the Iran-Contra chronology, telling the story of how Colonel North and Rear Admiral John Poindexter controlled secret operations that traded arms to Iran for hostages, and for money, some of which they diverted to the Contras.[40]

In November and December 1986, Secretary of State George Shultz obtained reports of the ongoing arms-for-hostages negotiations, and confronted President Reagan with the information. Although Poindexter testified that Reagan was already familiar with, and indeed had approved, much of what Shultz told him, Shultz testified that Reagan was very surprised and shocked. In any case, Reagan authorized Shultz to end the negotiations.[41]

On November 20 and 21, McFarlane, Poindexter, and CIA Director William Casey denied to congressional committees "that the United States knowingly participated" in certain of the arms shipments to Iran prior to a legally required presidential finding (as per the Hughes-Ryan Amendment) and that Poindexter destroyed a presidential finding "which would have exposed these statements as false."[42] Upon learning of an imminent Justice Department investigation, North and Poindexter destroyed additional documents, but failed in their efforts to conceal the diversion of funds to the Contras.[43] In a November 19 press conference, Reagan denied most of the salient facts concerning the events in question, perhaps as a result of "briefings" by Poindexter.[44]

Dissent vs. Security and the Executive-Legislative Balance

The Iran-Contra affair illustrates the potential for difficulty when the balance between the representative branch, in this case Congress, and the "efficient" managerial branch, in this case the White House and the NSC, is distorted.

Admiral Poindexter testified that he "thought Colonel North had acted properly in shredding documents concerning the arms sale and the contra supply operation,"[45] that his own "objective all along was to withhold from Congress exactly what the NSC was doing in carrying out the President's policy,"[46] that "his main regret was that he did not have a better damage control plan in the event the Congress and the press discovered what the National Security Council was doing,"[47] and that "he had done nothing wrong."[48] He characterized legislation like the Boland Amendments as "outside interference."[49]

Clearly, Poindexter did not understand the legitimate extent of Congress's role in foreign policy. In seeking a "unilateral" option from Poindexter, President Reagan also demonstrated a lack of understanding of that proper role.

House Speaker Jim Wright's meetings with Nicaraguan President Daniel Ortega in November 1987 went beyond the proper limits of the congressional role. Traditionally, the president is, as John Marshall said, the "sole organ of the nation in its external relations, and its sole representative with foreign nations."[50] In context, Marshall's statement meant that the president was the organ, or instrument, of the nation in carrying out the law.[51] Twelve sentences later, Marshall continued, "Congress, unquestionably, may prescribe the mode, and Congress may devolve on others the whole execution of the contract; but, till this be done, it seems the duty of the Executive department to execute the contract by any means it possesses."[52]

Oliver North cited *United States* v. *Curtiss Wright*,[53] a 1936 U.S. Supreme Court decision by Justice Sutherland, for the proposition that the president was to have sole control over foreign policy. Sutherland had quoted only the first part of Marshall's statement, thereby distorting its meaning, and was essentially reversed in the Steel Seizure Case in 1952.[54]

When Congress has made its policy clear, as in the second Boland Amendment's prohibition of military assistance to the Contras, the president and his advisers have no business evading that policy through secret means. North's deceptions and secrecy were intended to avoid political difficulties for Reagan's pro-Contra policy, not, as he testified, to avoid physical risks to operatives. When Congress did debate and later approve support for the Contras, "[o]perational details that would have put at risk the personnel conducting those operations were not publicly revealed."[55] North simply needed to protect the *policy* of military aid to the Contras by concealing it. Secret policy, contrary to the wishes of the Congress and indeed, as the polls indicated, contrary to the wishes of the American people, must be unacceptable to a democracy, while secret operations need not be.

In the case of the arms sales to Iran, North and Reagan were acting in contravention of Reagan's own stated policy, saying, as he did on June 30, 1985, "The United States gives terrorists no rewards and no guarantees. We make no concessions. We make no deals."[56] The secrecy cloaking the arms-for-hostages deals with Iran was necessary to sustain a policy that the American public would find outrageous, and that the president himself publicly deplored.

The findings requirements of Section 501 of the National Security Act, under the Hughes-Ryan Amendment and the Intelligence Oversight Act of 1980, were designed to guarantee that Congress would indeed be notified of policy initiatives in the covert-operations area "in a timely fashion." In the Iran-Contra affair, necessary findings were not made. Findings were designed to mislead as to the true object of the actions to which they purportedly applied, or to be so broad as to provide no meaningful information, or to attempt to override statutes or basic constitutional provisions, like Congress's control over appropriations. Findings were destroyed, or never provided to Congress.[57]

Section 501 of the National Security Act, if followed in letter and spirit, does provide a way to conduct covert operations consistent with democracy. But Poindexter, North, and Reagan did not understand that. Lies, deceit, violations of the rule of law played a significant role in enabling us to win World War II,[58] and probably must remain accessible as tools of foreign policy. But lies and deceit absolutely cannot be practiced on ourselves, on our own government. The philosophy of North and Poindexter was sharply challenged by Clair George, a veteran of thirty-two years of service with CIA Operations Division, who testified:

> . . . to think that because we deal in lies, and overseas we may lie and we may do other such things, that therefore gives you some permission, some right or some particular reason to operate that way with your fellow employees, I would not only disagree with, I would say it would be the destruction of a secret service in a democracy. . . . I deeply believe with the complexities of the oversight process and the relationship between a free legislative body and a secret spy service, that frankness is still the best and the only way to make it work.[59]

It does not make sense to advocate even some sacrifice of

representative government in the interest of security. The public should not permit, or else should not forgive, executive-branch foreign-policy making run wild, unfettered by congressional consultation and control. The tension between representativeness and efficiency in the service of security tends to be exaggerated. The tension between security, here expressed as government control of information, and the free flow of information may be more real. That latter tension produced the balanced provisions of Section 501, i.e., the requirement for real and meaningful consultation with Congress, or if necessary with only eight key congressional leaders. Sincere adherence to that compromise will honor representativeness while enhancing, not sacrificing, long-term efficiency, as both Shultz and Weinberger testified.[60]

The Iran end of the policy, of course, could hardly have been more harebrained. In that context, and according to the most credible witnesses involved, in many other such contexts, representativeness would not have been the enemy of efficiency.

Executive government has a tendency to try to control the flow of information, a tendency to which Poindexter and North were, in this instance, permitted to give free rein. Naturally, when Congress is not made privy to information about policy, it cannot debate that policy. In this context, the argument more precisely stated calls not for a free flow of information but for some flow of information to select representatives of the representative government. The benefits to be derived, limited though the "flow" may be in this case, nevertheless resemble the benefits John Stuart Mill ascribed to a fully free flow of information in the public marketplace of ideas: The deliberative body can test argument against argument, policy proposal against policy proposal, in an effort to arrive at the best alternative.[61] North and Poindexter claimed the need to shield their policies against partisan prejudice; they really needed to shield their policies against sane and reasonable questioning, under which such policies would not, indeed, have survived, nor should they have.

The Constitution wisely separated the powers of purse and

sword. Whatever technical legal arguments North and Poindexter can construct to justify the financing of policy implementation by the executive branch, independent of Congress,[62] such action violates the constitutional wisdom. Even such a strong advocate of executive power, and of such power in particular in the foreign-relations realm, as Alexander Hamilton warned:

> [T]he history of human conduct does not warrant that exalted opinion of human virtue which would make it wise in a nation to commit interests so delicate and momentous a kind as those which concern its intercourse with the rest of the world to the sole disposal of a magistrate, created and circumstanced, as would be a president of the United States.[63]

The Report of the Congressional Committees Investigating the Iran-Contra Affair concluded with a number of recommendations for change in the laws governing intelligence and covert activities.[64] More important, it concluded that the Iran-Contra affair "resulted from the failure of individuals to observe the law, not from deficiencies in existing law or in our system of government. This is an important lesson to be learned because it points to the fundamental soundness of our constitutional processes."[65] "Thus, the principal recommendations emerging from the investigation are not for new laws but for a renewal of the commitment to constitutional government and sound processes of decisionmaking."[66]

Had the officials involved in the Iran-Contra affair internalized an American constitutional value structure, the scandal could not have happened. Fairness and representativeness, in our system, require a faithfulness to the rule of law, at least within the territorial bounds of the United States. Representative government requires a respect for the institutional role of Congress, and liberty and equality require a respect for representative government.

If the Iran-Contra context appears to give this discussion too partisan a complexion, it should not. John F. Kennedy's Ex-

Com, dealing with the Cuban missile crisis, probably the most dangerous national-security situation the United States has ever faced, would not have been hurt by adherence to the letter and spirit of consultation with congressional leaders subsequently required by Section 501. As it happened, Republican Senator Kenneth Keating of New York was getting sometimes better information than ExCom was getting anyway;[67] the risk of additional leaks that might have been incurred by expanding the core group to include congressional leaders would have been more than offset by the benefits in experience, wisdom, and even relationships: Secretary of Defense Robert McNamara might well have had less trouble with Admiral George Anderson of the navy.[68]

Finally, the argument that Congress owns no more wisdom than the executive misses the point. The fundamental dilemma yields no better answer than consultation: We probably cannot know, in the abstract, whether the necessity for covert operations justifies their morality, or lack thereof, but we can test our theories against each other's arguments. Also, Congress has little ability to push an executive into international hostilities, as Grover Cleveland indicated.[69] Congress today, at best, can be only a brake on executive tendencies toward international conflict. If such conflict is warranted, the executive should, at least, have to persuade Congress. If the executive cannot persuade Congress, privately, of the justification for covert action, or cannot persuade the public, publicly, of the justification for overt action, or will not, then the likelihood of ultimate justification for such hostilities is slim. To guarantee ourselves that valuable safeguard against unwarranted hostilities, we must instill in our future public servants—our Norths and our Poindexters—a better appreciation and understanding of constitutional values.

Strategy, in military affairs, "is the very opposite of morality, as it is largely concerned with the art of deception," but grand strategy, which guides the ultimate purposes for which military affairs are undertaken, "tends to coincide with morality."[70] Executive strategists should at least internalize the constitutional values that will bring them to consult with Congress, whose natural concerns with grand strategy may correct the excesses of those who may have focused too narrowly on military strategy.

An alteration in the statutory structure of information flow, as proposed by Morton Halperin and Daniel Hoffman, would prohibit classification of, and would make "available not only to Congress but to the public," "[i]nformation necessary to congressional exercise of its constitutional powers to declare war, to raise armies, to regulate the armed forces" and so forth.[71] The enemy already knows that American forces are fighting with theirs; the American public should be informed as well. As in the Contra case, those who receive American military assistance do not hide that fact from those whom the American forces oppose; there is, again, no justification for hiding it from congressional leadership, and little justification for withholding it from the American people.[72]

On the other hand, the public does not need specific information about advanced weapons technology or intelligence operations, and Congress ordinarily does not need advance information about the details of military plans.[73] But the balance between security concerns, reflected in executive secrecy, and the free flow of information, necessary for informed dissent and debate, has shifted too far toward the former, and should be shifted back.

VI

First Amendment
Issues

Nazis and the First Amendment

Some aspects of our discussion of the Iran-Contra affair involved an assessment of the conflict between security needs, or the perception of security needs, and the free flow of information necessary for informed debate and dissent. Absent from that discussion was the element of majoritarian opposition to a dissenting message; indeed, a Congress most grievously deprived of information is the most majoritarian institution we have. Free speech, however, often conflicts with representativeness. It conflicts with deference to the will of the majority as expressed in legislation enacted by their representatives.

Security, in the sense of protecting the survival of the nation, supposedly needed to be balanced against dissenting free speech in the Communist party cases cited below in Chapter VII. The legislation in question there, such as the Smith Act rendering Communist party membership illegal, served no function at all in protecting the nation's survival. Similarly, while a few opponents of the Nazis' right to demonstrate feared at least a "potential" threat to the United States,[1] their perception was completely unfounded.[2] Even in Nazi Germany, the responsibility for the rise of the Nazis must rest with those who suppressed speech, not with those who would have protected it, according to the testimony of one refugee from Nazi Germany who was also an official of the American Civil Liberties Union. He noted that a ban by the government of Bavaria against speeches by Hitler served only to enhance his popularity when his supporters distributed "a drawing of Hitler gagged."[3] The Weimar government, notwithstanding the faulty history of those who claim it to have been a defender of free speech, "would occasionally prosecute those who were publicly critical of the descent into Nazism," such as George Grosz, the artist of *Ecce Homo*, for his ferocious paintings and drawings caricaturing the Nazis.[4]

What truly facilitated the growth of the Nazi movement in Germany was the failure of the Weimar government to prosecute the Nazis for their use of murder and assault: "[T]he lesson of Germany in the 1920's is that a free society cannot be established and maintained if it will not act vigorously and forcefully to punish political violence. It is as if no effort had been made in the United States to punish the murderers of Medgar Evers, [and] Martin Luther King. . . ."[5] "The Nazis did not defeat their political opponents of the 1920's through the free and open encounter of ideas. They won by terrorizing and murdering those who opposed them."[6]

So security, in the sense of national survival, is not at stake here. What is at stake here is security in the sense of protection against emotional injury.[7] Fear of some kind of emotional or psychological injury is a kind of "security" interest that underlies legislation intended to bar various kinds of expression. A group like the Skokie Jews, targeted by the Nazis, may also fear actual physical violence, although there was no basis for this fear in Skokie. If anything, there was more danger of violence against the Nazis by outraged Jews.[8] Before we address the emotional injury feared in the Skokie Nazi case, and the legitimacy of the response to it, we will examine the balance, more generally, between the free-expression value and the "representativeness" value that includes, in legislation presumably reflecting the majority will, protection of emotional and psychological security.

In political debate, a particular point of view may be deeply offensive, even frightening. Nonetheless, anyone can hand out leaflets on a public thoroughfare, setting his point of view forth. If he does so, neither an individual citizen nor a legislature can justifiably prevent this action based on the argument that people have a right to go to work without encountering ideas that disturb them. Even ideas that are deeply offensive at any given time may be so only because of transitory prejudice, however widely held. The unregulated "marketplace of ideas" is a traditional concept in American free-speech jurisprudence. Free competition among alternative policies generally should give eventual victory to the best and strongest ideas. Such competition requires constitutional protection for ideas that are unpopular but might, with time, prove meritorious and gain in popularity. Without constitutional protection, popular majoritarian legislative actions could ban the circulation of policy proposals that might eventually compete with the current conventional wisdom. So the majority, represented as it is by the government it selects, must, to use an academic metaphor, take the "required course" of unpopular minority viewpoints.

Sexually explicit photographs play no such role in the process of government unless, of course, they make a political argument of some kind. If so, they are then not primarily prurient in orientation. In response to public pressure on the legislature to address the proliferation of graphically illustrated sex-magazine covers on display in grocery stores in New York, the state Legislature amended the law prohibiting such displays on the street to add a prohibition against such displays "in any place accessible to members of the public without fee or other limit or condition of admission such as a minimum age requirement."[9] This law simply requires covering the pictures in question so that those who wish may avoid encountering them and incurring the kind of emotional or psychological injury they wish to avoid. Others who so desire may continue to locate publications with such pictures on their covers in "adults only" areas, or by their titles if in universally accessible areas. Such sexual material, then, also wins protection under the First Amendment, but as an "elective course": Citizens have a right to buy or sell it (perhaps after meeting a precondition, say, like being an adult) but are not required to encounter it if they do not choose to do so. A citizen accosted with such photographs on a public thoroughfare on his or her way to work does indeed have the right to have the purveyor removed.[10]

Even with respect to graphic sexual material, however, the exercise of competing speech—protest—appears to be a better answer. Protest more effectively pursues both values, free expression and protection of "emotional security"—the community interest in avoiding what it perceives to be emotional or psychological injury. When new management brought X-rated movies to a theater in the present writer's neighborhood, six weeks of daily picketing by a large contingent of neighbors brought enough economic pressure, by virtue of deterring those too shy to face their neighbors as patrons, to force the theater to change hands again, this time to management committed to showing non–X-rated movies. Other potential purveyors of X-rated fare received a clear message that the neighborhood in question was not a good investment for their business. Government may, as noted, properly place some limits on the sale and display of explicit sexual material, but our community action produced a far more satisfying victory as a competing exercise of First Amendment rights in the American constitutional tradition.

For some, perhaps for many, encountering Nazi propaganda
works a far more serious emotional and psychological injury
than any sexual material might inflict. Skokie, Illinois, is a
town whose seventy thousand residents include about thirty
thousand Jews, about one thousand of whom are European ref-
ugees, survivors of the Nazi holocaust.[11] In 1977 and 1978 it
was the subject of a well-publicized and well-litigated threat by
an American Nazi group, the National Socialist Party of America (NSPA), to demonstrate. This may well be the limiting case
in evaluating the balance between a majoritarian decision to
enforce "community security," on the one hand, and the free-
expression rights of a party whose expressions inflict serious
emotional trauma, on the other. The degree of trauma is such
that during the controversy, increases in serious physical ail-
ments, as well as in psychological complaints, were reported
among the Jewish population.[12]

In a serious and thoughtful study of the Skokie affair, Professor Donald Downs argues that the nature of the expression
involved was not such as to merit First Amendment protection.[13] The foundation for his argument is the "fighting words"
doctrine of Justice Frank Murphy's 1942 decision in
Chaplinsky v. *New Hampshire.*[14] Murphy said, "[S]uch utter-
ances are no essential part of any exposition of ideas, and are
of such slight social value as a step to truth that any benefit
that may be derived from them is clearly outweighed by the
social interest in order and morality."[15]

This approach, however, makes the speaker's rights dependent upon the audience's reaction: Impassioned oratory for one
audience may be "fighting words" for another. Thus, the
Court, on a similar theory, upheld the conviction of a Communist orator when he refused a police order to stop talking despite the angry heckling he provoked. The Court asserted that
he had "passe[d] the bounds of argument" and had "undertake[n] incitement to riot. . . ." While the Court denied that it
was permitting the police to be "used as an instrument for the
suppression of unpopular views," it appears that it did just
that.[16] Instead of defending the speaker's right to free expres-

sion, the police arrested him, and the Court gave this response its blessing.

The Court did not adhere to this approach with consistency,[17] and during the civil-rights and Vietnam protests substantially limited its impact. In *Cohen* v. *California*, for example, the Court indicated the inapplicability of the fighting-words doctrine to situations in which the audience had a reasonable avenue of escape from the offensive message.[18] In *Gooding* v. *Wilson*,[19] a black woman who screamed "White son of a bitch, I'll kill you. . . ." at a white police officer was convicted under a statute prohibiting the use, without provocation, of "opprobrious words or abusive language, tending to cause a breach of peace." The Supreme Court found the statute unconstitutionally vague and overbroad because its application would be too dependent on the subjective reactions of the subject of the comments.

The prevailing contemporary rule for political speech appears to be "content neutrality": near-absolute constitutional protection for speech, its offensive nature notwithstanding, as long as it does not constitute a real incitement to imminent and likely illegality, physically obstruct other lawful activity, or impose itself on an audience that wishes to escape and cannot.[20] This reflects the procedural-due-process, "optimalist" approach of the Warren Court,[21] which in the First Amendment area was continued by the Burger Court,[22] has been reaffirmed by the Rehnquist Court,[23] and gives application to the "participation-enhancing" constitutional theory of John Hart Ely,[24] to be discussed in Chapter VIII.

In response to NSPA's statement of intention to demonstrate at Skokie's village hall in protest against the Skokie Park District's denial of a demonstration permit to NSPA, the Skokie Village Board of Trustees enacted three ordinances prohibiting the wearing of the storm-trooper uniform, the distribution of material "which promotes and incites hatred against persons by reason of their race, national origin, or religion, and is intended to do so," and the issuance of permits for demonstrations with similar themes. The latter ordinance also imposed a $350,000 insurance-bond requirement on permitted demonstrations.[25]

The American Civil Liberties Union brought suit challenging the constitutionality of the ordinances, on behalf of the NSPA.[26] The court applied the content-neutrality rule, writing

> The Skokie ordinance punishes language which intentionally incites hatred. This standard is . . . subjective and impossible to clearly define. . . . The distinction between inciting anger with a social condition and hatred of the person or group perceived to be responsible for that condition is impossible to draw with requisite clarity, and depends to a great extent upon the frame of mind of the listeners. . . . A society which values "uninhibited, robust, and wide-open" debate [quoting *New York Times* v. *Sullivan*, 376 U.S. 255, 270 (1964)] cannot permit criminal sanctions to turn on so fine a distinction. . . .[27] [I]t is better to allow those who preach racial hate to expend their venom in rhetoric rather than be panicked into embarking on the dangerous course of permitting the government to decide what its citizens may say and hear. . . .[28] [T]he process of free debate [can] be relied upon to identify false ideas. . . . [G]overnment [can] not. . . .[29]

While Professor Downs agrees that the Skokie ordinances "may indeed have been vague,"[30] and would presumably agree that they may have been unconstitutionally so, he argues that the "content-neutrality" rule has been carried too far in creating a constitutional standard that appears to leave too little room for legitimate, necessary applications of the "fighting words" doctrine in situations, like Skokie, in which the primary thrust of the expression was to cause hurt. He would therefore restore some of the vitality of the *Chaplinsky* decision to foster "the basic communitarian norms of civility and protection which are also legitimate values of the polity."[31]

Specifically, Downs finds justification for restricting expression even in arguably political contexts when a reasonable person would determine that such expression, in the public forum involving race or ethnicity . . . is accompanied by the advocacy of death or violence . . . against that group . . . *or* . . . explicitly demeans or vilifies through reference to race or ethnicity . . . *or* so vilifies or demeans in a symbolic or implicit manner. . . ; *and* [is intended to cause harm, and was without] significant provocation; *and* . . . is directed at an individual, home, neighborhood, or community in such a way as to single out an individual or specified group as the definite target of the expression [emphasis in original].[32]

Downs makes a heroic effort to find a middle path between content neutrality and more restrictive alternatives offered by others. For example, he discusses "an approach to the First Amendment which takes virtue and natural justice into consideration," taken by a scholar who would permit courts to withhold First Amendment protection from speech which is not "consistent with virtue and justice" or "*could tend to* lead to anti-democratic results even in the very long term."[33] Such a standard could, of course, enable government to abridge any speech that threatened its hegemony, and Downs, recognizing this, rejects this standard.[34]

Rather than such a completely open-ended, subjective moral-rights approach, he draws on Kant's prohibition against the treatment of persons as mere means, but takes a "weak" Kantian position, as he calls it, allowing him to retain a large part of the utilitarian defense of free speech based on its special instrumental role in majoritarian democracy.[35] This permits only narrow restrictions on speech, as noted above, when the harm that would otherwise be inflicted purposely and directly on individuals would be great.[36] More fundamentally, he sees at stake "the equality premised on the essential dignity of the individual and the right to be treated in accord with this dignity."[37] Clearly, he rejects Ely's procedural-due-process interpretation of the requirements of equality, for that would support the content-neutral application of First Amendment principles, and calls instead for "substantive due process" protection of an "equal" right to "basic respect":[38] "Accordingly, when speech includes the *context* of targeting and the *content* of racial or ethnic vilification, it should be constitutionally abridgeable in the name of substantive justice."[39]

Unfortunately, such efforts to find a compassionate middle ground do not succeed in escaping the quicksand. When Downs reaches into the muddy waters of intuitionist, moral rights, substantive due process, and comes up, like Dworkin, with murky concepts like an "equal right to basic respect" to justify his propositions, like Dworkin he ends up jeopardizing too much liberty for the chimerical equality he seeks.

There is no way to protect people in a healthy functioning democracy against the emotional and psychological bruises of ferocious political battles without giving government, perhaps representing a temporarily enraged and vicious majority, too much power to repress dissent. The specific proposals Downs recommends, noted above, do this.

No such recommendations can rectify the fundamental flaws in the *Chaplinsky* decision itself. Words that "by their very utterance inflict injury,"[40] and under that ruling may therefore be deprived of constitutional protection, may by the very fact of their emotional power carry a message that cannot be communicated as effectively any other way. "Calling Lyndon Johnson a murderer for his role in the Vietnam War . . . or shouting four-letter words at 'Honkies' as an expression of black frustration and rage, may have moved us faster toward perceiving the truth of those issues than all of the more refined dialogue of the intellectual elites."[41]

Downs's limit on the application of his recommendations to racial or ethnic "vilification" doesn't help much either:

> The Washington Supreme Court admitted as much in *Crown Zellerbach* (*Centreras* v. *Crown Zellerbach Corp.*, 565 P.2d 1173, 1177 [Wash. 1977]) when, after listing all the racial epithets (Wop, Kike, Spick, etc.) that it regarded as currently beyond the pale of decency, it justified that judgment by observing, "changing sensitivity in soci-

ety alters the acceptability of former terms." To subject
people to punishment because they violate the "changing
sensitivities" of a particular community at a particular
time is to place freedom of expression on a precarious footing.[42]

Neither does the "intentionality" requirement solve the
problem. Downs argues that "intent" in this context would be
subject to proof and jury determination as in any other criminal context, and argues that the harm done to people in this
context justifies leaving such judgments to a jury.[43] One must
wonder, however, whether Downs would have been comfortable leaving that aspect of a case to a jury—say, an all-white
one—had Martin Luther King been on trial for intentionally
causing emotional injury to the residents of "the most intol-
erant white neighborhoods" of Chicago when he brought his
marchers there to demonstrate for open housing; "indeed,
there is reason to believe that Dr. King was not unhappy to see
national television news coverage of angry mobs of counter-
demonstrators hurling rocks at him and his supporters."[44]
If all that is left of Downs's prohibitions is the one against
murder or violence, hate groups will probably "clean up their
act" to eliminate any such direct references. In England,
where the Race Relations Act of 1965 has prohibited the cru-
dest forms of verbal assault, "this has been to the advantage of
[a racist leader], for whereas the former virulently racialist
language of his magazines had often alienated people who
might otherwise have subscribed to his views on racial matters, more moderate language had increased the circulation of
his publications."[45] And England, since the enactment of its
Race Relations Act, has been no "freer of racial conflict in the
streets than has the United States."[46]
We do well to heed the warning that only "in the face of the
most extreme—yes even the most odious—challenges," do we
"revitalize our understanding of what we are all about. If we
never hear the questions, we will soon forget the answers."[47]
Professor Downs, in his scrupulously fair presentation, pro-

vides a lengthy and comprehensive account of the ways in which the Skokie affair made substantial contributions to "revitalizing" the "understanding of what we are all about" for various participants, including the Holocaust survivors. Downs recognizes the ways that the conflict contributed to what he calls "republican virtue."[48] Nonetheless, he concludes that "the speech right extend[ed] too far at Skokie despite the beneficial results we found. . . ."[49] His effort to compromise free-expression values in the direction of an intuitionist, moral-rights concern for "equality (of which dignity and respect are constituent parts)"[50] provides his justification for that conclusion. But a Nazi-type government could not survive in a society of free and open debate. Protecting, nurturing, and enhancing that tradition, then, even at the price of emotional injury to individuals from time to time, must be paramount. Our utilitarian jurisprudence dictates a content-neutral protection of political expression, with which there can be no compromise.

Free Speech in Shopping Malls

An interesting and relatively unusual conflict is that between free expression and property. The other conflicts we have examined illustrated conflicts between an American constitutional value on one hand and a universal value, like security or efficiency, on the other. This one takes place between two American constitutional values that command especially strong loyalties in our culture.

American suburban life has changed over the past few decades. The shopping mall has arisen, quite visibly, as a new physical and social institution. In 1950 there were fewer than 100 in the United States; by 1985 there were more than 25,000.[51] This has had some real and potentially enormous impact on the exercise of First Amendment rights by those without the funds necessary to engage in paid advertising. To a significant extent, these malls have replaced the downtown or "Main Street" commercial business districts, where leafleters could cheaply and effectively communicate their messages to the public. Main Street is a public street, publicly owned; malls are privately owned, and under current law, may generally choose to prohibit or expel leafleters if they wish. Legal efforts by organizations wishing to preserve the usefulness of their First Amendment right to distribute leaflets by extending it to shopping malls run up against the property rights of the owners.

Traditional Anglo-American property rights have not, generally, conferred complete and absolute control. Eminent domain and various kinds of government regulations supersede the rights of private property owners. In the free-speech realm, the landmark precedent in this area is *Marsh* v. *Alabama*,[52] in which a company owned an entire town and refused to allow a Jehovah's Witness to proselytize on its property. The Supreme Court held that the company, in that context, was the functional equivalent of a local government and could therefore not abrogate First Amendment rights by removing the Witness. Her First Amendment rights took precedence over the company's property rights: "Ownership does not always mean absolute dominion. The more an owner, for his advantage, opens up his property for use by the public in general, the more do his rights become circumscribed by the statutory and constitutional rights of those who use it. . . ." And whether a town is publicly or privately owned, the public has the same right to expect "that the channels of communication remain free. . . ."[53] One right among the bundle of rights that usually constitute property ownership, the right to exclude persons performing activities disapproved by the owner, had to give way in order for the essential elements of American democracy to function.

When the first shopping-center case came to the Supreme Court, it decided, similarly, that since the center was the "functional equivalent" of the business street in a company town, the owner could not properly prohibit its union from picketing a store in it.[54] In subsequent cases, however, the Court retreated from this position, holding that shopping centers are not sufficiently equivalent to public areas to require the application to them of First Amendment rights.[55] In 1979 the California Supreme Court held that the California constitution protected First Amendment rights in the shopping-center context. The shopping-center owner appealed the decision to the U.S. Supreme Court as a taking of his property without due process, barred by the Fifth and Fourteenth Amendments, and as a forced statement, by virtue of the activity on his property, that he approved of such activity, in violation of his own First Amendment freedom of expression. The U.S. Supreme Court affirmed California's right to prefer the First Amendment rights of expression to property rights, and rejected all the shopping-center owner's arguments, since the First Amendment exercise there did not "unreasonably impair the value or use" of the shopping center and did not coerce the owner into saying or not saying whatever he chose.[56] But the Court in no way indicated that the federal Constitution provided the protection that the California court found in the California constitution. The Court's earlier finding of federal free-speech protection in shopping malls was not to be revived.

In 1980, leafleters from Shad Alliance and Paumonok, organizations opposing the operation of the Shoreham Nuclear Power Plant on Long Island, attempted to hand out their flyers at the Smith Haven shopping mall in Suffolk County, Long Island. This mall is one of only eighteen in New York with over one million square feet of interior space. It covers 97 acres, 85 of them for parking, and contains about 130 stores and businesses. It has permitted various public-service groups to use its premises, from free health clinics to the League of Women Voters to the Scouts, but has never permitted any distribution of leaflets, nor did it permit distribution by Shad Alliance and Paumonok.[57]

In *Shad Alliance* v. *Smith Haven Mall*, the New York Court of Appeals noted that "structurally and functionally, a shopping center is very different from the 'company town' in *Marsh* v. *Alabama* . . ."[58] and is therefore "not the functional equivalent of a government. . . ."[59] The Court of Appeals found no basis in the New York State constitution for going beyond the protection of free speech, as against private property, offered by the federal Constitution.[60] The court argued that for it to read the free-speech provisions of the New York State constitution[61] as impinging on a private party, when there was no precedent or other historical basis for such a reading, would "signify 'a determination by the court that it, instead of the legislature, will settle conflicting interests among citizens. . . ,'"[62] i.e., the conflict between those urging their expression rights and those urging their property rights. "A disciplined perception of the proper role of the judiciary, and, more specifically, discernment of the reach of the mandates of our State Constitution, precludes us from casting aside so fundamental a concept as State action in an effort to achieve what the dissent perceives as a more socially desirable result."[63]

But Chief Judge Sol Wachtler, in dissent, would impose a procedural value, not a particular substantive value: He seeks a process-oriented jurisprudence here, a participation-enhancing, "clearing the channels of change" approach that pursues the vision of participatory democracy more clearly than in any other case we have yet encountered:

Free speech rights are only valuable if there are adequate means of communication available to those who wish to express a view. Inexpensive channels of communication which provide direct access to large numbers of people are often essential for effective expression [citations omitted]. To this end, the distribution of leaflets or handbills in places where people gather has long been recognized as vital for the preservation of a meaningful freedom of speech. . . .

. . . [B]ecause the Mall, though privately owned, has, through its size, nature of use and broad invitation to the public, become the functional equivalent of a traditional public forum, and because a complete denial of access will have a significant adverse effect on the dissemination of ideas in the community, any requirement of state action

under Article I, [section] 8 has been satisfied, and the Mall should not be able to ban the distribution of leaflets on its premises. The mall owner, of course, would be entitled to adopt time, place, and manner restrictions on the leaflet-ting designed to prevent any interference with the commercial functions of the Mall. . . .
. . . In the past, those who had ideas they wished to communicate to the public had the unquestioned right to disseminate those ideas in the open marketplace. Now that the marketplace has a roof over it, and is called a mall, we should not abridge that right.[64]

While this case does not fit under our Third Rule ("No person shall be deprived of the exercise of otherwise available First Amendment rights on the basis of the political point of view expressed in that exercise"), the participatory rights-oriented jurisprudence urged here would certainly support the dissent. However, since the dissent was in fact only a dissent, the next best thing was for the legislature to take up the invitation of the majority to "settle conflicting interests among citizens." As the majority noted, the Supreme Court in *PruneYard* "acknowledged that, in certain circumstances, a State may recognize broader free speech rights as a matter of state law without offending any Federally guaranteed rights enjoyed by the property owner."[65]

Thus, Assembly Bill Number 846, of the 1989–1990 session, introduced by the author, would provide "the right of free speech and the right to petition in the common area of a shopping center containing at least two hundred fifty thousand square feet of gross leasable area," "subject to reasonable time, place, and manner regulations promulgated by the management thereof," and in a way that "shall not unreasonably interfere with such shopping center owner's reasonable investment-backed expectations. . . ."[66] It has not yet become law, but its supporters in the legislature will persist until they prevail.

VII

Organized Crime Control Act

For several years, New York's law-enforcement community energetically supported my legislation to create an Organized Crime Control Act for greater prosecutorial efficiency and effectiveness. New York's civil-liberties community had resisted the enactment of such legislation, regarding it as detrimental to the fair trial process. Their battle exemplified the struggle between fairness and efficiency; the result was a classic and happy compromise.

In 1986, the Organized Crime Control Act (OCCA) became law in New York State, recognizing the newly defined state crime of "enterprise corruption."[1] OCCA, a "little RICO," provides state prosecutors with their version of the powerful federal crimefighting tool, the Racketeer Influenced and Corrupt Organizations (RICO) Act of 1970.[2] State and local prosecutors far outnumber federal prosecutors, and in New York several of each had testified to the need for a state version of this weapon. For all the publicity surrounding the well-known federal cases, most of the work has to be done by state and local prosecutors if it is to be done at all.[3]

The New York law-enforcement community strongly and unanimously endorsed the new New York law, but they preferred earlier drafts to the bill finally enacted.[4] They also preferred the federal prototype and other states' "little RICOs." The final bill, however, cut out the questionable provisions contained in those other existing statutes that engendered a mass of appellate and scholarly criticism.[5]

The press attempted to portray the process that produced this result as a conflict between proponents of a "tough" bill and proponents of a "weak" bill.[6] The reality, of course, was far more complicated and far more interesting. The prosecutors, allied with other law-enforcement personnel and the Republicans who lead the New York State Senate, wanted the powerful tool that is available to prosecutors in other jurisdictions in order to protect New Yorkers most effectively against the physical, financial, and moral harm inflicted by criminals of every kind. The Democrats who lead the New York State Assembly, allied with civil libertarians, wanted to limit the potential for prosecutorial abuse noted in the scholarly literature and protect New York's tradition of fair trial.

But the two sides significantly shared many desirable values. Fairness is a deeply held American value, especially in the trial context, and particularly among government professionals,[7] a category that included both sides in the negotiations. Obviously, government professionals also share an interest in protecting citizens against crime as efficiently as possible, understanding "efficiency" as the most productive use of resources for the optimization of desired values.

Initially, the prosecutors resisted complaints that their proposals raised "fair trial" problems serious enough to require major changes, and the Assembly leadership doubted that fair trials could accommodate the prosecutors' felt need for greater efficiency. The prosecutors doubted the Assembly leadership's commitment to crime-fighting, and the Assembly leadership doubted the prosecutors' commitment to fairness at trial. That the two sides did eventually reach agreement testifies to the reality that they did indeed share values.

The two sides had to travel a considerable distance before reaching agreement, however. At one point in our negotiations, in mid-June 1986, the negotiators identified thirty-one points of disagreement. This was by no means at the beginning of the process. I first introduced a draft of the bill in early 1983, and began suggesting amendments to bring the two sides together shortly thereafter.[8]

The first draft was based in part on federal RICO, under which a defendant may be indicted if he invested in, acquired an interest in or control of, or conducted or participated in an "enterprise" through a "pattern of racketeering activity" consisting of at least two acts of such activity (from among a compendium of possible predicate crimes) committed within ten years of each other.[9]

Our New York law, as it finally emerged, has much more specific requirements, including knowing participation in a criminal enterprise, and three acts of "enterprise corruption," as we call it, two of which must be felonies. There are numerous additional differences from RICO, and from our own first draft.[10] The difficult progress from the first draft to the final draft required resolving many issues separating the prosecutors from the Assembly leadership.

However, one issue—deciding which defendants could be prosecuted together at the same trial, an issue lawyers call "joinder"—really captured the core of the philosophical debate in RICO and OCCA. That issue goes to the heart of the concept that produced federal RICO in the first place, and the resolution of that issue in New York's OCCA was paradigmatic for the way the other issues were resolved.[11] The analysis that follows, of the principles that guided the two sides to agreement, should be useful to those who would replicate our success with this bill or other controversial criminal-justice legislation.

Traditional Joinder Limitations
and Organized Crime

The constitutional right to due process of law requires that guilt remain "individual and personal." From this follows "the right not to be tried en masse" for an agglomeration of distinct and separate offenses committed mostly by others.[12] "It is difficult for the individual to make his own case stand on its own merits in the minds of jurors who are ready to believe that birds of a feather are flocked together."[13] Therefore, joinder rules seek to protect the defendant from the "spillover effect" or transference of guilt from one defendant to another because of the associative link that the prosecution, by joining them together as co-defendants, has created between them.

Joinder was traditionally permitted only when defendants had, by the nature of their own actions, joined themselves together by acting in concert. If the defendants worked on the same crime together, they were deemed to deserve any prejudice toward the one that resulted from association with the other. "The evidence indicates appellants committed the crime in concert, therefore, it is generally proper to try them together."[14]

Conspiracy law did permit prosecutors to go somewhat further. Persons who did not know each other and did not commit the same particular criminal acts could nevertheless be tried together as co-conspirators if there was "a single agreement to commit one or many crimes." For a conspiracy charge to succeed, prosecutors had to show that one particular agreement defined the shape of the conspiracy.[15]

The adoption of the corporate structure enabled organized

crime to take advantage of these principles and escape even the broader conspiracy basis for joinder: "A single agreement or common objective cannot be inferred from the commission of highly diverse crimes by apparently unrelated individuals."[16] Prosecutors found this a serious bar to making organized crime cases. Presumably, organized-crime groups do not generally spell out conspiracy agreements, nor would they make them available to prosecutors if they did. Instead, courts have looked to certain metaphors to define a complex, multiparty conspiracy.

The "chain" conspiracy requires mutual interdependency within each link, knowledge of the existence of remote links, and awareness of a single unified purpose. The "wheel" conspiracy involves independent individuals or groups ("spokes") dealing with a common figure ("hub") and requires interaction and agreements between the spokes in relation to a common illegal object.[17] Either has characteristics that may not exist in the context of highly diversified organized-crime activity.

Subgroups or cells may be kept separate from each other, and may yet commit crimes that help the overall organization. A gambling operation and an illicit drug-selling operation, for example, could each provide emergency cash reserves for the other through some central higher-up coordinating body without the membership of one operation ever meeting the membership of the other. Furthermore, higher-level beneficiaries of criminal acts and participants in lower-level operations need never meet each other.[18]

Given the traditional restrictions on joinder and rules of conspiracy, prosecutors were barred from presenting some large-scale and particularly awesome patterns of criminal activity at one trial, before one jury. "A prosecution concerned only with convicting an individual for one underlying offense deemphasizes the crime's severity when committed by a member of a criminal group as part of a pattern of racketeering activity."[19] As a result, juries were not in a position to make accurate assessments of the impact of certain criminal organizations, since their operations could never be portrayed fully and in context to the same set of jurors.

From the perspective of fairness to defendants at trial, the pre-RICO law worked fairly well. Defendants who were not working toward the same specific criminal goals and who did not know of each other's existence could not be indicted together and made to stand trial together as co-defendants in the same case. Such defendants, therefore, would not suffer from jury prejudice against one based on the moral turpitude of another.

However, this protected the fairness value only to a limited extent. After all, defendants who did commit crimes together and who therefore could face trial together might well be of significantly different levels of criminality, with one somewhat unfairly making the other look worse to the eyes of a jury. The pre-RICO joinder restrictions prohibited such unfairness only when the defendants did not act in concert. Therefore, legislators and others legitimately questioned the cost of this marginal protection of the fairness value in terms of the efficient pursuit of other generally held social values.

The costs were considerable. First, and less significant, holding several trials instead of one cost extra time and money. This was simply and clearly inefficient. Second, and more significant, prosecutors couldn't display to juries the complete picture of an organized-crime operation, and therefore couldn't show the true extent and nature of the harms in question. Two defendants who knowingly played key roles in a criminal organization that benefited them both but was purposely structured to withhold their identities from each other could not be indicted and prosecuted together. Thus, society's interest in optimizing desired values, including fair trials but also including the protection of citizens against criminals through effective prosecutions of organized crime, was not well served by the pre-RICO joinder law.

The RICO Response and the
Response to RICO

In the late 1960s, the public became much more aware of the scope of organized crime and became very concerned about the vulnerability of legitimate business to its predations.[20] When the ordinary business owner, for example, discovered that a competing organization was in fact an organized-crime subsidiary capable of using terror tactics to make its point, calling the police was not a very attractive alternative to compliance. In the ordinary case, at best the complainant could hope for criminal convictions against some participants, usually low-level ones, followed by prison terms for those participants. The criminal organization, however, normally continued to pursue its goals, if not against the same business owner, then against others. If the convicted participants ranked high enough in the criminal organization, they might have continued to direct its operations from prison. If, as was more likely, they were only "soldiers" or "associates," others would replace them. When they emerged from prison, they might be promoted. While they served time, their immediate families would be supported.[21]

In response to this threat and other damage to society attributable to organized crime, Congress in 1970 enacted RICO. Combatting "the infiltration of legitimate business by organized crime" was its primary purpose.[22] Its drafters, foremost among them G. Robert Blakey, well understood how organized crime had benefited from traditional joinder rules, and attacked that problem head-on. Thus, instead of the "single agreement to commit one or many crimes" required by *Braverman*,[23] a RICO-defined "enterprise" indictment recognized a connective link among the defendants, sufficient for a joint trial, from alleged common involvement through "a pattern of racketeering activity."[24]

Thus, RICO became a highly effective enforcement response to the evolutionary step in the character of crime that had occurred by the 1930s with organized crime's adoption of the corporate structure. Prior to RICO, prosecutors could be barred from demonstrating to a jury the scope and context of an organized-crime operation. Prior to its enactment, the argument that defendants were involved in several different conspiracies, not one, and that prosecuting them together could work to the substantial prejudice of their rights, could well have persuaded the judge to chop the indictment into several different cases, to the great detriment of the prosecution when attacking one single criminal organization. "Prior to the enactment of the RICO statute," said the court in *Elliott*, "this argument would have been more persuasive." But "[t]he RICO net," said the court, "is woven tightly to trap even the smallest fish."[25]

RICO was without question a brilliant and major step forward. Like other important innovations, however, it was criticized for doing too much, particularly in the expansive way in which it has been interpreted.[26] The critics have all argued, *inter alia*, a point that then Assembly Codes Committee counsel Jim Yates, representing the Assembly leadership, made forthrightly in 1983 in response to early drafts of the New York bill: "It's two misdemeanors, a felony, and a coat of paint." The pattern requirement in our early drafts and in the federal law, he claimed, was so loose as to be no requirement at all. Such a pattern could include a very wide-ranging assortment of unrelated acts and actors. Under the federal law and our earliest drafts, he argued, prejudicial joinder could take place with very little justification in the action of the defendants themselves. Defendants whose own actions had not in any meaningful way "joined themselves together" could be joined together by prosecutors using RICO.

Traditional joinder and conspiracy principles required interdependence among the criminal actions making up the crime or conspiracy. In order to charge the defendants jointly, the various criminal actions on which the charges were based had to add up to one overall scheme. Scholars and judicial critics contrast such "interdependence" requirements[27] with RICO's "pattern" requirement, construed by many courts not to require interrelationship among the predicate acts.[28] While most courts require that the predicate crimes be related to the affairs of the "enterprise,"[29] they cannot very well require that the enterprise be anything much if "enterprise" is defined as the group of people that got together to commit the acts charged.[30]

By the time *Elliott* was decided in 1978, a transformation

in the understanding of RICO had taken place. Notwithstanding periodic recognition that the principal goal of RICO, as enacted in 1970, had been to prevent the infiltration of legitimate business by organized crime,[31] courts now often read the "enterprise" element to include those whose "patterns of racketeering activity" are simply their method of doing business in the course of conducting their own, criminal enterprise.[32] Thus, the Fifth Circuit broadly defined the "bare essentials" of a RICO charge as follows: "Being associated with a group of individuals who were associated in fact, [the defendants] each directly and indirectly participated in the group's affairs through the commission of two or more predicate crimes."[33]

Commentators often criticize the "illegal enterprise" theory because of the paradoxical effect of eliminating the independent significance of the "enterprise" element. Where the infiltration of legitimate business occurs, the legitimate business "host" assures the continuous criminal scheme. But, "[i]n contrast, an illegal operation generally includes a group of people with a constantly changing membership, a loose organizational structure, and a stop and start existence. Frequently, the mere existence of an illegal enterprise does not supply continuity because, unlike a stable, continuing business, the parties to an illegal operation are likely to come together temporarily for single purpose ventures."[34]

Thus, the possible elimination of the "enterprise" element threatens the connective link in which RICO defendants should be commonly participating for joinder purposes. The statute, so construed, allows for unfair joinder, and further provides the basis for Yates's more general complaint that OCCA, in its earlier forms, might likewise have been a "coat of paint" providing harsher penalties for no more than the particular underlying crimes proved.[35]

From the point of view solely of efficiency, RICO works extremely well. Groups of criminals, even if loosely linked, can be prosecuted at a single trial, in the course of which each connecting link between criminals can be shown. The full and complete picture of criminal activity can be presented to a jury with no exceptions for defendants who may not have known or worked directly with other defendants. At the prosecutor's discretion, potential defendants may be dropped from the case and convinced to testify against their fellows instead of facing indictment themselves, while the defendants to whom they are the only link may nonetheless be forced to stand trial.[36] While prosecutors may not always use this tool, it does give them the ability, at least in theory and often in practice, to conduct their cases with great efficiency.

From the perspective of fairness at trial, RICO leaves a lot to be desired.[37] In theory, and arguably in practice, RICO may be used to obtain convictions in mass trials of defendants who would not otherwise have been convicted, were it not for the prejudicial presence of their co-defendants. A minor criminal, tried on his own, would likely elicit from a jury no more than a conviction on an appropriately minor charge. The same "little fish," branded a racketeer and linked by a RICO indictment to defendants who are more obviously, easily, and accurately portrayed as racketeers, may be seen by a jury in a more ominous light and may receive accordingly harsher penalties. For similar reasons, the American Law Institute Model Penal Code recommends conspiracy joinder provisions similar to the pre-OCCA New York State joinder rules.[38]

Since under RICO defendants need not know their co-defendants, need not have worked toward a common specific criminal purpose with them, and in most jurisdictions[39] apparently need not even have known of or benefited from their common participation in an overall organization, RICO is not consistent with the tradition of fair joinder. Generally, fairness requires that if a defendant is to suffer in the eyes of a jury from his associations with others, he must have knowingly done something with those others in the expectation of criminal gain.

Negotiating Joinder

As noted above, even my initial 1983 draft of OCCA, prepared by the New York State attorney general's office with the blessing of New York State prosecutors generally, in many respects responded to the criticism that RICO did not comport with notions of fairness at trial. The American Bar Association had issued a list of criticisms of RICO, with recommendations for reform, and the prosecutors had incorporated a number of those recommendations in our first draft. Thus, the prosecutors accepted the basic legitimacy of the "fairness at trial" value. The Bar Association recommendations they adopted included requirements that at least one triggering criminal act be a felony, that the criminal activity have taken place within five years of prosecution (instead of ten, as in RICO), and that the predicate acts must have occurred in separate incidents.[40] These requirements were at the expense of prosecutorial efficiency and in the interest of fairness at trial.

The prosecutors came to the negotiations, however, feeling that they had already arrived at a reasonable balance between fairness at trial and prosecutorial efficiency, with the exception of a few points that they were willing to concede readily and early in the negotiations.[41] They tended to discount the seriousness of the Assembly leadership's concern that some members of the prosecutorial community might use the liberal joinder provisions of RICO-like early drafts of OCCA to gain convictions through prejudicial mass trials of some defendants against whom convictions could not otherwise be obtained. The prosecutors who actually negotiated the bill assumed that other prosecutors shared their own real commitment to fair-trial values. Given their assumption that prosecutorial abuse was therefore unlikely, they felt that narrowing the joinder provisions unnecessarily sacrificed an additional measure of efficiency.

The success of the Assembly leadership in persuading the prosecutors to accept additional sacrifices in the interest of fair-trial values, rested on their convincing demonstration of serious concern that such values were still jeopardized in early drafts. Without question, those persuasive efforts were greatly assisted by their making it clear that there would be no agreement at all otherwise, and the prosecutors would get nothing.

At the same time, the prosecutors were not prepared to settle too cheaply. At least one of their principals, a highly prominent and influential district attorney, had garnered considerable media attention by attacking the Assembly leadership for balking at this legislation, and seems to have been prepared to continue doing so had the negotiations failed. For its part, the Assembly leadership had some interest in answering charges against itself of insufficient concern for the needs of prosecutorial efficiency, and so had its own incentive to negotiate to an agreement.

Still, the Assembly leadership came to the negotiations doubting, to some extent, the real need to increase prosecutorial efficiency in this manner, and skeptical whether it could do so without making serious sacrifices of fair-trial values. The Assembly leadership, reacting to criticisms of RICO, took pride in New York's relatively strict "pre-RICO" joinder rules and valued those rules as a bulwark of fair-trial values. The fact that the Assembly leadership finally accepted a significant liberalization of those rules demonstrated its own commitment to prosecutorial efficiency (once the prosecutors convinced Assembly representatives that prosecutorial efficiency really required such liberalization) and the prosecutors' skill in arguing that fair-trial values would not thereby be seriously jeopardized.

Finding a compromise that enhanced prosecutorial efficiency without jeopardizing fair-trial values recalled charting the course between Scylla and Charybdis.

In January 1985, the prosecutors and I willingly responded to Assembly leadership concerns by amending the then-current draft, A.229, to add to the "pattern" definition the requirement that persons who committed the three requisite predicate acts must, for indictment as co-defendants in an OCCA prosecution, also be associated in a criminal enterprise. A "criminal enterprise" would be defined as "an enterprise with purposes that include engaging in criminal activity as that term is defined [in the substantive list of predicate crimes in OCCA]."[42] This would exclude the joint charging of individuals related to each other through some legitimate business or association.[43] Every subsequent draft of OCCA, including the final law, rested heavily on a definition of criminal enterprise.

This was far from enough to satisfy Assembly leadership concerns. What, indeed, did our "criminal enterprise" requirement entail? Neither under the amended 1985 bill (A.229B) nor under the federal RICO Act would the prosecution have to show that the defendants knew each other or knew any one defendant in common, nor would they have to show associations through a traditional "wheel" conspiracy with a central leader and subordinate "spokes," or even a "chain" conspiracy with mutual interdependency and a common goal.[44] Jim Yates objected that "Tinkertoy" connections would still suffice for prosecutions under this draft: In 1980, A committed a crime with B; in 1979, B committed a crime with C; in 1978, C committed a crime with D; in 1977, D committed a crime with E, so now a prosecutor can make them all defendants (except, say, D, who is now a witness for the prosecution) in one grand OCCA trial, since the criminal enterprise is composed of and defined by the various crimes. Of course, each defendant would have to have committed three "related" crimes under our bill, but Yates's point that each defendant need have associated with only one of the possible co-defendants was well taken. (For a graphic comparison of the effects of RICO and OCCA on a real organized crime group and on a "Tinkertoy" group, see the chart at the end of this chapter.)

So in A.229D (the "D print," or the fifth draft of what started the 1985–1986 session as A.229 and went through amendments transforming it into A.229A, A.229B, and so forth), the definition of "criminal enterprise" was changed to "a group or association of persons engaged in criminal activity and having a continuity of existence, structure, and criminal purpose beyond the scope of individual criminal incidents." This would guarantee that the criminal enterprise, to the extent it provided linkage, would reflect serious and significant interconnections among its participants. The criminal enterprise would have purpose beyond the particular crimes alleged in the indictment.

However, although the D print now defined the criminal enterprise in a way that made it a real entity, the requirement linking the potential defendant to that entity was still weak. Section 460.10(4) of the D print expressed the linkage requirement by defining "pattern of criminal activity," the triggering phrase for indictment under the act, to include the three requisite crimes performed "with intent to further the common scheme or plan or with knowledge of the criminal enterprise." Knowledge, Yates argued, and I agreed, was a weak and vague standard. The "bottom line" for the Assembly leadership became the following standard: The three requisite crimes had to have been performed "with intent to participate in or advance the affairs of the criminal enterprise."

This, to me, refined the law to where it should be. Organized crime had profited from joinder principles by use of the cell structure, allowing criminals who really did benefit from their position of cooperation with other criminals to avoid being tried with those other criminals by purposely maintaining artificial separations, by never dealing directly with their counterparts. Federal RICO knocked down the joinder wall, but knocked it down a little too far: Minor figures who did not really know of or intend to advance the affairs of the criminal enterprise could also be tried together with more destructive defendants. Now we struck the right balance: If a defendant knowingly benefited from participation in a structured criminal operation, even if he or she didn't personally know his co-defendants or commit the same particular crimes with them, that defendant had joined himself in fact in the operation, and no proper legal principle should bar his joinder in law. But there were to be no exceptions: For a prosecutor to charge defendants with enterprise corruption, he or she had to prove the separate criminal-enterprise connection among the defendants whether they had conducted a criminal enterprise or infiltrated or controlled a legitimate one.

Accepting the uniformity of this standard was the hardest pill for the prosecutors to swallow. They had hoped to replicate the federal model for prosecutions involving the corruption of legitimate enterprise. The two sides left the negotiations without agreement on this issue, knowing that if the prosecutors finally refused to accept the Assembly position, all our efforts would have been in vain.

First, though, we had reached a tentative agreement on one other point. We split the difference between the Assembly leadership's desire to require all the defendants to be chargeable under existing New York joinder rules,[45] and the prosecutors' desire to avoid any such requirement: Each defendant would have to have been joinable with at least one other defendant under existing joinder rules, so that, for example, the two of them might have committed particular crimes together.[46]

Conclusion

On June 26, 1986, after obtaining the Assembly leadership's agreement to pass some technical corrections to A.229E and some language making clearer what the Assembly felt was already the bill's effect, that is, that its provisions could be used against those in a criminal enterprise who were attempting to corrupt legitimate organizations, the Law Enforcement Council, the prosecutors' official voice for this purpose, released a letter unanimously endorsing our bill.[47] With additional changes for three typographical errors, it was renumbered A.11726 on July 1. On July 2 at midnight, the Assembly passed it, as did the Senate about three hours later, on the last day of that legislative session. A little over three weeks later, with the governor's signature, it became law.

In August 1988, a New Jersey jury acquitted twenty defendants in a federal RICO prosecution after a twenty-one-month trial.[48] One influential editorial page opined, "The mere presence of so many defendants and lawyers in one courtroom guaranteed an atmosphere of disorder and distraction."[49]

That acquittal suggests that perhaps we didn't lose very much efficiency in striving for more fairness. Prosecutors seeking larger and larger racketeering cases may reach a point of diminishing returns. This may provide yet another example of the felicity of American constitutional values, with fairness complementing efficiency, just as, in the foreign-policy discussion in Chapter V, we found dissent complementing security.[50]

With experience, we may be able to develop an even better law. As of now, however, New York has an Organized Crime Control Act, a powerful and effective crime-fighting tool that meets the highest constitutional standards of due process and fair trial.

Fairness and Efficiency
of Various Joinder Models

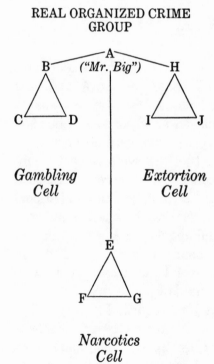

REAL ORGANIZED CRIME
GROUP

A ("Mr. Big")
B   H
C   D   I   J

Gambling
Cell

Extortion
Cell

E
F   G

Narcotics
Cell

DOUBTFUL ORGANIZED
CRIME GROUP
("Tinkertoy Joinder")

A+B B+C 1979

1981,
1980

C+D   D+E 1977
1978

1975 F+G   E+F 1976

1974 G+H   H+I 1973

Here F is "Mr. Big" and is given immunity. Dates indicate when the predicate crimes were committed.

Has continuity of existence, structure, and criminal purpose beyond the scope of individual criminal incidents. Individual participants are tightly connected with the organization: Each has performed these crimes "with intent to participate in or advance the affairs of the criminal enterprise." However, members of one cell do not know members of other cells, and are not involved in planning particular criminal schemes with other cells.

Each participant has committed two criminal acts. All the criminal acts, taken together, constitute a "pattern of racketeering activity."

PRE-RICO: Somewhat fair, inefficient

3 trials: A-B-C-D, A-E-F-G, A-H-I-J

FAIRNESS: A, B, C, and D joined together, or at least conspired together, willingly and knowingly, to plan or commit particular crimes. If D looks worse than he is in the eyes of a jury because of his association with A, it's his own fault.

EFFICIENCY: Society will not be able to have a jury, its representatives, examine the operations of those

PRE-RICO: Somewhat fair, inefficient

5 trials, at minimum: A-B, C-D, E, G, H-I

FAIRNESS, EFFICIENCY: No one can be tried with anyone he or she doesn't know or share particular criminal goals with.

interconnected crime groups at one trial, and will be unable to assess accurately the overall impact of the organization. Therefore it may be unable to impose appropriate penalties, and may thus lose excessive resources to the organization's predations. Also, three trials cost more than one.

RICO: Unfair, very efficient

One trial

FAIRNESS: A can be persuaded to testify against everyone else in return for immunity. Although B, C, and D know no one else who will be indicted with them, they may suffer prejudice from those associations.

EFFICIENCY: Society can examine the entire scope of this criminal organization, to society's benefit.

RICO: Unfair, very efficient

One trial, or maybe two, if A's acts are especially minor— except in the Eighth Circuit, where five trials may again be required after *U.S.* v. *Anderson,* 626 F.2d 1358 (1980)

FAIRNESS: A never heard of E or G but may suffer prejudice by association as E and G's co-defendant.

EFFICIENCY: Society can try all of these crimes at once, and increase the likelihood of each defendant's conviction.

OCCA: Somewhat fair, somewhat efficient

One trial

OCCA: Somewhat fair, somewhat efficient

Five trials

FAIRNESS: Each defendant voluntarily worked with at least one other defendant, and knowingly joined with all the others to aid a criminal organization to achieve its goals.

EFFICIENCY: Society can show the entire scope of this criminal organization in one trial, unless it prefers to grant a major actor immunity in return for information.

FAIRNESS: No one can be tried with anyone with whom he has not voluntarily joined in aiding a criminal organization to achieve its goals.

EFFICIENCY: When the defendants are not meaningfully linked to each other, society must provide separate trials.

PART THREE

Competing Theories of American Government

VIII

Constitutional Theory

With the constitutional tradition so powerful a force, the way Americans resolve many key issues depends on the way we interpret the Constitution. Constitutional theory, then, far from being a dry and dusty subject, actually affects critical issues in the lives of Americans: working conditions, birth control, voting rights, crime and punishment, among many others.

From the late nineteenth century until 1937, the Supreme Court struck down as unconstitutional hundreds of state laws, enacted by state legislatures, regulating working conditions. The Court based these decisions on the general theory that depriving a business of the right, say, to hire children for fourteen-hour workdays seven days a week took away from both the business and the children their respective rights to enter contracts. Since legislatures took away these "rights" without trials and, in the Court's opinion, without adequate justification, the Court decided that they were taken away without "due process of law." In a well-known example, *Lochner* v. *New York*,[1] the Supreme Court decided to strike down a New York statute that forbade bakeries signing workers to contracts requiring more than ten-hour workdays.

In reality, the Court was imposing its economic theory on the nation. The Court may have argued that it found the process used to enact these laws inadequate, but in truth, the Court was rejecting the substance of the legislation, not the process that produced it. Legal scholars call this kind of jurisprudence "substantive due process," when the Court imposes its economic or social views through its power of judicial review of legislation,[2] as opposed to "procedural due process," in which the Court is truly concerned with procedure and process values, not substance.

By 1937, the Court was regularly overturning federal New Deal legislation passed by Congress at the urging of President Franklin Roosevelt, as well as state legislation. Roosevelt, frustrated and angry, tried to get Congress to increase the size of the Court beyond its nine members to enable Roosevelt to appoint enough new members sympathetic to his own views to form a new majority. Congress refused, but the Court seemed to get the message, and became much less aggressive in striking down social-welfare legislation.

In 1938, for example, in a decision typical of its new stance, *United States* v. *Carolene Products*,[3] the Court refrained from striking down the Federal Filled Milk Act, which prohibited the interstate shipment of fake milk made from skim milk and nondairy fat products. The *Carolene Products* decision would be virtually forgotten but for its fourth footnote, probably the best-known footnote in legal scholarship. In that footnote, Justice (later Chief Justice) Harlan Fiske Stone addressed the question of when the Court should be more aggressive in overturning legislation by finding it unconstitutional:

There may be a narrower scope for operation of the presumption of constitutionality when legislation appears on its face to be within a specific prohibition of the Constitution, such as those of the first ten amendments, which are deemed equally specific when held to be embraced within the Fourteenth.

It is unnecessary to consider now whether legislation which restricts those political processes which can ordinarily be expected to bring about repeal of undesirable legislation, is to be subjected to more exacting judicial scrutiny under the general prohibitions of the Fourteenth Amendment than are most other types of legislation.

Nor need we enquire whether similar considerations enter into the review of statutes directed at particular religious, or national, or racial minorities: whether prejudice against discrete and insular minorities may be a special condition, which tends seriously to curtail the operation of those political processes ordinarily to be relied upon to protect minorities, and which may call for a correspondingly more searching judicial inquiry.[4]

The "political processes" references of the fourth footnote suggested some solutions to what became the central problem of constitutional interpretation: If the Court could not or should not impose its substantive views of society through judicial review, how should it apply the Constitution? What "neutral principles," not biased toward one or another ideology or socioeconomic theory, could guide the Court in applying the nonspecific, open-ended provisions of the Constitution, like the due-process or equal-protection clauses of the Fourteenth Amendment?[5]

The fourth footnote influenced at least two modern responses to the problem, with subtle but important differences between them. With the "optimalist" approach of John Hart Ely and Chief Justice Earl Warren, the Court, in deciding whether to intervene between legislatures and the public, leaned more toward intervention when necessary to prevent the exclusion of groups and individuals from the political process. Under the "functional contract" approach of Alexander Meiklejohn and Justice William Brennan, the Court would go further, making participation in the political process not just a value to be weighed more heavily, but the central value of the nation, in order to make government by the people as real as possible.

At least three other major approaches offer themselves. Justices Felix Frankfurter and John Marshall Harlan took the "realist" approach, deferring to legislative judgment whenever possible. Robert Bork also claims that approach.

Liberal natural-rights and moral-rights theorists like Ronald Dworkin rejected the call for neutral principles, and supported the unabashed new liberal "substantive due process" jurisprudence of Justice William O. Douglas. The "individualistic contract" of Justice Hugo Black sought the protection of individual liberties as the highest priority of the Court, for their own sake, more than for the sake of self-government by the people.[6]

No such taxonomy can fully capture the jurisprudence of a prolific and intellectually creative justice. Brennan, for example, fits into the functional-contract category much of the time, and I will follow Professor Edelman in so categorizing him. But Brennan spoke as a liberal substantive-due-process advocate in arguing that the death penalty must always be prohibited as cruel and unusual punishment.[7] Nonetheless, the categories make for easier intellectual handling and are generally and roughly, if not always, correct.

These approaches can be split and grouped a different way. The optimalists (Ely and Warren) and the realists (Harlan, Frankfurter, and Bork) share a view of American democracy that practically scoffs at the notion that we govern ourselves in any serious way beyond merely voting for our leaders. They note that fierce conflicts among well-organized interest groups characterize our political process and produce public policy. They therefore reject as unrealistic the old view of American democracy as a sort of New England town meeting, in which citizens argue, debate, and finally agree on considered policy judgments. They see that most citizens will, at best, vote, choosing among candidates for leadership who have themselves worked out policy positions with interest groups. Since voting (i.e., choosing which group of leaders shall lead) constitutes the only real remaining part of self-government for citizens, the realists and the optimalists want to give the legislative branch, the part of government most directly controlled by voters, as much power as possible. That is why Harlan, Frankfurter, and Bork frequently urged the Court to avoid overturning legislation. While Ely would give, and Warren did give, the Court more leeway in overturning legislative decisions that make the legislative process less representative of the people, as in voting rights, dissent, and reapportionment cases, they also gave some deference to legislators because legislatures at their worst are more accountable to voters than is the Supreme Court.

Hugo Black, also, the individualistic-contract theorist, limited judicial intervention to where it was needed to protect individual rights, more than to assure full-fledged citizen participation in self-government. He, too, seemed to think judicial deference to legislatures protected democracy better than judicial intervention overturning legislative decisions in order to guarantee fuller political participation, although he would do the latter when he thought it necessary to protect the individual.

The liberal substantive-due-process theorists, like Dworkin and Douglas, care relatively little about deference to the voter and thus to legislatures. They happily give the Court the power to impose its views on justice over the contrary views of legislatures. They happily give the Court the power to impose its views on justice over the contrary views of legislatures. In doing so, they neither nurture citizen participation to restore New-England-town-meeting notions of democracy, nor defer to legislatures to safeguard the power of that branch of government most accountable to the voter at the next election.

The functional-contract theorists, Meiklejohn and Brennan, operate out of the premise that if citizens don't argue, debate, consider, and produce public policy themselves, they should and can. They were far more willing to have the Court override legislatures when legislatures tried to limit the power of the citizen to examine the range of policy alternatives and to impose his or her will on those in government. Meiklejohn and Brennan, therefore, gave the most reliable support to voting rights and to dissent.

Realist Theory

It may be consoling to see this process as a real-life version of the Benthamite utilitarian calculus. If voters really pick the parties who best further their interests, victory will go to those who reflect as nearly as possible the net aggregate of the voters' interests. However, the reality at best provides only a rough approximation of this model, since distinctions among candidates' policies are often unclear, and voters often choose candidates even when they know they do not share their policy preferences and interests.

Since, in this theory, only the vote connects the public to their government, democracy depends heavily on protecting the power and role of the legislatures, those representative institutions that voters control most directly. Thus, realist theorists would use judicial review very sparingly, since the voters have relatively little influence on the Court, in this view an antidemocratic institution. Justice Felix Frankfurter, an adherent of this view, said simply, "Courts are not designed to be a good reflex of a democratic society."[8] In the extreme version of this view, the electoral process, not constitutional rules, provides all necessary political protection for freedom. Courts, then, merely intrude into the democratic process.

Thus, when Congress made membership in the Communist party illegal under the Smith Act in 1950, it abridged freedom of expression. But for Harlan and Frankfurter, that was an acceptable decision by Congress to balance the interests involved: free speech and assembly on one side, and national security on the other.[9] They took similar positions in the cases in which prosecutions of NAACP members under various state laws came to the Court.[10] Thus, it was up to "politically elected officials" to decide how much political freedom citizens should have, just as it was up to them to make other policy decisions.

Frankfurter and Harlan would even leave the rules of the political election to the politically elected officials: They resisted efforts to involve the Court in reviewing malapportionment cases, describing reapportionment as a "political thicket" best left to politicians, not courts.[11]

In searching for "neutral principles," Robert Bork finds only the "original intention" of the Framers of the Constitution, arguing that any alternative gives judges too much power to make policy. However, given the unlikelihood that the Framers intended such an extreme degree of control over the future,[12] Bork's "realist" theory would seem to leave some room to include what Bork himself would *hope* the Framers intended. Bork explicitly rejects a natural-rights theory, and he certainly rejects the functional-contract theory. Unlike Meiklejohn, he would have followed Frankfurter and Harlan in the Communist party cases, where membership in the party was illegal.[13]

But Bork appears to be even less sympathetic than Frankfurter and Harlan to the argument for the protection of "political" speech for Communist party members. He not only rejects the need for a showing of "clear and present danger" to justify suppression, he rejects the need for any kind of balancing test with respect to the Communist party case defendants. Membership in the Communist party was illegal. For Bork, once the legislature has deemed something illegal, doing it violates the legitimate decisionmaking process. In his view that process is completed in the legislature.[14] Bork doesn't consider that such activity could be necessary to create the public debate that will eventually show the law in question to have been unwise.

The functional-contract theory, of which more later, teaches that the use of political rights benefits everyone, by bringing the widest possible range of choices to the attention of the decisionmaking majority. Bork ignores this. For him, constitutional rights function in a zero-sum game: If some citizens gain rights, others must lose an equivalent quantum.[15] Bork's opposition to the functional-contract theory goes deep and to its roots in Mill: At one point, he notes sarcastically, ". . . one may complain today that the Constitution did not adopt John Stuart Mill's *On Liberty*."[16]

Like Harlan and Frankfurter, Bork rejects Court intervention in reapportionment cases: He scoffs at a "right to equality" beyond what he sees as the specific racial-equality intentions of the Fourteenth Amendment drafters, and he rejects the idea that the Article IV, Section 4, guarantee of a republican form of government requires the one-person one-vote rule.[17] He does find readily discoverable the intention of the Fourteenth Amendment drafters to bar state-enforced discrimination based on race, and thus justifies the decision in the great 1954 school desegregation case, *Brown* v. *Board of Education*.[18] He finds no comparably "discoverable" constitutional principle barring discrimination when not enforced by the state.[19]

Bork is probably at his strongest when attacking Douglas's opinion for the Court in *Griswold* v. *Connecticut*,[20] the famous "privacy" decision striking down laws banning contraceptives—the case that laid the groundwork for the later *Roe* v. *Wade*[21] abortion decision. In *Griswold*, the plaintiff challenged his conviction, asserting the unconstitutionality of a Connecticut statute prohibiting the disbursement of contraceptives even to married couples. Justice Douglas "discovered" that the privacy-related aspects of the First, Third, Fourth, and Fifth Amendments, together with the "reserved powers" provision of the Ninth, cast "penumbras," shadows, out of which an "independent" right to privacy emerged,[22] on the basis of which he found the Connecticut law unconstitutional.

Bork noted:

> The Court, we may confidently predict, is not going to throw constitutional protection [of like kind] around heroin use or sexual acts with a consenting minor.[23]

On the basis of what neutral principles could Douglas limit

this new right of privacy to cases like *Griswold?* Could it be said to apply only to married couples? To the use of contraceptives? To sex?

Bork had good support here from Justice Black's dissent. Black conceded immediately that the Connecticut statute was not only ill-advised but "offensive." But he found no basis for holding it unconstitutional. Black excoriated the kind of natural-law reasoning Douglas used "on the basis of the court's appraisal of what laws are unwise or unnecessary," and invoked the specter of pre-1937–style substantive due process.[24]

Another theoretical school, the optimalists, like Bork, rejects the right to privacy as discovered by Douglas "out of nowhere"[25] in *Griswold.* Nonetheless, they are able to find a principled basis for more political expression than Bork can accommodate, based on the need to guarantee the fair and proper workings of the mechanisms of democratic choice to which Bork is so deferential. Bork, however, remains a purist, unwilling to enter upon that slippery slope of judicial intervention beyond what he sees as the clear mandate intended by the Framers.[26]

Optimalist Theory

In addition to the late Chief Justice Earl Warren, the list of optimalist justices should probably include Potter Stewart and Tom Clark. They were willing to throw out malapportioned legislative districts to achieve "effective majority rule," so that the electoral process would remain meaningful. In their view, however, sometimes the one-person one-vote standard would lose out to such other factors as regionalism and representation of various economic sectors.[27]

Chief Justice Earl Warren, in *United States* v. *Robel,*[28] wrote a classic optimalist opinion with respect to the provisions of the 1950 Subversive Activities Control Act barring Communist party members from working in defense plants, balancing national-security needs against the "preferred" freedoms needed for full political participation as implied by the *Carolene Products* footnote four. Warren held the provisions unconstitutional only because they were unnecessarily restrictive, since there was no demonstrated need to limit the exercise of free-association rights of those working in nonsensitive positions, or of those who were theorists with no interest in damaging American society. In principle, i.e., with a properly and narrowly drawn statute, Warren could have upheld restrictions on the activities of those who had chosen to join the Communist party. The Court majority made similar determinations regarding state loyalty oaths.[29]

John Hart Ely, in *Democracy and Distrust*,[30] rejects substantive due process much as Bork does, and as Black did in his dissent in *Griswold*, arguing that if one cannot accept the jurisprudence of the pre-1937 Court, one cannot accept the "value imposition methodology" of *Roe* v. *Wade* either.[31] But unlike Bork, Ely finds a third alternative to either original intent or to substantive due process with its roots in natural law:

> For the constitutional document itself, the interpretivist's Bible, contains several provisions whose invitation to look beyond their four corners—whose invitation, if you will, to become at least to that extent a noninterpretivist—cannot be construed away.[32]

Ely thus derives a theory of constitutional interpretation from what he sees as the key overall themes of the Constitution, indicated most strongly by the free-speech and free-press clauses of the First Amendment, the cruel and unusual punishment clause of the Eighth, the due-process clauses of the Fifth and Fourteenth, and the privileges and immunities and equal-protection clauses of the Fourteenth.[33]

The "general constitutional themes" are, of course, those of participation in the democratic process. Ely gives prominence to footnote four of the *Carolene Products* case in highlighting areas of special concern for the Court in promoting participation in that process.[34] With the support given to citizen participation by the Warren Court in the reapportionment cases and the political-freedom cases, the "deep structure" of the Warren Court's constitutional decisions may well make Earl Warren the ultimate optimalist. Ely dedicated his book to Warren, and Ely's own democratic theory, as near as is discernible, promotes the optimalist view.

Ely, like the realists, sees the people exercising their power only by voting among competing candidates for decisionmaking, instead of by deciding things themselves.[35] Ely skeptically rejects the premises of participatory democracy: "[T]here is no consensus to be discovered (and to the extent that one may seem to exist, that is likely to reflect only the domination of some groups by others)."[36]

Therefore, Ely does not always make participatory self-government paramount, but rather remains committed to balancing tests, as in *U.S. v. Robel*.[37] Certainly he favors the protection of participatory-process values, weighted heavily in favor of protecting speech and with the Court as a quite active "referee."[38] But he does not place the protection of political speech at the very center of majoritarianism. The only ones who do so are those who want to make participatory democracy more real and more powerful, the functional-contract theorists, whom we will review later.

Still, we should not undervalue the commitment of Ely and the optimalists to free-expression values: *Brandenburg* v. *Ohio*[39] protects advocacy of illegal action, short of incitement to violence on the spot, and Ely, if anything, worries that it doesn't protect unpopular speech strongly enough to withstand the next wave of national paranoia.[40] Bork, by contrast, thinks *Brandenburg* gives far too much protection.[41]

Liberal Substantive Due Process

Ronald Dworkin, who considers himself a natural-rights theorist,[42] dominates the field of liberal substantive-due-process theory. He has very little respect for legislative determinations because he doesn't even credit the general concept of public sovereignty,[43] much less the legislature's representations of it. The Jeffersonian notion of self-government, with its basis in individual liberty, has little value for Dworkin. He would have the Court impose a particular social theory, that of John Rawls, when interpreting the due-process and equal-protection clauses of the Constitution. Since he has little respect for legislative determinations, he approves of the Court overturning those determinations if they conflict with Rawlsian theory, which stresses equality at the expense of liberty.[44]

Dworkin makes it clear where his attitude toward the voter would take his jurisprudence in discussing the *Roe* v. *Wade*[45] decision invalidating anti-abortion laws in 1973:

> It does not follow from the fact that the man in the street disapproves of abortion, or supports legislation making it criminal, that he has considered whether the concept of dignity presupposed by the Constitution, consistently applied, supports his political position. . . . [I]t is not to be taken for granted that political preferences, expressed casually or in the ballot, have been subjected to that form of examination.[46]

Dworkin calls the core of Rawlsian theory "equal concern and respect," and claims to find it in the American constitutional tradition. He claims to need the highly aggressive role for judges that he prescribes in order to protect individual rights against majority tyranny.[47] Madison and the Framers, by contrast, urged reliance on competition among factions within the democratic process for that purpose.[48] Dworkin has far less confidence in democracy.

Dworkin attempts to drape the mantle of constitutional legitimacy over his own Rawlsian ideology. But this is a fraud. Dworkin seems to suggest, for example, that the right to property should not exist;[49] the Framers, however, were very serious about protecting property rights, and most Americans continue to feel the same way.[50]

Even within his own equality-oriented value structure, Dworkin stumbles. He regularly urges "principled" decisions favoring minorities against majority opposition, in order to bring treatment of minorities up to equality with others. But this requires disregarding the principle of equal treatment implicit in the voting process: If the views of three voters prevail over the views of ten, we are not treating voters as equals. Each of the three has, in effect, been given voting power much greater than each of the ten.

Dworkin thus gives judges great power at the expense of legislatures, but also at the expense of the Constitution. Judges determine rights, which are supposed to be permanent. Legislatures merely determine policy, which may be changed. Dworkin's principles would have judges imposing equality of material resources. While Dworkin denies this,[51] the main thrust of his presentation points inexorably in that direction. The government, then, will have to compel some to give up property to raise the level of others. Legislatures do this now, through taxes, but those are adjustable as legislatures change policy from year to year. If courts do it, under claims of "right," much more permanent power will be in the hands of a branch of government not usually accountable to the voter. Citizens will have far less protection against arbitrary power that they will not control. This is precisely what the Constitution was designed to avoid.[52]

More generally, Dworkin seeks readings of the Constitution that will enable or ennoble judges to propel us toward "the good society." The Framers felt differently. They learned from Locke that government aims should be modest, derived from the right of self-preservation, and not too intent on enforcing virtue. The Framers did not expect the Court to "guarantee a good society," but only to "help prevent a bad one."[53] Dworkin would have done better, with respect to the Court, to pass along the advice of the poet Thomas Gray, "Let not ambition mock their useful toil." The ambition Dworkin has for the Court could have it take us down the road to tyranny.

Justice Douglas was the premier liberal substantive-due-process advocate on the Court. During the "Red scare" of the

McCarthy era in the 1950s he saw the optimalist, preferred-freedoms balancing approach fail to protect individual rights. Powerful currents of paranoid public opinion resulted in exaggerated concerns about national security and tilted the balance too far against the interest of full participation for all in the political process.

Douglas responded not by sanctifying political participation, which would have elevated "process" values (safeguarding participation in the political process), but by sanctifying individual rights for their own sake, elevating "substantive" values which might otherwise have been the *results* of a political process. Thus, for Douglas, the individual was primary; the Constitution itself, majoritarian government, any government, were merely the tools. While Douglas believed judges should exercise self-restraint with respect to economic and social management designed by legislators and administrators, he had no real qualms about the nondemocratic character of the Supreme Court when it came to the use of judicial review to promote "the maximum feasible self-fulfillment of the individual,"[54] which he thought was its proper use.

"Balancing" might be appropriate for legislatures, but not for courts; legislatures are supposed to balance interests against each other, but freedom is more than an interest, should not be treated as an interest, and should be beyond the reach of balancing.

The right to vote, for Douglas, stood foremost as a personal right. Therefore, the Supreme Court could rightfully void as an illegitimate act any discrimination against an individual in voting. Douglas strongly supported the one-person one-vote rule of *Baker* v. *Carr*, and consistently voted to end exclusions from voting based on military service, lack of property ownership (or parenthood, in school-board elections), or lack of property-tax–payer status in bond-issue votes. In voiding the poll tax, Douglas's opinion ignored precedent except to overrule it.[55] Based on his version of moral-rights theory, he deemed equal voting participation simply a right.

But since his voting-rights theory was strictly individual-oriented, Douglas had no fixed position with respect to the problem of equalizing group voting power. Thus, in dissent in *Wright* v. *Rockefeller*,[56] he opposed the existence of Representative Adam Clayton Powell's congressional district with the argument that racial boundaries are irrelevant in getting the best representation, and in dissent in *Whitcomb* v. *Chavis*,[57] he called for the creation of heavily black districts with the argument that black voting power would otherwise be diluted.[58]

His concurrence in *Brandenburg* v. *Ohio* illustrated Douglas's complete abandonment of the optimalist, preferred-freedoms balancing test for political-expression cases, in favor of his moral-rights position of absolute protection for ideas, expressed in speech not "brigaded with action," i.e., speech other than incitement to criminal activity, or in symbolic acts.[59] He supported the dissenters in all the Communist party and NAACP cases.

Douglas's and Dworkin's positions, like the older natural-rights theories, run into problems because they are subjective and arbitrary, much as Bentham and Mill pointed out, and too narrow in their assumptions to provide sufficient guidance for consistent and principled decisionmaking, as we saw in Douglas's apportionment decisions. This latter problem emerged even more vividly in his privacy decisions.

Douglas, "the creator of much of the Court's case law on privacy,"[60] and the justice whose most basic assumption of maximal self-fulfillment for the individual must include a strong privacy right, wrote opinions in libel cases "noticeable for their lack of concern for privacy."[61] In *Time, Inc.* v. *Hill*,[62] a family had been held at gunpoint by convicts for several days, and as a result received a great deal of publicity, which they disliked enough to move to another state to avoid more. Years later, without their permission, *Life* magazine featured them in a story about a play which *Life* said was based on the family's experiences, but in fact depicted much worse experiences.

In his concurrence, creating a plurality opinion that prevented the Hill family from recovering damages, Douglas said, "It seems to me irrelevant to talk of any right to privacy in this context."

In *Gertz* v. *Robert Welch, Inc.*,[63] he made his priorities even clearer:

> Unlike the right of privacy which, by the terms of the Fourth Amendment, must be accommodated with reasonable searches and seizures and warrants issued by magistrates, the rights of free speech and free press were protected by the Framers in verbiage whose prescription seems clear.

To justify Douglas's opinion for the Court in overturning state law in *Griswold*, privacy should have been a "real" right, not a "sometimes" right. But the "right" of privacy may well be as tentative as Douglas indicated in the *Gertz* case. Professor Edelman seemed appalled by "[t]his viewpoint from the Court's leading advocate of the right of privacy!"[64] Because if it is indeed so tentative, then Douglas had no business pretending that the state law the Court overturned in *Griswold* really foundered on bedrock constitutional principle.

When fighting to establish the right of privacy in *Griswold*, two years before *Time, Inc.* v. *Hill* and nine years before *Gertz*, Douglas found "penumbras" and "emanations" in the Bill of Rights to do so. A substantive-due-process jurisprudence, like that of Douglas and Dworkin, will entail such devices, and will inevitably trip over them. (Note that Douglas disavowed substantive due process in *Griswold*, but his approach seems functionally equivalent, and the concurrences in that case, especially Goldberg's, did rest explicitly on substantive-due-process claims.)

Functional-Contract Theory

Justice William Brennan discovered a different theory to justify a firmer grip on freedom of expression than the optimalists provided, but with a broader foundation in political theory than the rights-based theory Douglas grounded rather narrowly in the Declaration.

Alexander Meiklejohn rejected, at least normatively, the pluralist-realist notion of control by elected leaders merely competing for popular support through elections. He argued, as Mortimer Adler does today,[65] for the reestablishment of a far more active role for the citizen than merely voting. In reviewing the Federalist Papers and the Tenth Amendment's reservation to the people of powers not otherwise enumerated, and drawing an analogy to the role of Congress as outlined in Article I, Section 2(1), Meiklejohn found and offered a restored vision of popular involvement in issue and policy formation, with the people seen, once again, as truly sovereign and self-governing, and the Congress, president, and the rest of the apparatus of government as no more than the people's servants.

Madison argued powerfully that representative bodies, not the public itself, should make policy,[66] and Meiklejohn's approach may at first seem inconsistent with Madison's arguments. But between robotic representatives mechanically transmitting their constituencies' desires, and apathetic constituents turning over all responsibility for their interests to their representatives, lies a wide range of possibilities. Meiklejohn sought an active, interested public that debated issues and policy with vigor, but did not contradict Madison's argument that the policies thus developed and transmitted to representatives should receive further assessment and transformation by those representatives.

Meiklejohn's approach stresses process values, but those who argue that substantive values cannot truly be separated from process values might well use Meiklejohn's approach as illustrative. Process values for him vibrate with the energy of liberty, equality, and rights. While I consider his participation-enhancing theory a process-value theory, those who categorize it otherwise can certainly be forgiven for considering his degree of commitment to process as virtually substantive.

In contrast with Douglas, who saw the social contract under the Constitution as a guarantee of natural rights, Meiklejohn saw the basic contract as a guarantee of self-government.[67] To the extent that self-government exists ultimately to produce "wise decisions,"[68] his theory has a utilitarian aspect, but the contractarian guarantee of self-government predominates.

Justice Brennan adopted this "functional" contract approach, and had no hesitation in applying judicial review to maintain the integrity of the contractual guarantee.

Brennan strongly supported the one-person one-vote doctrine of *Baker* v. *Carr*. He joined in the more recent opinion by Justice White in *Davis* v. *Bandemer*,[69] which held that the courts may hear and remedy cases of nonracial, partisan gerrymandering, a concept implied by the functional-contract theory, although the facts of *Davis* itself were not held to justify such intervention.

But the thrust of the theory goes far beyond voting. If the people are sovereign, Congress has absolutely no right to restrict the people's deliberations by restraining political speech, just as the First Amendment says: No balancing is needed; the Framers have already selected the appropriate balance. So the Smith Act, the Subversive Activities Control Act, and other such statutes in the Communist party cases were clearly unconstitutional.[70]

Sailors in ancient times had a maxim: "Living is not necessary; seafaring is necessary." In a nation dedicated to self-government, security is not necessary; freedom is. In practice, of course, "no clear and imminent security threat was prohibited by statute or evident in the indictments" underlying the Communist party cases.[71] In practice, maximum freedom seems also to protect security best. The Framers designed the American experiment for self-government, but self-government seems to help self-preservation as well.

Thus, the loyalty oaths that certain states required of public

employees[72] were unconstitutional not because they were unnecessarily broad restrictions in the balance against "preferred
freedoms," but because legislatures simply have no right to impose an "idea test" on the people or any part thereof. The Constitution, with this reading, allows *no* interference with
political activity, defined as rational debate and discourse in
peaceful forums. Security restrictions based on physical danger
to the nation are legitimate, but not security restrictions based
on beliefs. Thus, J. Robert Oppenheimer, proven loyal to the
United States, could never have been denied security clearance
had this view prevailed.[73]

The theory has some boundary problems. In its earlier for-
mulations, it did not include protection for expression apparently unrelated to political discourse, such as obscenity,
blasphemy, incitement to criminal action, and private libels.
Brennan's rule in *Roth* v. *United States*,[74] denying protection
to pornography that lacks "redeeming social importance," reflects the Meiklejohn approach, but that rule can be difficult to
apply.

The functional-contract approach underscores the importance of public forums.[75] Meiklejohn thought we should create
centers for the discussion of public policy in every municipality.
Streets, parks, and other public meeting places should be open
for demonstrations, which may be the only vehicle for unpopular groups without resources to communicate their views
effectively. Reasonable time, place, and manner restrictions
are valuable, in this view, as they increase society's ability to
provide effective forums through rational scheduling.[76]

The functional-contract theory tends to describe what should
be; the competitive, pluralist paradigm probably does a better
job of describing what is, at least for the moment. We don't
really live in a society that operates like the old New England
town meetings, if indeed they even existed in the idealized way
we imagine them. Further, Meiklejohn may have overesti-
mated how much time and energy the American citizen would
be willing to offer to the commonweal. But his vision of the
proper role of the citizenry is an ennobling one. And Mortimer

Adler, who argues that "citizenship" is the highest office in a democracy, continues to educate the American public to assume that role.[77]

It may not be necessary to adopt a contractarian approach in order to reap the benefits of this theory. If Americans seek self-government as our ultimate goal, we probably do take a fundamentally contractarian approach. But if "the ultimate interest of the self-governing process [is] . . . wise decisions. . . ," which may be sought for a wide variety of reasons, values, and benefits, we can characterize our approach more accurately as utilitarian, although a different brand of utilitarian than the pluralist, realist, competitive paradigm. Edelman argues that a more utilitarian functional test would serve us better by avoiding absolutes,[78] and in the Pentagon Papers case[79] Brennan did take a balancing position more utilitarian and less absolute, perhaps, than Meiklejohn would have preferred. Brennan indicated that he would approve even prior restraints on political expression upon "proof that publication must inevitably, directly and immediately cause the occurrence of an event kindred to imperilling the safety of a [troop] transport already at sea. . . ."[80] A direct, straightforward balance against survival values, like that one, Edelman felt, was "consistent with functional contract theory,"[81] and appears to be a more traditionally utilitarian approach.

Meiklejohn's functional contract has little in common with the Rawlsian contract. The parties to Rawls's contract seek to maximize their respective self-interest; the parties of Meiklejohn's contract seek self-government, and they are not necessarily attempting to aggrandize their personal interests in so doing. Rawls derives egalitarian unselfishness from selfish, and perhaps even grudging, considerations of calculating individuals; Meiklejohn sees an intrinsically and unstintingly communitarian contract, even if it does not necessarily result in so much equality. Finally, the Rawlsian contract smuggles in a "moral law" tilt toward distributional equality; Meiklejohn's contract tilts toward liberty more than toward material equality.

Individualistic-Contract Theory

Justice Hugo Black's jurisprudence also seemed to reflect a contract theory, but his contract, instead of being primarily for the preservation of self-government, appeared to be designed primarily for the preservation of individual rights. Black saw a society less rosily communitarian than Meiklejohn's, although perhaps not as bleak as that of the realists.[82] Meiklejohn thought we could all be civil enough toward each other to work out a good deal of our policy differences among ourselves; the realists thought that all meaningful policy formation came out of the clash of competing interests; Black thought he'd better make sure that individuals weren't hurt or crushed in the policymaking process, and that a good deal of judicial effort could be justified in striving for that assurance.

For Black, individuals did not so anxiously desire to talk politics with each other, or did not so willingly sacrifice their peace, quiet, and privacy in the interests of hearing novel points of view on political matters expressed by noisy obnoxious demonstrators creating a fuss, bother, and nuisance. His dislike of street protest recalls Madison's dislike of "passions."[83] But his atomistic view of society more accurately sets forth the present than does Meiklejohn's picture. The individual will influence political leaders by more than merely voting, but given the large size of electoral units, the right to vote retains its primacy as the key to democracy: Not everyone—indeed, few—will be heard among the citizenry in policy debate.

The Court must defend those provisions of the Constitution that provide unique protection against tyranny, so Black approved of energetic judicial review in that context, but otherwise judges should refrain from policymaking. The Constitution guarantees liberty primarily for the individual, only secondarily for the purpose of self-government, and individual rights must prevail over group interests, underscoring the identification of Black's approach with the contract theorists as opposed to the pluralists.[84] The right to vote, therefore, must prevail over regionalism, economic representation, or other group interests. Therefore, Black strongly supported Warren's one-person one-vote rule in *Reynolds* v. *Sims*.

Black, of course, defended an absolute right to political beliefs, including advocating—but not inciting to—violent overthrow of the government.[85] In real security-risk cases, though, such as investigations into beliefs and associations required for appointments to truly sensitive positions, Black had a tendency to concur silently in upholding state policy.[86] Black's theory could not justify the investigations, but he voted for them anyway.

He had no problem protecting nonpolitical speech like pornography ("though he personally abhorred it"):[87] With his individual-rights contract approach, he simply found it to have absolute protection. As suggested earlier, he had a bigger problem with privacy. In *Time, Inc.* v. *Hill* he would have ignored the privacy interest and dismissed the suit, his "absolute" protection of free-expression rights making it impossible here to recognize any right of privacy at all, notwithstanding his general attachment to privacy as a value.

He was not generous in his view of appropriate public forums, believing that government had no obligation to provide a place for the exercise of free expression. This might have reflected inadequate appreciation on his part of the difficulties facing groups that lack financial or other resources. More likely, though, it reflected his view that rights are for the benefit of individuals, not for the benefit of any particular societal function, and therefore individuals must manage to exercise them as best they can.

Since Black understood that demonstrations had to be regulated, and since he would not regulate speech, he drew a sharp distinction between them, refusing to consider demonstrations, which he considered conduct, within the range of protected free expression. Ironically, Harlan, in balancing the rights of demonstrators against the rights of those the demonstrations would annoy, ended up voting to allow more demonstrations than Black.[88]

Black's jurisprudence may, finally, fail to promote participatory self-government. Black refused to allow himself, as a judge, the power to overturn legislative enactments unless the enactments violated individual rights as he saw them in the Constitution. This approach reflected his respect for the representative branch of government, and thus for the voter. With that approach, his jurisprudence, if incomplete, was at least finite, bounded, and rational.[89]

IX

Administrative
Theory

Administrative theory is only a subset of constitutional theory. It is a very important part, however, because the vast preponderance of American government is government by administrative agency. In budgetary terms, for example, everything else—Congress, the courts, the White House—takes up about 2 percent of the budget, with the rest funding the agencies.[1] Therefore, administrative theory effectively guides most of American government.

Richard Stillman has traced the genealogy of various theories of public administration to, respectively, Hamilton, Jefferson, and Madison.[2] The discussion that follows interweaves the work of various other historians, classifiers, analysts, and creators of public-administration theory.

The Hamiltonian Tradition

The colonists had before them the English model of crown, lords, and commons, with administration seen as the province of the crown, although in reality English administration was under the King-in-Parliament, as their cabinet system demanded. Parliament's dominant party formed a government by supplying the king's ministers, up to and including the prime minister, and the king's ministers headed the administration. This was, of course, an impossible model to follow without a king, and the colonists could make only a weak analogy between king and president. Nonetheless, it was the closest available model, and it greatly influenced Hamilton's concept of public administration, which dominated the early years of independence.

Hamilton sought a strong national government. Fearing the masses, he envisioned a strong executive as the locus of concentrated and centralized power.[3] In arguing that Congress had the power to charter a national bank, he devised the theory that in addition to express and implied powers, the government must have "resulting" powers. Hamilton's expansive reading of the "necessary and proper" clause of the Constitution was based on disregard for the notion of sovereignty of the people. For Hamilton, sovereignty was clearly in the government, not the people.[4]

Hamilton's position quite contradicted the theory he and Madison, as authors of *The Federalist*, had used to justify the system of checks and balances among the legislative, executive, and judicial branches as set forth in the Constitution. The Anti-Federalists sought legislative supremacy. Their reading of the British model was that king, lords, and commons, each a part of the legislature, made the legislature a microcosm of society. For the United States, they argued, with the whole people represented in the legislature, our legislature ought to be supreme: The legislature, including representatives of all strata, already reflected an appropriate balance. The Federalist answer was that the people, not the legislature, retained sovereignty, and the other branches would check legislative power in the interests of individual rights.[5]

Separation of powers and checks and balances did not preclude blending of powers. The Federalists intended the Senate to have far more significant executive power than it actually attained. One draft of the Constitution gave the Senate the sole treaty-making power, and the sole power to appoint "ambassadors and judges of the Supreme Court."[6]

The kind of civil servants the Federalists hired also reflected their confidence in a strong executive branch. A leading scholar calls the period of Federalist domination of the civil service—from 1789 to 1829, much longer than Federalist domination of American politics, which ended in 1800—"government by gentlemen."[7] Public administration was expected to be conducted by an elite, with long tenure in office, much on the British model.

The Federalists lost their hold on national politics in 1800, although some of their civil servants were left in place for a few decades longer until Andrew Jackson began to apply what Stillman calls Jeffersonian principles to federal personnel practices. Those Jeffersonian principles were in the ascendancy until an increasingly complex society, in the 1880s, called for the level of professionalism that Hamilton tried to implant in a much simpler era.

By the 1880s, however, the federal government had much more to do than deliver the mail, which had been responsible for much of the expansion of federal government in the first half of the nineteenth century.[8] The rather complex field of railroad regulation, for example, had been left to the states in the big years of railroad expansion from 1850 to 1870,[9] although federal regulation of interstate transportation was obviously more appropriate. Tremendous rural and foreign migration made American cities grow between 1880 and 1900 faster than they had ever grown before.[10] In a wide variety of areas, regulation of interstate commerce among them, a professional civil service was needed.

Civil-service reform, as an issue, took on great moral force because of the corruption and inefficiency that gradually grew from Jackson's democratization and politicization of federal employment. "Get rid of patronage" was the theme.[11] Thus, the Pendleton Act of 1883, requiring selection by competitive examination and merit, heralded the era of "government by the good."[12] The Industrial Revolution hastened the transformation of all areas of society from a basis in personal, informal relationships usually constrained by birth, to a basis in impersonal, formal relationships determined by achievement, especially in the United States.[13] Time-and-motion studies of business heralded the age of efficiency.[14] The "rational-legal ideal-type bureaucracy" was said to function, despite its human components, with the efficiency of a machine,[15] and civil service was to be conducted in a "businesslike manner."[16]

From 1906 to 1937, civil service could be described as "government by the efficient."[17] What Stillman described as a resurgence of Hamiltonianism, starting in 1883,[18] inspired the "managerial" approach to public administration,[19] with efficiency the value to be maximized. Leonard White and Luther Gulick, public-administration scholars of the latter part of the period, would argue that the focus of public administration should be management, not law; leadership, not rules; execution of programs, not legislation.[20]

Long before his presidency of the United States, Woodrow Wilson, as a highly influential political scientist, attacked the separation of powers as manifested in the abuse of power by congressional committees.[21] With increased industrialization, the end of the early agrarian homogeneity of the nation, and a real potential for legislative stalemates among the new battling economic interests reflected in Congress, Wilson's attack on "congressional government," in his book by that name, responded to some real need for a stronger executive in the Hamiltonian mold. Separation of powers to protect the people's

sovereignty was doubly foolish, he argued, because the people
have no sovereignty: they are not the governors; they merely
consent to be governed.[22]

Wilson was ahead of his time in the sense that the "realist"
democratic theorists were still decades away. But their theory,
that political leadership alternatives would compete for blocs of
votes in a pluralist environment, with the "people" playing no
role beyond choosing among alternative policy proponents set
before them, was anticipated by Wilson.

Wilson theorized that the legislature expresses the will of
the people (which is not necessarily the majority's opinion by
any means, but is in fact defined by what the legislature
chooses to do), and the executive carries out that will.[23] Wilson
stressed the separation of *functions*, but preferred the British
model, where *powers* aren't separated at all, the ministers
being members of Parliament.[24] "Checks" against excessive
power, provided in the Constitution to protect the rights of the
people, by means of separation of powers, at Madison's urging,
were of no concern to Wilson.[25]

Essentially, Wilson would save the nation from majoritarian
folly by wise executive administration instead of by checks and
balances limiting the scope of victories among countervailing
forces.[26]

The judicial branch, similarly, would be subordinate to the
legislature and the executive, as in the British model.[27] Again,
we see the roots of the "realist" democratic theory which led to
the judicial deference of Harlan and Frankfurter.

But Frankfurter had a far more powerful Hamiltonian influence that was much closer to his own roots in government. The
most enormous expansion of executive power to that time was
under Franklin Delano Roosevelt's New Deal, where Frankfurter started in government, and the Brownlow Report was
its theoretical justification. The Brownlow Report has been
called the "pinnacle" of the managerial approach. Like the
ideal-type bureaucracy, its premise was pure "merit": There
would be no "politics" in good administration, which was equivalent to efficient administration.[28]

In truth, the Depression did warrant an expansion of White House staff and improvements in budget, personnel, and planning.[29] The post-1937 civil service was called "government by managers."[30] But Brownlow justified a degree of executive supremacy that went far beyond the balance recommended by the Framers, and beyond a balance healthy for the constitutional tradition. John Rohr says, "As disciples of Brownlow, we came to believe that the buck *should* stop with the president until Richard Nixon put the buck in his pocket. Then we knew something had gone wrong."[31]

Mosher's description of "government by managers"[32] reflects the reality that "efficiency" isn't enough: To carry out complex policy initiatives in a complex world, a government needs not just functionaries but managers who can make adjustments to policy and who can exercise judgment and flexibility. But federal employees were never thought to be under the sole control of the executive branch: Their responsibilities are created by Congress as Congress creates the law, and while the president may impose duties, ultimately they are "subject to the control of the law, and not to the direction of the President."[33]

The Brownlow Report said that ". . . the whole executive power" is placed in the president. This was clearly untrue. The House and the Senate have part of the executive power in declaring war, approving treaties, confirming appointments, and other matters.[34] Hamilton never went as far as Brownlow: This was more Hamiltonian than Hamilton.

The rhetoric of the Report dutifully recited the president's accountability to Congress, but this invocation of the checks and balances tradition was not very reassuring inasmuch as the Report also stressed the president's role as leader of his party and of Congress.[35]

The Brownlow Report reflected changes in society that did justify a much stronger, more managerial public administration. In its enthusiasm, however, it neglected the value of constitutional checks on executive power, because administrative power need not be executive-branch power. Indeed, the Report explicitly excoriated the independent regulatory commissions because they were not fully subject to presidential control.[36] Limits on each branch, and competition among the branches, were designed to protect individual rights. The Brownlow Report, however, in its opening statement of purpose, described the goals of American government in social-welfare terms, without any clear reference to liberty, in terms more reminiscent of Bismarck than of Jefferson or Madison.[37]

Subsequently, forces in American society moved to create some degree of resurgence of limits on executive power. At the same time that street riots and elite pressures were imposing democratic limits on executive power by forcing executive government to open up to grass-roots participation in Lyndon Johnson's War on Poverty, executive management-control theorists were bringing their new management tools like Program Planning Budgeting Systems, Management by Objective, and Zero-Base Budgeting to bear at both the federal and local levels.[38]

After some of the judicially imposed limits on executive agency action appeared in the early 1970s, the executive-power proponents won several more victories. The Supreme Court moved to limit some "intrusions" into the "administrator's domain" in the late 1970s and early 1980s, "warning against judicially-imposed procedural requirements for rulemaking not mandated by statute, admonishing judges to consider costs."[39] While the impact of these Supreme Court decisions was only marginal, and was probably only meant to be marginal,[40] overall the Hamiltonian strain in public-administration theory remains strong. But it must co-exist with other strains.

The Jeffersonian Tradition

Jefferson was more committed to protecting the sovereignty of the people than a strong central government, at least when he wasn't president. His vision of an agrarian, low-density society wasn't far from the reality of America through the first few decades of the nineteenth century.

The Jeffersonian concept of civil service—volunteerism in administration, highly decentralized, with narrow discretion[41]—was, of course, never entirely applicable at the federal level. However, Jackson's version of a Jeffersonian civil service was egalitarian, representative, and politically responsive. Jackson concluded, probably not inaccurately for his time and place, that bureaucratic work did not require long experience or impressive credentials. In a simpler era like his, this may have been so. Under Jackson's presidency, his policy appears to have engendered little corruption. The image of the "spoils system," which he is said to have started, and under which a new administration would award federal jobs as the "spoils" of the campaign, derived from his successors. Mosher's designation of the system starting with Jackson in 1829 and lasting until 1883 as "government by the common man"[42] seems generally accurate.

Jeffersonian administrative theory fit well with the legal concept of the "delegation doctrine." The people elect Congress to represent them, and retain the power to replace Congress every two years. Under the Constitution, the people delegated their own inherent legislative power to Congress. Congress was supposed to make policy on the people's behalf by legislating. If the people didn't like what their representatives to Congress did, they could replace them with new representatives. If Congress delegated its power to a third party (i.e., a civil servant), the people might not even know immediately who the third party was. The people might not be able to fire that third party the way they could "fire" Congress, by electing new members. At best, the next Congress, if it included a majority so inclined, could do the firing (unless a sympathetic president, perhaps a new one, fired the civil servant first). If Congress had arranged for civil-service tenure, the civil servant might be shielded from being fired at all. Clearly, the people would have less direct control over this third party than they had over Congress.

Thus, ancient legal tradition held that the power delegated by the people to those it chooses as its representative cannot then be delegated by the representative to another.[43] Americans presumably learned this view from Locke.[44] The usual first American legal citation for the principle is to Justice Joseph Story: "A delegated authority cannot be delegated."[45]

Yet, the same year the Constitution was adopted, delegating the people's inherent legislative power to Congress, Congress gave to a group of clerks the power to decide who was eligible for veterans' benefits based on service in the Revolutionary War.[46]

Traditionally, the Court tried to satisfy Jeffersonian concerns by explaining that Congress was not truly delegating legislative power. Rather, since Congress could not possibly make every petty rule needed to guide every bureaucratic decision, it would merely legislate broad policy mandates, and agencies would fill in the necessary administrative details. This theory was still preferred as late as 1932.[47]

With postal service among the main executive responsibilities until the Civil War, a strong central executive government was not necessary. As Woodrow Wilson was later to report, the legislative branch dominated government. Popular representation was the dominant value in public administration, although it is doubtful whether Jackson's changes really increased responsiveness at the federal level. Locally, however, informal, partly voluntary, and not very managerial government may well have been responsive to community needs, where the Jeffersonian "New England town meeting" ideal was still close to reality.[48]

With the Civil War, the Industrial Revolution, and urbanization, the demise of Jeffersonian public administration was inevitable and the rise of the Hamiltonian strain succeeded it. With the need for increasingly complex decisionmaking by civil servants, the plausibility of the old justifications for delegations of power waned. The new theory claimed that the legislature's delegation of its policymaking authority to civil servants was acceptable so long as the delegation was constrained within standards prescribed by Congress.[49] Twice, in response to President Roosevelt's National Industrial Recovery Act, the

United States Supreme Court held that the standards provided by Congress were too broad.[50] The second decision overturned a New Deal delegation of power to the president to approve virtually any "code of fair competition," essentially giving him untrammeled control over the entire economy. The result is that since 1935, no delegation to the president has been held too broad.[51]

"Representativeness" in the civil service never entirely faded. A 1967 study of career bureaucrats showed a distribution of party and policy orientations substantially similar to that of Congress.[52] By 1967 the United States had to some extent reacted against the excesses of Hamiltonianism in the FDR administration. The requirement of "maximum feasible participation of the poor" in the poverty programs of the 1960s[53] was a resurgence of representativeness; Stillman suggests that the egalitarian theme of John Rawls's *A Theory of Justice* (1971) and the criticism of an overstrong executive in Arthur Schlesinger's *Imperial Presidency* (1971) also reflected the Jeffersonian resurgence.[54]

Congress further reacted against excessive executive dominance with increased use of legislative-veto provisions in the 1970s, the Freedom of Information Act, and sunshine and sunset legislation.[55]

The Jeffersonian tradition, along with the functional-contract theory of Alexander Meiklejohn and Supreme Court Justice William Brennan, reflects belief in an activist people who truly retain sovereignty. The Jeffersonian tradition can complement the liberal natural-rights theory of Justice William O. Douglas too, so long as popular majorities do not end up violating individual rights.

Managerial efficiency, though, does not reflect the Jeffersonian tradition. Jeffersonianism more closely resembles the "political approach," placing a higher value on representativeness, responsiveness, and accountability.[56] The 1978 Federal Civil Service Reform Act, while it implemented the long-awaited Hamiltonian managerial goal of the Brownlow Report of separating the civil-service merit system from personnel management,[57] also proffered a "representativeness," the Jeffersonian policy "to provide a Federal workforce reflective of the Nation's diversity."[58]

The Jeffersonian political tradition would take representativeness to mean a replication of society's values, while the Madisonian political tradition understands representativeness more in the sense of replicating society's "pluralistic free-for-all."[59]

The Madisonian Tradition

Madison feared the people and unbounded majoritarianism, as did Hamilton, but he also feared an overstrong executive, as did Jefferson. Madison deserves primary credit for the system of mutually limiting powers, "checks and balances."[60] He opposed Hamilton's call for a nationally chartered bank. He argued that the federal government could only do things "necessary and proper" to the carrying out of the enumerated, express powers, in contrast to Hamilton's ingenious theory of "resulting" powers.[61]

The Madisonian tradition in public-administration theory did not have its own independent expression until the rise of what we now call the "open model" organization theorists, the human-relations school, in the 1920s, who were reacting against the bureaucracy and efficiency experts and against Woodrow Wilson's approach.

When the sociologists discovered, in their research among employees at the Western Electric plant in Hawthorne, Massachusetts, that the rational-self-interest–based production strategies indicated by the efficiency theorists didn't work, they began to identify the informal group processes that motivate human behavior.[62] Emotions, the irrational, and "politics" were all relevant to behavior; individuals were not simply rational calculators of self-interest. Interest *groups* had their own patterns of behavior, which justified a more "political" style of management than the nineteenth- and early-twentieth-century "efficiency" theorists would approve.

In this view, "government by managers" might be considered Madisonian. Hamilton, in contrast, resembles the efficiency or "closed model" theorists, who inspired "government by the efficient." Madison appears closer to the interest group or "open model" theorists,[63] who would be more comfortable with "government by managers."

Representative bureaucracy, with faction countering faction within it,[64] now also looks more Madisonian than Jeffersonian, as indicated by Brandeis's comment in his dissent in *Myers* v. *U.S.*,[65] that "separation of powers [exists] . . . not to promote efficiency but to preclude the exercise of arbitrary power."

Justices Earl Warren, Potter Stewart, and Tom Clark were pluralists, but gave special weight to those values that protect the integrity of the political process so that as many groups as possible may have a chance to participate in a fair balancing process. Their constitutional theory seems particularly consistent with Madison's views. Madison's dislike of passion and fundamental concern for human rights also link him with the jurisprudence of Hugo Black.

Public-administration theories can also be classified as managerial, political, and legal, fitting nicely with the executive, legislative, and judicial branches.[66] At the same time, the managerial classification fits with Hamiltonian approaches, and the political classification fits with Jeffersonian or Madisonian approaches. However, the legal classification must be treated separately.

The Legal Tradition

This legal tradition is arguably Madisonian, if individual rights are protected by law only because the major power centers in society are offset by each other just enough to leave some law to protect the individual.

Justice Black's individualistic contract might fit here too:

Courts should protect individuals' contractual right to speak out politely when they wish, and to be let alone when they wish. But Earl Warren's optimalist approach also uses legal intervention to obtain fairness in the political process, and more than incidentally, protects rights. If "[p]ublic administration joins together what constitutional principle keeps apart,"[67] this legal tradition is what protects the rights of individuals against excesses of efficiency or representativeness.[68]

A "welcome corrective" to the disregard of individual rights in the Brownlow Report was the Attorney General's Report four years later. The most important outcome of the Attorney General's Report was the Administrative Procedure Act (APA) of 1946, with its provisions for hearing rights, procedural due process, and rulemaking protection.[69] Most important, the APA guaranteed access to the bureaucratic decisionmaking process, and thus became a crucial vehicle for making the bureaucratic process partly one of public participation.[70] From this point of view, the "legal" tradition protecting individual rights and the Jeffersonian tradition protecting democratic control merge in the APA. Public input is greatest in the rulemaking process, less in the adjudicative process, and least in discretionary exercises. Since rulemaking also provides the clearest form of notice to interested parties as to what the agency will require by law, continued calls by administrative-law scholars for more rulemaking, less adjudication and less discretion, even beyond the requirements of the APA,[71] also merge the Jeffersonian and legal traditions.[72]

With the best mechanisms of legislative control, government employees will inevitably have the authority to make millions of decisions that no legislature, and no legislator, could efficiently or even sanely review. Much must be left to discretion and judgment by the decisionmaking bureaucrat on the front lines who must actually handle the real-life cases. But where should the line be drawn?

A leading administrative-law scholar supplies the example of the police officer who arrests a boy who threw a rock and broke a window, but who gives a second boy just a warning for the same act.[73] Should the officer be instructed always to apply the same penalty for the same offense? What if the officer knows both boys, and knows that although neither has been arrested before, the first one has been a troublemaker while the second has never been in trouble, has a dying parent, and was merely influenced by the other boy? Taking away the officer's right to use discretion in such cases could result in lowering the quality of street-level justice. Yet, there will inevitably be some inconsistency, some injustice, some abuse of such discretion.

Penalties might also vary, equally justly or equally unjustly, were the cases tried or plea-bargained before a judge. The judicial structure, though, with the defendants assured some power in the adversary process, better satisfies our customary vision of justice.

The vast preponderance of agency decisions, however, are informal decisions like those of the police officer. There is no written record of the "process" that leads to such decisions, and therefore no possibility of "review" of such decisions in the legal sense. For example, fewer than 3 percent of the 1.9 million audits the IRS performed on 1970 tax returns resulted in administrative appeals.[74] Hundreds of thousands of taxpayers paid more money without going through any process that would have provided a reviewable record. Similarly, welfare recipients appeal only a small percentage of New York State Department of Social Services decisions affecting them.[75] Thus, discretionary action plays a major role in the workings of American government.

Agencies tend to resist the publication of explicit policy guidelines for the exercise of discretion because they perceive that such publication makes them vulnerable. Consider the bureaucrat conscientiously trying to monitor the activities of the finance companies. The bureaucrat might well plead that the lawyers for the finance companies would be able to find loopholes in virtually any set of published rules.[76]

Some regulatory agencies such as the Securities and Exchange Commission and the Federal Trade Commission must and do, however, promulgate rules that have the force of law.

They follow formal rulemaking procedures that are detailed in the laws enacted subsequent to the federal Administrative Procedure Act. These laws require that the agencies formulate and publish such rules only after appropriate public notice and public hearings.

However, when agencies launch proceedings against individuals who are said to have violated those rules, sometimes those individuals argue that the activities in question were not clearly prohibited. The issue is whether such "questions of first impression" can legitimately be decided by an administrative-law judge adjudicating such a proceeding, or whether fairness dictates that an explicit rule must be published first.

For example, the Securities Act of 1933 and the Securities Exchange Act of 1934 prohibit misrepresentations and manipulative or deceptive practices in the sale or purchase of stock. Section 10b of the 1934 Act permits the Securities and Exchange Commission to prescribe such rules as may be necessary to protect investors or the public. Rule 10b-5, promulgated under that authority, generally and broadly prohibits fraud in stock transactions.

A broker sold shares of a corporation's stock based on information from a member of the corporation's board, information that had not yet been made public. The SEC had not at that time promulgated any rule stating that such an action was prohibited. However, the SEC argued successfully that the broker should have known that his action contravened the spirit and general intent of the two Securities Acts. Should this policy decision of the SEC have been implemented through adjudication, as it was in this 1961 case,[77] or should it have been implemented through the rulemaking process?

Various efforts have been made to determine the appropriate domains of each. However, no definition seems quite right. It seems intuitively and obviously fairer for agencies to lay down new law in advance, so that all parties have notice of what they may and may not do. But as was evident in the case cited above, and as the Supreme Court had previously made clear,[78] agencies need not do so. The rationale for this is also fairly clear: Agencies simply cannot anticipate every way some person may invent to violate the spirit and intent of the law the agency was designed to enforce. Therefore, if the spirit and intent are at least reasonably clear, agencies may, through adjudication, find a newly invented scheme illegal. In general, "an administrative agency can rule on a question of first impression in an adjudicative context."[79]

The "judicialization" of the administrative process that has occurred in recent years in the United States has its costs and benefits. We use administrative agencies in the first place because hearing examiners, or administrative-law judges, by specializing in matters of one particular sort and by dispensing with many of the formalities of the regular trial process, can operate much more quickly and efficiently than the court system. The growth of "due process" protection for the individual who comes before an administrative tribunal obviously undercuts the speed and efficiency to be found there. Procedural due process can mean, among other things, the right to counsel, to notice, to cross-examination, and to a hearing on the record. To the extent that courts require administrative agencies to adopt such protection, they make the role of agencies more like their own.

For many years courts refused to impose such protective requirements on administrative agencies. In *Wilkie* v. *O'Connor*,[80] a New York court held that the government's restrictions on its grants of welfare had to be accepted by the recipients: "In accepting charity, the appellant has consented to the provisions of the law under which charity is bestowed."

But this attitude eventually changed. The 1970 decision in *Goldberg* v. *Kelly*,[81] a case in which a welfare recipient went to court to challenge a cutoff of welfare benefits pending a hearing, marked the historic turning point toward more due-process protection. Justice Brennan, writing for the Court, stated that welfare benefits "are a matter of statutory entitlement for persons qualified to receive them" and as such, may not be withheld from a recipient for an alleged violation of a condition of eligibility without a prior hearing. Within three years,

Goldberg v. *Kelly* was followed by decisions providing judicial
protection in varying degrees to government employment, un-
employment benefits, public housing, licenses, and even government contracts.[82]

As the expansion of the due-process right to a hearing grew
into other administrative areas, the government's vulnerability
to legal attack brought about significant financial and social
costs. With every increase in the range of judicially enforceable
rights, society pays a price in terms of resources it must de-
vote to litigation. The benefits of managerial decisionmaking
are lost to the judicial decisionmaking process; the more due-
process protections are required in administrative hearings,
the less managerial and the more "judicial" they become.

The further reaches of the expansion of due-process procedural rights to administrative hearings, in the welfare rights
area, for example, have been of somewhat dubious value.[83] Despite the case law on the books, welfare recipients have been
casually and regularly denied access to their own case files, the
opportunity to introduce relevant items into evidence, intelligi-
ble transcripts, and even adherence to federal regulations.[84]
Free legal representation for the poor, necessary to convert
such rights into realities, was hardly available in 1977,[85] and
the Reagan administration, of course, reduced the availability
of such counsel even further by reducing the budget for Legal
Aid.[86]

In some areas, the "new property" doctrine of *Goldberg* v.
Kelly, transforming what had previously been considered privileges into rights, or at least into "entitlements" with attendant
protection in terms of administrative hearings, seems to have
been a sound and sensible response to changing conditions. As
the Supreme Court has recognized, for many people today a
driver's license is a necessity, not merely a privilege, and must
not be taken away except by the due process of law.[87] Obviously, the point is not that a license is more important than
subsistence. Rather, for many, including welfare recipients,
the full-blown panoply of trial rights as announced by the
courts does not necessarily constitute the most helpful arma-

ment. Far more critical are the will and the resources to make the enjoyment of some of the most basic of those rights a reality. Indeed, the recent trend has been toward less formal procedures in administrative hearings, such as the decision of the District of Columbia Court of Appeals that a full evidentiary hearing was unnecessary over less than one hundred dollars in a medical-benefits case. Rather, the form the hearing "may take is flexible and can be adapted to the particular situation."[88]

Encouragement for other methods of reducing the trial-type adversary nature of agency proceedings and indeed, of courtroom proceedings themselves, has been growing. For example, a well-considered 1982 publication sets out detailed guidelines for avoiding litigation by settling contract claims against the government.[89]

In *Ashbacker Radio Corp.* v. *FCC*,[90] the Court held that when two or more applications for permits or licenses are mutually exclusive, the FCC must conduct a comparative hearing of the applications. The FCC had promised the "challenger" a hearing after the process of granting the rival application was to be completed, but the Court rejected that approach as a meaningless gesture. *Ashbacker* illustrates the role of administrative agencies in allocating scarce resources in our society. There, the FCC and the Court both recognized that granting both petitions would have been the least effective distribution of resources, because the two radio stations would have drowned each other out in static. The question, however, is whether the equitable principles upon which the Court's decision was based provides for the most effective and efficient distribution of resources. The answer is obviously no. The economic manager directs resources and energies; the judge declares rights. Those roles are not equivalent.[91]

A Tradition of Balance

John Rohr suggests that the bureaucrat act as a "balance wheel" among the three branches;[92] that the Public Administration, as he calls it, should strengthen whichever branch needs support in view of constitutional values. In this respect, Rohr continues to call for the internalization of constitutional norms, as he did in his earlier work.[93] Thus, if Congress, the president, and/or the courts give the bureaucrat mixed signals, that bureaucrat should follow the Constitution, to which he or she has taken an oath.[94] The people ratified the Constitution slowly, over time, in a serious, deliberative mood. Bureaucrats should obey Congress, for example, not primarily because Congress is elected but because the Constitution requires obedience in the situation in question. That constitutional requirement outweighs even a majoritarian decision, which may be but a passing passion of the moment.

A high-ranking counsel in the Energy Department took it upon himself, in a situation in which he apparently had no direction at all, to decide that four million dollars in surplus funds should be given to religious institutions for them to use to alleviate the burden of heating bills on the poor.[95] One can imagine that this effort to improve distributional equality might have reflected the jurisprudential influence of John Rawls, perhaps as applied to constitutional thinking by Ronald Dworkin, were the case at hand judicial, rather than administrative.

> Sufficient heat is certainly a basic need or primary good, but [this bureaucrat's action, unauthorized by anyone except himself] cannot convincingly be linked to the needs of democratic decisionmaking . . . [and] abridges the polity's right to decide what harms or injustices it wishes to remedy or to what other uses it wishes to put the surplus funds.[96]
> [T]he kinds of primary goods that Rawls and other proponents of liberal equality propose (such as basic amounts of housing, health care, or education) [cannot] be legitimately provided if a connection to political choice [cannot] be firmly established. Rawlsian notions such as the "difference principle" or the "veil of ignorance" and the con-

ception of justice that follows from them have no privileged place within a democratic conception of responsibility.[97]

This suggests a need for "a broader understanding of the bureaucrat's place within a more encompassing set of political institutions and processes."[98] Like Ely in the judicial arena, John Burke commends to those in the administrative arena a process-oriented structure of constitutional values.[99] Burke explicitly recognizes the Nuremberg exception to orders from those who are more accountable politically, but argues that such situations, in which one receives orders that are outrageously violative of fundamental ethical principles, are rare.[100] Furthermore, the process values that Burke argues can be derived from "the enterprise as a whole,"[101] to which one owes obligations at least as great as to one's personal superiors, would probably cover such cases, although Burke does not make this argument.

Burke utterly rejects Dworkin's preference for the utilization of substantive rights in "hard cases," however, in administration as well as in jurisprudence: "[A] procedural sense of fairness . . . may be more positively protective of rights since it does not independently grant or take away rights."[102] Burke illustrates his point with Dworkin's treatment of the deFunis case, where Dworkin's "right to equal concern and respect" results in forcing Dworkin to justify rejection of the (white) deFunis from law school based on his race, while Dworkin simultaneously attempts to assert the supremacy of individual rights over policy goals.[103]

Burke argues for a more Jeffersonian approach here, in calling for the supremacy of the democratic political process over the bureaucrat's own decision of what substantive values he thinks the constitution calls for: That is, the Energy Department counsel should have sought a decision from those in positions of greater democratic accountability. Citing Rawls's book as a resurgence of Jeffersonianism[104] may have been right in terms of equality, but wrong in terms of representativeness.

Even Jerry Mashaw, who goes to great lengths to construct a substantive, neo–natural-rights "dignitary model" to inform "due process in the administrative state," as he called his book, believes "that we should give ourselves law primarily through nonjudicial institutions of private and public ordering, and that the compromised character of public life necessarily limits the degree of constitutionalization that will accommodate our constantly shifting needs to mediate the clash of individual and group interests."[105]

PART FOUR

The Constitutional Tradition in American History

X

Components of the Tradition

While the major themes of seventeenth- and eighteenth-century political philosophy powerfully shaped the general outlines of the American constitutional tradition, the particulars of English and American history reinforced certain elements and contributed others. The same philosophical context could have produced a wide range of alternative value systems; history selected from among them. In so doing, it provided the conceptual components of the utilitarian framework that best guides American policymaking.

Representativeness

Representativeness, the rule of law, and dissent were sown in England, but grew into very different shapes in American soil. The roots of representativeness in England were visible in the religious developments of the sixteenth and seventeenth centuries. Henry VIII's break from Rome placed him and his successors, rather than the pope, at the head of the Church of England. The new Anglican Church remained hierarchical and authoritarian, so Protestant reform could attack it quite as vigorously as it had attacked the Roman Catholic Church. In the late sixteenth century, for example, Cartwright of Cambridge "declared unlawful all forms of church government save the Apostles," and then fled to Holland.[1]

The Bible provided authority for Cartwright and for the English church reformers who followed him. These reformers used the Bible to expand the ability of an individual not in a formal position of authority—not a bishop, not a king, not even a duke or baron—to raise a credible challenge to formal authority based on individual interpretation of the written word; in this context, the written Word.

The Calvinist tradition used the Bible itself for ample evidence "that covenanting was the Lord's chosen method for social and religious combination,"[2] noting the post-Flood covenant with Noah,[3] the post-sacrifice covenant with Abraham,[4] and the Mosaic covenant with the Jewish people.[5] Presumably thus inspired, a few brave sixteenth-century souls tried to create their own church separate from the Church of England. They were stopped by "the authorities of London." Some participants were imprisoned, since they were obviously rejecting and at least implicitly attacking the official state church. Their "temerity" in establishing their own church appeared at the time "preposterous."[6]

By the early seventeenth century, however, Congregationalism had its own established tenets. Important among them were the separation of Church and State and the ability of like-minded individuals to join together in a covenant to form their own church, by free consent of the participants and guided by their individual interpretations of Scripture. The individual's right to make his own judgment necessarily underlay this theory. But this was not merely theory: The theory was implemented, and Congregationalists established churches.[7]

In 1603 reformers within the Anglican Church, perhaps in an effort to preempt the Congregationalists, called on James I to replace their bishops with elected ministers. James I understood the implications of this kind of reform. After refusing, he told the bishops, "If you were out, and they in place, I know what would become of my *Supremacie. No Bishop, no King.*"[8]

The Pilgrims fled to Holland to escape persecution. Holland, however, was too permissive for their tastes, so they arranged to move to America. Those arrangements required a corporate form to attract the necessary capital from London merchants. Thus, the Pilgrims, who had already covenanted with each other to constitute themselves as a church, now joined with each other in a second agreement as fellow stockholders in what was mostly their own business company. They landed at Plymouth Rock, far north of the area in Virginia that their London backers had arranged for them, and as far as they knew, completely out of touch with European civilization. Therefore, they formed yet a third agreement among themselves, this one for self-government beyond religion or business, but obviously influenced by the two previous covenants. They agreed "to combine ourselves into a civill body politick" under the terms of the Mayflower Compact in 1620. Numerous subsequent New England settlements organized themselves under similar covenants and compacts.[9]

In 1638, the Fundamental Orders of Connecticut established a government not just for the people party to it, but for the Commonwealth, providing for a legislature, a governor, judges, and other appurtenances of government. This created the first written constitution in history.[10] It was not radically different from other New England covenants. Thus, well before Hobbes and Locke set down their theories of civil societies organizing themselves by agreement and compact, American colonists were actually doing it.[11]

Joint-stock companies, such as those utilized by the Pilgrims, as well as by the East India Company and the Hudson's Bay Company, played major roles in colonization. The early Congregationalists no doubt took the covenanting idea from the Bible, but probably made conscious use of the joint-stock-company form.[12] So American colonists formed both church and company by constituting an entity out of various individual persons.

As opposed to the Virginia Company, whose charter remained in London, the officers of the Massachusetts Bay Company decided to transfer its charter to the colonies. ". . . [T]he charter of the corporation became with some modifications the constitution of the Commonwealth." By 1634, membership in the Company had grown to two hundred. A few active members, not officers, reviewed the charter and noticed that the power to make laws was theirs, not the officers'. They convened a meeting of the membership, only twenty-four of whom attended, and enacted some laws. More important, they provided that from then on a smaller number of deputies elected by the whole membership would make the laws. "Representation was . . . a convenient method of exercising fully legal rights in a corporation."[13]

This was obviously a fundamental step in building the idea that laws were to be made by the people's representatives, and that the ultimate source of authority was the voting population—each with one equal vote. While some scholars have cautioned against reading too much modern thinking back into early colonial history,[14] this form of representation was clearly an advance, and not just in theory; it happened. It differed considerably from the British system, where members of Parliament then frequently "represented" boroughs far away from where they lived, upon their party's recommendation. To this day, members of Parliament have a more tenuous connection with their constituencies and are relatively more beholden to their parties instead, compared with their American counterparts in Congress.[15]

Representativeness plays a much weaker role in France, for a second example. Unlike American bureaucrats, French bureaucrats have inherent power to make laws on their own (the *pouvoir réglementaire*) without any delegation of power from the legislature.[16] This power was said to have eased the transition from free France to the Nazi Vichy government in 1940.[17]

The Rule of Law

It should be noted that the events of 1634 in Massachusetts derived from common members of the corporation reviewing its charter. These corporate charters—no corporation could trespass beyond the powers set out in them—continued to build into the American consciousness the legitimacy and authority, if not the sanctity, of the fundamental written document.[18] The religious tradition of scriptural interpretation, in which the theologian "applied his logical faculties" to the document and then applied his interpretation to the real-life problem before him,[19] created legalistic habits in the colonies. This led Edmund Burke to complain, a month before the American Revolution, that the lawyerliness of the colonists was responsible for the American tendency to react as though harm had been done to them on the basis of principle, without "an actual grievance." No other country, he thought, had so many students of law, a "science" which creates the tendency to "anticipate the evil, and judge of the pressure of the grievance by the badness of the principle. . . . They . . . snuff the approach of tyranny in every tainted breeze."[20] Clearly, the authority of the written word helped to reinforce the concept of the rule of law, with its attendant concepts of fairness and equality before the law.

The great battles of the seventeenth-century English Civil War, culminating in Cromwell's victory, were fought largely in the name of the rule of law. Those battles greatly interested the settlers just then creating New England.

To James I at the end of the sixteenth century the alternative to inherited succession to the crown by divine right was

anarchy and destruction. If the people think the king has violated his contract with them, God is to provide whatever remedy is appropriate, not the "headlesse multitude."[21]

Sir Edward Coke, the great antagonist to James I, answered
that commands of the king fell null and void if in conflict with
higher law, natural law, or, as he put it, "common right and
reason . . . which God at the time of creation of the nature of
man infused into his heart. . . ."[22]

Coke's position eventually prevailed, but not without an outraged response from his own sovereign, James. In 1608 James
convened the judges of England, including Coke, who was then
Chief Justice of the Common Pleas, and announced that he
could overturn any of their judgments if he so chose. Coke de-
murred, quoting Bracton that while the king is under no man,
he is "under God and law," infuriating the king.[23] In fear of
martyring Coke, however, James instead "kicked him upstairs"
to the post of Chief Justice of the King's Bench, but the king
could neither co-opt nor deter him, and Coke found additional
opportunities to reject the king's claims of legal supremacy. In
1616, James finally removed Coke from the bench altogether.
But by 1628 Coke, by then seventy-seven years old, was a
leader of Parliament in the reign of Charles I, who ascended to
the throne upon James's death in 1625.[24]

Under Coke's direction, the 1628 Parliament enacted the Petition of Right, prohibiting the imposition of taxes without parliamentary approval and prohibiting imprisonment without a
demonstration of cause. Charles assented to, but ignored, the
Petition. Generally, throughout the rest of his tenure, Charles
attempted to defend the principles of divine right and absolute
royal supremacy that his father had propounded, but with less
diplomatic skill. Charles's stubborn defense of those principles
against the rising tide of English constitutionalism resulted in
the rebellion of Oliver Cromwell's Puritans, civil war against
Charles's Scots allies, the defeat of the latter, the trial and execution of Charles in 1649, the generally unhappy rule by
Cromwell as Lord Protector until his death in 1658, and finally
the restoration of the monarchy with Parliament's invitation to

the son of Charles I, who had been exiled to France, to return as Charles II in 1660. But Charles II and his successors governed as constitutional monarchs, not as absolute monarchs.[25]

The Levellers were the ideologues of Cromwell's revolution, although they never really exercised power during the Interregnum, and had little influence on English thought. However, the American concept of the separation of the people from the government, with the people as sovereign, had roots in the Levellers' 1649 Agreement of the People, with its idea that those who agree to the basic covenant, compact, or constitution, and their successors-in-interest, comprise the people-as-sovereign.[26]

The reality of the Interregnum in England from 1649 to 1660 was far less inspiring than the rhetoric of the Agreement of the People; indeed, the Agreement was nothing more than a draft, "quietly shelved by the Rump Parliament to which it had been presented."[27] Successive Parliaments were virtually meaningless as checks upon Cromwell's executive power. The democratic and libertarian theories, sentiments, and rallying cries of the period later exercised more influence in the colonies than they did in England. Invoking "English" principles of that era for their own constitution-building needs, later American colonists "were pitting the myth of the seventeenth century against the reality of the eighteenth and then transferring the qualities of the mythological seventeenth to their own assemblies."[28] Thus, in American theory, derived in this odd sense from seventeenth-century English history, government merely serves the state. It may make laws, but it does so only within the confines of the basic agreement.

Some American colonists were to argue that while those in Great Britain had agreed to the sovereignty of Parliament in the course of the Glorious Revolution of 1689, the American colonists, already here by then, were not party to that agreement. As a result, Jefferson and others argued that while the various portions of the Empire were of necessity under one monarch, they might well be under separate legislatures.[29]

The power of the "rule of law" concept seemed to increase

with distance from the human sovereign. New England hanged
Quakers for their views and thus hardly exemplified toleration
as well as, say, Pennsylvania.[30] Still, even New England "continued to cherish the doctrines and exemplify the principles of
the English rebellion, long after the Restoration and the apparent failure of the Radical and Puritan cause." Locke wrote
about the right to revolution when the monarch violated the
law; the Americans, of like mind, rebelled "in defense of law."
Americans, like James Otis in the 1761 Writs of Assistance
case, which condemned those English writs as illegal and
therefore void, knew the words of Coke, that "in many cases
the common law will control Acts of Parliament and adjudge
them to be utterly void." Whether Coke's dictum was good English law in 1761 was irrelevant; Americans knew the dictum
and thought it was good law.[31]

In 1765 Parliament inflicted the Stamp Act on the American
colonies, requiring the purchase of tax stamps for all sorts of
printed materials, from legal documents to playing cards. The
proceeds were used to raise money to pay for British troops in
the colonies. The American response reinforced and refined the
concept that different institutions of government properly play
different roles, although most usually attribute the idea to
Montesquieu. The Continental Congress of 1774 acknowledged
that Parliament had the power to regulate American sea commerce, because an Empire's legislature would need such regulation of international trade among its component parts (this
may have been inconsistent with Jefferson's argument, noted
above, of equal and independent legislatures), but denied that
Parliament could justifiably impose a tax on the American colonies.[32] The opposition across the water, in Parliament itself,
argued that the power of Parliament was total and complete.
In fact, governmental powers in the Empire had already, of
necessity, been fragmented. Colonial governors governed, with
Parliament only occasionally "meddling."

This brought the conceptual issue into sharp focus. When
Americans designed their own government, it was with a very
strong consciousness of the desirability of separation of

powers. McLaughlin stresses the federal division, between national and state governments,[33] but it seems likely that this consciousness helped further the distribution of powers among the governmental branches as well. Otherwise, the eighteenth-century view of sovereignty was that it was absolute, ultimate, indivisible. Blackstone was correctly cited for this proposition, and Hamilton echoed it. Yet Hamilton subsequently defended the federal division of powers, and the distribution of powers among the branches, with the argument that each is "sovereign with regard to its proper objects."[34]

Histories of the ancient republics made the Framers very nervous about the republican form of government. The tyrannical policies of George III, not the form of government, provided the justification for revolution as set forth in the Declaration of Independence. Hamilton noted that the Greek and Italian republics were so replete with violations of natural rights as to disqualify the republican form of government from any consideration were it not for recent "great improvement" in the theory of republican government.[35] A key "improvement" was David Hume's insight that the many diverse clashing interests in a large republic would likely produce better safeguards for rights than a small republic, which might be more susceptible to domination by a more cohesive collection of interest groups.[36] Madison wanted a national republican government with veto powers over state legislatures.[37] His failure to achieve that result disappointed him. Nonetheless, he defended the Constitution as it was finally designed, arguing that it went far enough in the direction of the large republic so that various self-interested factions would neutralize each other, preventing tyranny of the majority, and permitting "rational men to promote the public good."[38] Another "improvement" was Madison's division of governmental roles, for ambition "to counteract ambition."[39]

But what kind of tyranny worried the Framers? What kinds of rights did they fear might be curtailed? We have seen the rather limited legal and theoretical foundations for free speech and press at the time. Various laws sharply limited property rights as well. Price restrictions on bread or on moneylending, for example, limited the use one could make of one's own money in terms of allowable business return on investment. Sumptuary laws limited the items one could buy for enjoyment to those within the confines of the aesthetics, morality, and economics of the time. Categories of real-property tenure and the laws of nuisance and eminent domain limited the ways one could use or dispose of one's land.[40] ". . . [N]either liberty nor property was a right, singular; each was a complex and subtle combination of many rights, powers, and duties, distributed among individuals, society, and the state."[41]

Nonetheless, colonial Americans and the English held a much different concept of private property than that prevalent in other realms. Central government controlled business in Mogul India, Ming China, and the Ottoman Empire and left far less room for the independent exercise of control over property than did the relatively free market of even medieval Western Europe.[42] The enormous influence of the Byzantine Empire over Russia during Russia's formative years around A.D. 1000 imprinted on the Russian psyche the Byzantine idea that the State properly exercises great control over commerce: "[U]nlike the European merchant . . . the Muscovite enjoyed no independence and could not form companies or guilds." This tradition paved the way for the acceptance of communism in Russia almost a thousand years later.[43]

Thus, Western Europe had a relatively strong tradition of private control and independence with respect to property. Rights to real property were even less "encumbered" in the frontier conditions of colonial America[44] than in England. Individual freedoms of speech and press pose more of an analytic problem.

Dissent

The Levellers of the 1640s also rallied to the call for freedom of political expression,[45] and this call had far more impact on eighteenth-century America than on seventeenth-century England. England's separation from Rome substituted the English monarch for the pope as the source of the imprimatur required for book publication without subjection to criminal penalties. Printing was a state matter. A 1637 decree of the Star Chamber codified the prepublication licensing requirements that had replaced the imprimatur. Parliament under Cromwell and then under the Restoration repeatedly reenacted the terms of the decree. It was not until 1694 that the free-press advocates of the period achieved their highest goal, abolition of prior restraint on publication, when Parliament ceased renewing the licensing requirements.[46]

Freedom of speech meant that the monarch could not punish members of Parliament for statements made during proceedings of the House of Commons. Although Professor Maitland claimed that there was "statutory recognition of the freedom of debate" under Henry VIII,[47] other scholars believe that even this modest version of freedom of speech in England did not truly emerge uintil Elizabeth I and was not guaranteed until the English Bill of Rights of 1689.[48]

It is likely that Blackstone meant little more than these concepts of free speech and free press when he wrote that liberty of the press was essential to a free state, but his statement, which became "an eighteenth century cliché,"[49] may have meant more to the colonists than it did to Blackstone.

The famous 1735 trial of John Peter Zenger for seditious libel set a royal governor against a colonial jury who found Zenger innocent, basing their conclusion on the premise that Zenger's negative comments were true. This advanced considerably over the English law, which didn't accept truth as a defense against the charge of seditious libel until 1843.[50] The Zenger principles obviously fell short of guaranteeing freedom of expression: Had a hostile jury disliked what Zenger had to say, they doubtless would have convicted him. The Zenger decision represented, in essence, a victory of the jury over the Crown. That victory, however, was burned into the American consciousness as a victory for free expression. After 1776, fellow citizens *became* sovereign, so to speak, and free expression almost inevitably came to mean something more: freedom to say what the jury disliked. In any event, with the Zenger verdict, freedom of the press already meant more than the freedom from prior restraint that the English had won in 1689.[51]

According to Benjamin Franklin, colonial printers "impartially" published whatever made them money, except "bad things," which, it seems, were things that they thought might be unlawful. What was unlawful were "private, blasphemous, obscene or immoral, and seditious" libels.[52] Prior to the Zenger decision, in nonprivate libels, truth could not be used as a defense because the perceived harm of endangering the peacefulness of society made the statement's truthfulness irrelevant. This was all, of course, at least a century before John Stuart Mill's analysis of freedom of expression in *On Liberty*.

The evolution in thinking that would eventually produce *On Liberty* had begun. After the Stamp Act, the colonial press criticized Great Britain ferociously. The habits of a critical press persisted during and after the Revolution, lambasting American state and federal public officials and policy decisions "as contemptuously and scorchingly as it had against Great Britain. . . "[53]

The Sedition Act of 1798 established criminal penalties for criticism of administration policies. Its authors intended it to curb such criticism. Instead it produced a firestorm of criticism itself as an attack on liberty, and American history so remembers it. However, its drafters incorporated the Zenger principle of truth as a defense, and added the requirement that malice be proven, greatly anticipating, by many years, comparable advances in English law. Yet, it "played the villainous role here";[54] widespread public protests rose up against it, and it was not renewed upon its expiration in 1800.[55]

Apparently, the public was reacting against the experience of suppression: The legislation itself did not regress in terms of the official legal theory of free expression of that time. In the Revolutionary period, the fundamental concept of seditious libel (i.e., that mere words against the government could constitute a criminal assault) still flourished. The colonists had not hesitated to engage in "the tarring and feathering of a Tory editor because of his opinions," reflecting, as Leonard Levy wrote, "a rather restricted meaning and scope of freedom of the press."[56]

Levy, the foremost modern student of eighteenth-century free-expression thinking, greatly influenced modern scholarship with his 1960 book, *Legacy of Suppression*. In explaining his change of heart and change of title in the revised 1985 version of the book, *Emergence of a Free Press*, Levy wrote,

> Some states gave written constitutional protection to freedom of the press after Independence, others did not. Whether they did or not, their presses operated as if the law of seditious libel did not exist. To one whose prime concern was law and theory, a legacy of suppression came into focus; to one who looks at newspaper judgment on public men and measures, the revolutionary controversy spurred an expanding legacy of liberty. . . . If the press freely aspersed on matters of public concern for a generation before 1798, the broad new libertarianism that emerged after the enactment of the Sedition Act found a continuum linking prior experience with subsequent theory. If a legacy of suppression had existed at all, the realms of law and theory had perpetuated it, not the realms of practice.[57]

Levy cautions against overreaction to his newer book, and maintains that the tolerance of widespread seditious libel does not prove that there was a free press: "So long as the press *may* be subjected to government control . . . the press cannot be free—or is not as free as it should be."[58] But he concludes, ". . . [A]n antiquarian historicism that would freeze [the First Amendment's] original meaning has not guided its interpretation and was not intended to";[59] whatever the Framers' understanding was, they had intended to be read expansively:

> The First Amendment injunction, that there shall be no law abridging the freedom of speech or press, was boldly

stated if narrowly understood. The bold statement, not the narrow understanding, was written into the fundamental law. . . . What they said is far more important than what they meant.[60]

When he analyzed freedom of expression in *On Liberty*, John Stuart Mill was both reading the American past and writing the American future.

Equality and Democracy

Equality, like representativeness, came to mean something much beyond the versions of it that the colonists took from England. As the scope and power of the equality principle expanded, it transformed the American republic into an entity increasingly resembling a democracy, although the Founders feared democracy.

Equality in its earlier, more modest form, challenged the older theory of the "great chain of being," with all of creation hierarchically arranged, including a human subsystem with monarchs at the top and everyone else arranged in order below. Locke's theory of the civil compact, in contrast, provided for equality "to the extent of being signatories to the agreement"; all citizens were "equal voices, equal wills."[61]

The Founders utilized Lockean principles in their arguments for independence, and against Britain. Equality before the law provided justification for insurrection, since Americans were denied the benefits that other Englishmen were granted by the common law. Most notoriously, Americans sent no representatives to the Parliament that taxed them. Furthermore, English courts ruled against the validity of general, unlimited search warrants against Englishmen in England. But customs officers obtained and utilized such warrants in the colonies.[62] Such unequal treatment provoked a rallying cry for "equality."

But the Framers did not attempt to organize American society under strongly egalitarian principles. Following Locke, they were entirely comfortable with inequality of property, so long as it resulted from equal opportunity to exercise individual ability. Equality before the law and equality of treatment by government merely provided a means to the greater end of civil peace, necessary for private liberty. Private liberty could be exercised in areas outside the scope of government, where inequalities would properly develop: in commerce, for example.

Even in the public sphere, equality emerged on new and shaky ground. In Massachusetts and some other colonies, religious leaders tried to create virtual theocracies.[63] While theocratic control faded with the Revolution, the Massachusetts constitution of 1780 did retain property qualifications for voting and officeholding.[64] Equal rights under law obviously did not yet mean equal rights to make law.

Slaves, of course, had neither equality before the law nor equality of opportunity. The Framers appear to have acknowledged that slavery was wrong, but saw it as a necessity to create the Union. "Slavery was an evil to be tolerated, allowed to enter the Constitution only by the back door, grudgingly, unacknowledged, on the presumption that the house would be truly fit to live in only when it was gone, and that it would ultimately be gone." Jefferson took that position, although he did not believe it possible for freed blacks, en masse, to live under the same government as their former owners.[65]

Even in the South, the law continued to reflect, uncomfortably, a presumption against slavery. Throughout the South, the killing of a slave was generally considered murder.[66] But slavery was an institution to which the southern states were unalterably committed. Given their political power, Jefferson or Lincoln, lacking absolute or despotic power, could either yield to the prejudice of the time or "get out of politics altogether—and leave it to the *merely* prejudiced."[67]

An evangelical movement in the 1740s, especially in Virginia, democratized the spirit of colonial Christianity. New England Calvinism produced a somewhat rigid social structure with the autocratic doctrine of the "elect," those whose success in this life marked them as candidates for heavenly reward. The 1740s movement, with its sweeping theme that piety and grace are available to anyone at anytime, was a strong egalitarian democratic influence.[68]

The Revolutionary rhetoric of equality, directed against England, unleashed additional egalitarian sentiment, disturbing established patterns of deference. Initially, upper-class colonials may have talked more freely in egalitarian terms than they otherwise would have because of the habitual electoral deference given to the gentry and higher classes by the lower classes. However, the power of the rhetoric of equality of rights took the application of the concept well beyond the apparent intentions of the Framers.

After the Revolution, domestic quarrels proliferated, most dramatically with the 1786 Shays's Rebellion of indebted, overtaxed farmers. The Framers were extremely nervous about the potential for tyranny by the masses, although they remained equally nervous about tyranny by autocrats. Since they generally acknowledged the people as the ultimate source of sovereignty, legitimacy, and authority, the only available solution lay in balancing one class against another. Liberty, therefore, meant government "as an honest broker among a variety of propertied interests." Otherwise, rule by the masses would result in expropriation and the destruction of liberty. Thus only the propertied could be trusted with the reins of government. The propertied, however, were a relatively large group at the time. When the Framers thought of "the people," they probably envisioned the "yeomanry," the large class of small property owners. As the propertyless parts of the middle class and the even poorer urban proletariat increased dramatically as a percentage of the population, American political thought became increasingly democratic.[69]

During the Constitutional Convention, which was closed to the public, the Framers freely expressed their profound reservations about empowering the masses. As soon as they had to begin the public process of winning popular support for ratification, they returned to democratic rhetoric. "Men who only a few months earlier had voiced deep misgivings over popular rule now tried to outdo their opposition in expressing their enthusiasm for the people."[70] Property qualifications for voting began their inevitable fall in New York, where they were repealed in the state constitutional convention of 1821.[71] By the mid-nineteenth century, suffrage extended to virtually all adult white males.[72] A few decades into the nineteenth century, the better-established classes appear to have become convinced that the (white) lower classes could be trusted with the vote. This came out of the realization that most Americans expected to be rich someday, and therefore supported safeguards against potential majority decisions to trample the wealthy minority. In supporting laws that "explicitly placed limits on the majority,"[73] Americans provided some protection for other minorities as well. Even Lincoln felt obliged to warn against violent jealousy against the rich in these terms: "Let not him who is houseless pull down the house of another; but let him labor diligently and build one for himself, thus by example assuring that his own shall be safe from violence when built."[74]

Then, as now, the American attachment to personal ownership of property competed with the American goal of equality.[75]

Virtue, Self-interest, and Property

Hume thought that countervailing interests more effectively guarded against tyranny in a large republic with more interests than in a small republic with fewer interests. That theory addressed one problem Madison and other Framers had anticipated based on their review of ancient republics. A second problem involved even more subtlety.

A like-minded citizenry, uniformly loyal to some established set of moral values, would probably produce a stable republic,

free of violent clashes and strife. But starting with a heterogeneous, independent-minded, and self-interested population,
enforcing the imposition of homogeneous values would have en-
tailed a probably futile effort. Furthermore, a people strongly
and almost uniformly attached to a particular set of moral values will probably act unjustly to any who do not share those
values. Thus, the Framers addressed the problem of designing
a republic simultaneously stable and just.

Classical theory, dating from Aristotle, taught that the goal
of government is to produce the most virtuous possible citizenry. The Framers rejected this view.[76] They foresaw that
the government powers requisite to this task would be enormous, and would likely include oppressive brainwashing. While
ambitious self-interest was to grow to extraordinary propor-
tions among Americans in the nineteenth century, it already
occupied a substantial place in the American character in the
eighteenth. The colonies, except Massachusetts, "were all
founded with the incentive of a very high degree of appeal to
the interests themselves . . . in the first half of the seventeenth
century."[77] By the eighteenth century, America's population
would obviously resist the sacrifice of private interests for public virtue. To reorient the public to accept as its highest priority the *public* welfare, the Framers might well have needed
to create a highly authoritarian state utilizing extremely harsh
policies. Mao used such policies in twentieth-century China to
produce the social order he sought.[78]

For a republican model closer to their liking, the Framers
looked to small, self-sufficient, homogeneous polities probably
akin to Swiss cantons. The American polity was large and heterogeneous, even then. The Constitution, therefore, needed to
accommodate American conditions with republican goals. Instead of direct participation, as in the canton, the Constitution
provided for representation; instead of individual autonomy, individuals held rights against the state; substantive consensus
was replaced by procedural consensus; and perhaps most important, public norms were replaced by private norms, and
shared values were replaced by self-interest.[79]

Aristotle's Christian successors would have had the State encourage "grand, dramatic, character-ennobling" virtue, a kind of virtue likely to lead to violent differences of opinion. Locke, in defining, narrowing, and separating out the function of the government from that of the polity, left responsibility for the higher, more dramatic virtues to the nongovernmental parts of the polity, like private educational establishments. The Framers, following Locke, held the role of government only to be the protection of "commodious self-preservation" for the citizenry.[80] Thus, Locke said, "however strange it may seem, the lawmaker hath nothing to do with moral virtues and vices."[81]

In the classical view, "commerce was seen to undermine the manly virtues without which a republic could not survive."[82] By contrast, the Framers clearly designed American government to promote and protect the pursuit of private interest,[83] but foresaw that enlightened self-interest would promote more subtle virtues. In a commercial republic merit, not artificial aristocracy, would be the ruling principle. Indeed, Toqueville reported, fifty years later, on the dominance of enlightened self-interest, not classical virtue, in motivating Americans' efforts on behalf of their own local communities. Unpaid mayors and aldermen made small sacrifices of their time and money for the welfare of their communities, but those sacrifices served their own best interests.[84]

The Framers, therefore, abandoned what were in any case "unrealizable ethical perfections"[85] in return for stability and liberty.

The success of this strategy required the taming of emotionally powerful religious forces. Religious concepts of the role of the State had motivated the destabilizing internal and external European wars in a way the Framers hoped to avoid.

The Puritans sought liberty to serve Christ. The Declaration of Independence reflected and encouraged a new way of thinking. "Life, liberty, and the pursuit of happiness" meant the liberty to pursue happiness each in his own way. Like the Congregationalists reading the Bible for themselves, Amer-

icans were to read the Declaration for themselves. As Cal-
vinists felt themselves each permanently and personally
responsible for their relationship with God, Americans were to
feel themselves each permanently and personally responsible
for their relationship with government. Men understood that
they now must make government "respond to the kind of lives
they wanted to live."[86]

Jefferson's commitment to freedom of religious expression
advanced the "privatization" of religion. As key facilitators in
the long American process of taking religious doctrine out of
and away from the legitimate sphere of government, the Framers reduced the likelihood of internal religious wars. This also
inevitably removed from government the role of "improving"
the citizenry by inculcating it with the "true" faith. There was
to be no "true faith"; government's aims would be more modest. Government's "first object," said Madison, was to be the
"protection of different and unequal faculties of acquiring property."[87] This would have been shocking to preceding genera-
tions for whom government's chief goals were Aristotelian in
the Christian context, i.e., to promote virtue as defined by
some particular form of Christianity.[88]

The passion that in Europe had frequently been devoted to
the pursuit of religious truth, with resulting bloodshed, here
attached to the pursuit of property.[89] The availability of a land
relatively abundant in natural resources,[90] and the relative
abundance of land itself, surely helped. Turning Americans
away from devotion to strict and harsh religious demands and
toward the pleasures of material acquisition may have contributed to the rapid decline in prosecutions for sexual or religious
offenses (the latter including blasphemy, profanity, and failure
to attend church) in seven Massachusetts counties. Between
1760 and 1774, 51 percent of the prosecutions there were for
such offenses. In the early nineteenth century, with no major
changes in the laws on the books, "the rate of prosecutions for
these crimes declined almost to nothing."[91] Crimes against
property, burglary and theft, became the major prosecutorial
focus. "During and for a generation after the Revolution it was

a common complaint of the clergy that the virtues of simplicity of life and dedication to religion were getting lost in a welter of lust for private gain."[92]

"Equality of opportunity" was a strong mid-nineteenth-century theme. Indeed, many Americans availed themselves of very real economic opportunity. "Opportunity" really existed, but "equality" gave the phrase moral authority in the mouths of Americans. That authority derived from the Revolutionary rhetorical tradition and perhaps also from the use, very popular then, of the biblical story of universal descent from Adam and Eve.[93]

Nineteenth-century America devoted itself overwhelmingly to commerce and the acquisition of property. Andrew Jackson coined the phrase "equal protection" in his 1832 message vetoing the rechartering of the Bank of the United States: "If [Government] would confine itself to equal protection, and as Heaven does its rains shower its favors alike on the high and the low, the rich and the poor, it would be an unqualified blessing." Jackson's commitment was to extend equality of opportunity under the protection of government to "every social or economic class." "It fell to a later generation than Jackson's to extend the obligations owed by government to members of every race or heritage."[94]

Andrew Jackson, at least within the constraints indicated, sincerely believed in equality of opportunity. He vetoed the rechartering of the Bank of the United States in rejection of the notion that government should create unequal, and better, opportunities for some.[95]

In the later years of the nineteenth century, however, American government facilitated "the release of individual creative energy,"[96] more than it refereed among various kinds of property ownership in a hands-off, laissez-faire style. As a contrast to the older English monarchical model, decentralization of power seemed to require that the control of property, to the extent possible, be placed in private hands rather than in a central government. Government would play a major role in coordinating that placement. Article IV, Section 3, of the Con-

stitution says, "The Congress shall have the power to dispose
of and make any needful Rules and Regulations respecting the
Territory or other property belonging to the United States."
Grants of federal land to the railroad companies built the interstate transcontinental railroad system in the 1860s.[97] Throughout the nineteenth century, the states regularly expropriated
land from private owners, with compensation, "to allocate resources, to influence the structure of entrepreneurial activity,
and even to provide effective subsidies for favored types of
business enterprises." By the 1820s, Americans commonly accepted as a point of law the eminent-domain power of the sovereign to take private property for public purposes, as long as
the original owner received fair compensation.[98]

For Americans, the unhappy experience with England
emphasized the value of limits on government's power to decide how property would be used. The energy of nineteenth-
century American development brought irresistible support for
the use of law to facilitate development, not just to protect
property, and the two goals could come into conflict.[99] Even
voluntary, informal associations of Americans "jerry-built"
legal institutions for such purposes as resolving disputes over
land claims. The courts would not hesitate to put their imprimatur on such ad hoc arrangements once they had been in
place for a while. Nineteenth-century legislatures, reflecting
public perceptions, saw "property as an institution of growth
rather than merely of security," and went so far as to grant
"franchises for private capital development," while retaining
"standard reservation[s] of legislative authority to amend or
repeal what they gave."[100]

The Civil War, requiring as it did new long-distance rail
transport of soldiers and supplies and large-scale manufactur-
ing, probably hurried the concentration of economic power.
The Supreme Court further accelerated this process in 1886,
when it applied the Fourteenth Amendment provision for due
process to corporate "persons." This enabled the Court to
strike down state legislation "interfer[ing] with the private accumulation of capital."[101] With corporate access to "oppor-

tunities" not open to ordinary, noncorporate persons, equality of opportunity became less a reality than it had been, but corporations and other persons claimed the "equal protection" of the law.

This began a series of important changes in the American legal concept of property. Justice Oliver Wendell Holmes wrote, in dissent, "By calling a business property, you make it seem like land, and lead up to a conclusion that a statute cannot substantially cut down the advantages of ownership existing before the statute was passed."[102] By facilitating "the private accumulation of capital," this redefinition by the Supreme Court "hastened the industrialization of the American economy."[103]

Supreme Court majorities in this period from the end of the nineteenth century until 1937 couched their policy of protecting private property against government interference in terms of natural-law theory, with reference to the natural rights of property ownership. The courts thus prevented legislatures from limiting the power of industrial monopolies on those occasions when legislatures were so inclined. Workers and farmers suffered at the hands of concentrated economic power. Their representatives, first the agrarian Populists of the late nineteenth century and then the urban Progressives of the early twentieth century, sought restoration of the equal-opportunity doctrine, and eventually turned to a more utilitarian theory to defend themselves, the natural-rights theory having been appropriated by the opposition.[104] The Progressives turned "to the power of national institutions to dominate that of the great private corporations."[105]

Their success came with the New Deal, when the government finally began to accept a role as counterbalance to, instead of facilitation for, the great private interests. As a result, starting with the New Deal, the proportion of American wealth held and controlled by government grew enormously. Individuals now pay a substantial portion of their income to the government. That portion is therefore no longer available to the individual. "The taxpayer is a participant in public insurance,"

such as Social Security, "by compulsion, and his ability to care
for his own needs independently is correspondingly reduced.
Similarly, there is no choice about using public transportation,
public lands for recreation, public airport terminals, or public
insurance on savings deposits. . . . [G]overnment is the sole
supplier."[106]

Thus, another shift in the allocation of power was warranted.
Ordinary citizens had seen themselves at the mercy of powerful private forces prior to the New Deal. The New Deal empowered government to control those private forces, but in the
process gave government a much greater degree of control
over the lives of ordinary citizens as well. In response, citizens
(or at least scholars purporting to speak on their behalf) demanded a counterbalancing increase in the level of rights protecting individuals against government power.

Thus, older courts had held that welfare was a privilege,
mere "charity" that could be conditioned on whatever rules
government chose to set.[107] The "privilege doctrine" was overturned by the landmark holding of *Goldberg* v. *Kelly*,[108] that
welfare grants were a kind of property that could not be taken
away without due process of law. *Goldberg* v. *Kelly* and its
numerous progeny in case law created another major change in
the American definition of property, once again changing the
boundaries within which "the owner has a greater degree of
freedom than without." In feudal times, all property belonged
to the Crown, which was then equivalent to the State. Gradually, land ownership devolved to private individuals through
royal grants. Now, entitlements to money grants, like welfare,
would also come to be "owned" by private individuals, and not
by the State.[109]

The problem is that government may have to tax one set of
citizens in order to provide these entitlements for another set
of citizens. A 1960 study of skilled workers, such as a machine
operator who was also a part-time janitor, found that such
"workers tended to feel that a man should be allowed to keep
the goods of fortune, and that one who had made a million dol-

lars had deserved his reward." As Pole concludes, "a genuine egalitarian ideology would conflict with the American system of incentives."[110] Americans will not countenance an unequivocal commitment to equality of results.

While Americans share common core ideas of property, the boundary lines around its definition remain controversial.

XI

Evidence of the Tradition

There was a United States Constitution before there was a United States. The Framers of that Constitution wondered whether, as Hamilton put it, we could arrange a better government for ourselves and our descendants by "reflection" and design or whether "accident and force" must ultimately prevail.[1] The design for the country was the Constitution. It worked.

Not everyone accepts this conclusion. A prominent law professor wrote that the constitutional tradition in America pales into insignificance in comparison with an unwritten constitution with its "nasty little secret" that the government is above the law, and that a "government of laws and not men" is merely an "idealistic cliché."[2] A respected constitutional lawyer added that the "falsity" of "notions of government by law, not people," including "judicial subservience to a Constitution," was "exposed" long ago.[3]

Better historians than those just quoted have also rejected the tradition of the Constitution as the critical factor in American society and history. Daniel Boorstin argued that political parties, more than the Constitution, played the important formative role.[4] David Potter pointed to material abundance as the key.[5] Charles Beard stressed economic relationships.[6] Frederick Jackson Turner pointed to the frontier.[7] Their arguments have long been accorded the respectful attention they deserve, and need no further discussion here. However, the evidence supports at least equally well a critical historical role for the Constitution. Yet the Constitution sometimes seems to serve more as the target of revisionist critics than as the subject of affirmative statement.

The evidence indicates that political parties in the United States have tested their actions and their platforms against the constitutional tradition. When they have passed the test, they have gained the mantle of legitimacy. When they failed, they paid a high political price; sometimes, as with the national ambitions of the Federalists, the results were fatal. The first bellwether year in American political history was 1800. That year, the Federalist party, which had provided the first twelve years of presidential government in the United States, lost in large measure on the basis of public reaction against its 1798 Sedition Act's infringement of freedom of speech, perceived by the public as repressive, and therefore unconstitutional.[8] The Federalists were never to regain national dominance.

Both sides perceived themselves as fighting the Civil War to defend constitutional principles. The South saw the dominant Northern attitude toward states' rights as "revolutionary,"[9] and their own stronger version of states' rights as bedrock constitutional principle to be defended. The North saw secession by the South as a threat to the Constitution, which Northerners identified with law and order.[10]

Franklin Roosevelt's court-packing scheme failed, but the eventual constitutional success of his program of vast increases in the magnitude of federal executive government was far more significant. The twenty years of Roosevelt-Truman Democratic government so cemented into American constitutional tradition the legitimacy of large-scale federal executive power that even succeeding Republican administrations made no significant effort to cut back such power or basic programs operating under it. These extensions of federal executive power had posed serious, basic, and major constitutional issues, but they were decisively legitimized by the post-1937 Court decisions in their favor. Judicial review, as well as the system of party government, communicated such legitimacy to the American people.

The unwillingness of some American critics to accept the magnitude of the role of the Constitution and its tradition may stem from a "purloined letter" effect or from "missing the forest for the trees": It is so obvious, it is overlooked. Or it may come from an unwillingness or inability to compare the characteristics of other nations; or from the allure of revisionism and cynicism, which do after all sound somewhat more sophisticated than reaffirmation of the virtues of the United States and its Constitution.

Of course, the cup may be half full or half empty. The cynics are to some extent right: The Constitution has from time to time been "altered or disregarded in the name of necessary response to crisis," but the fact that its moral suasion more often prevails is a far more significant and remarkable phenomenon.[11]

One cynical observer suggested in 1982 that a majority of the Supreme Court then dared not overrule the publicly disliked holding of *Miranda* v. *Arizona*,[12] the criminal defendant's "right to warnings" case, only because the Court feared a reaction "too harmful" to the Court's legitimacy.[13] The cynical observer intended to demonstrate the weakness of precedent and the rule of law. But his illustration suggests a different conclusion. Even though the public dislikes the *Miranda* decision, it has so much legitimacy as law, and even more so as constitutional law, that the Court dares not risk its own legitimacy by attacking it frontally.

There are four aspects of the constitutional tradition in the United States. The first consists of those commands of the Constitution that have been clearly understood from the beginning, without historical development or judicial interpretation. The separation of the federal legislature into two houses, the House and the Senate, provides an example of one such command. The requirement of a presidential election every four years is another.

The second aspect is those general concepts and values that the Constitution reflected, crystallized, and continues, permanently, to inject back into the American polity: representativeness, the rule of law, dissent, property, liberty, equality. Their general form does not change, but their specifics evolve. The extent of freedom of speech understood to have been implied by the First Amendment has changed with the years. The implications of the Commerce Clause have grown so much and so consistently that each generation would likely be surprised were it confronted with the following generation's interpretation.

The third aspect consists of those results of judicial interpretation which have been accepted by the public, whether immediately or gradually, as correct and authoritative. The validation of congressional power to make Treasury notes legal tender was one example of this aspect.[14] The prohibition against legally mandated segregation, more recently, was another.

Each of these first three aspects of the constitutional tradition includes a method, accepted by the American people, by which certain powers or actions of the government are made legitimate, and others illegitimate, in their eyes.

The fourth aspect, closely related to the "rule of law" value in the second aspect, consists of faith in a written document as an effective blueprint for a society, which stems from the even stronger faith in the power of the (generally unexamined) Constitution itself. The most notorious example of that faith was the Prohibition Experiment under the Eighteenth Amendment. Faith in the power of the Treaty of Versailles to create an effective League of Nations, or in the Atlantic Charter to institute an era in which Franklin Roosevelt's "Four Freedoms" would be taken seriously by the entire planet, are other examples. Manifestations of the attitude created by this faith can also be found throughout the history of voluntary associations in America, an enormous proliferation of clubs based on charters and constitutions, worthy of notice by Toqueville in 1835,[15] and so numerous that General Henry M. Robert had reason to publish his *Rules of Order* of parliamentary procedure for the use of such clubs.[16]

These comprise the constitutional tradition in the United States. That the Constitution itself has been violated often does not controvert the thesis that its tradition has been and is a dominant force in American life.

The United States operates, by and large, under the rule of law. The Supreme Court, through the process of judicial review, serves as chief oracle of the law, and reports of the Court's unpopularity in that role occasionally surface. Yet five attitude surveys conducted between 1962 and 1966, shortly after two Supreme Court decisions prohibiting prayers in public schools,[17] showed popular support for the Supreme Court.[18] Indeed, in one of the studies, using Minnesota data, nearly half the respondents who approved of prayer in schools still seemed to approve the Supreme Court decisions, suggesting "some sort of halo effect from the symbolic image of the Supreme Court."[19] A 1965 Seattle study concluded, "However measured, the attitudes were supportive of the Supreme Court."[20]

Visitors have noticed the unusual degree to which law operates in everyday American life. Toqueville said, "Scarcely any political question arises in the United States that is not resolved, sooner or later, into a judicial question."[21] This is because judicial review of legislation makes the Constitution the supreme authority—the Constitution, not the president, and not any legislative or political body.[22] Another French observer, some fifty-six years later, in 1891, wrote, "In the United States it is the American people which was the artificial element, and, so to speak, created from above. Here, it is not the nation which made the Constitution, but the Constitution which created the nation."[23]

Americans are a litigious people: We constantly look to the law to resolve disputes.[24] It has been argued that a heterogeneous people like ours needs this tool particularly to resolve political disputes, because "only a *constitutional* bridge, buttressed by judicial review, can effectively span the gap between politically warring factions. . . . [M]ajoritarian legislation is not adequate to the need."[25]

The Constitution gives law its special power to legitimize government policy and political or social change, and can destroy efforts to implement government policy or social change that cannot be harmonized with the constitutional tradition. That power was impressively demonstrated in the impeachment proceedings against Richard Nixon, in the Steel Seizure Case against President Harry Truman,[26] in the national acceptance of the New Deal, and in the racial-integration cases. The history of constitutional protection of dissent and civil liberties, and the failures thereof, does provide evidence that the Constitution has been disregarded, on occasion, in the name of "necessary response to crisis," but it more impressively demonstrates that the constitutional tradition has prevailed against what would in other countries have been the crushing force of "reasons of state."

Legitimacy and the
Constitutional Tradition

The Nixon impeachment proceedings demonstrated the depth and strength of the national commitment to constitutional legal process in times of political crisis. The House of Representatives debated the matter in the language, and over issues, of constitutional law. If the House had voted to impeach, the senators trying the case would have sworn a special oath, under the "Rules for Impeachment Trials" in the Senate manual, to do "impartial justice according to the Constitution and laws," i.e., without regard to party or politics.[27]

Lawyers for Nixon and the special prosecutor waged battle in court for control of the Watergate tapes.[28] Processes of law resolved a momentous question of national politics. This seemed a reasonable approach in the United States, through our long practice in the habit of resolving political questions by law. Within the same general period of time, the British had held a general election which gave Prime Minister Edward Heath neither a clear mandate to remain in office nor a clear signal to resign. Unlike Nixon, Heath had done nothing wrong; the problem was purely political. It was, however, a "constitutional dilemma" for the British. "But no one in Britain would have dreamt of putting the question to a court."[29] It seems to have been peculiarly American to have resolved the question of our leader's fitness to continue in office over questions of law debated in a court and in a legislature.

In England, Walter Bagehot long ago noted the dichotomy between the symbolic power of the Crown and the operational power of the prime minister.[30] As the actual operation of a government involves the practice of politics, which is often unromantic and disillusioning, the English government retains its legitimacy, its symbolic power, through the Crown. Only the prime minister need dirty his or her hands in the politics of government. Some see the legitimacy of American government as vulnerable because the symbolic and operational power must both reside in the president. By virtue of the symbolic power of the Constitution, the government of the United States retains its legitimacy, whatever the president may do, as the Nixon proceedings demonstrated. The president only administers the Constitution. He may tarnish or even destroy his own symbolic power through malfeasance in office, but he cannot tarnish the symbolic power of the Constitution, and he therefore cannot destroy the central integrity of American government legitimacy.

The outcome of the impeachment proceedings illuminated another facet of the constitutional tradition as well. Nixon had unleashed an unprecedented assault on that tradition by approving crimes like burglary and wiretapping, by abusing the Internal Revenue Service, the Federal Bureau of Investigation, and the Central Intelligence Agency for his personal and political vendettas, and by utilizing preventive detention against the May Day demonstrators. As a result, Henry Steele Commager wrote that Nixon's resignation was "no voluntary act. . . . It was forced on him by a ground swell of public outrage, by a popular ralliance to the Constitution comparable to that which swept the North at the time of Fort Sumter, and by a Congress that after long vacillation finally responded to the standards of duty and the obligations of the Constitution."[31]

One constitutional scholar argued that the law has never stood in the way of top government officials during national emergencies, except for the Steel Seizure Case,[32] which he dismisses as a "sport."[33] There, the Court voided President Truman's Korean War emergency order mandating federal control and operation of the steel mills, holding it an unconstitutional taking of property without due process of law. Apparently the writer did not think it significant that the Court, with no economic or military power, could by the force of its legitimacy and moral suasion thwart the president, the most powerful political leader in the country.

Robert Dahl argued that the Court usually loses major battles against Congress or the president. Still, even he conceded that the Court has been quite effective in delaying the implementation of presidential and congressional policy decisions for years, and even for decades. He agreed that the Court plays an essential role in conferring legitimacy, in conjunction with its responsibility to set "higher standards of justice and right than the majority of citizens or their representatives might otherwise demand."[34]

Millions of people supported Franklin Roosevelt's New Deal programs, but millions opposed them too. When the Court first struck down his National Industrial Recovery Act as unconstitutional,[35] he was thwarted, at least with respect to the programs in question. Later, the Court changed, and his programs changed too (never again did he attempt a delegation of congressional power to executive agencies as broad as the one that was attacked in the *Schechter Poultry* case),[36] and the Court upheld his efforts.[37] The Supreme Court alone could have imparted such legitimacy to the New Deal.[38] The degree to which it did so was illustrated by Republican presidential candidate Dwight D. Eisenhower in a 1952 speech: "We accept as part of these social gains the fact that Americans must have adequate insurance against disaster. No one counts that thing a political issue anymore. That is part of America."[39]

But what of social change still embroiled in controversy for Americans? What, in particular, about the great U.S. Supreme Court school-desegregation decision, *Brown* v. *Board of Education*?[40] In 1954 the Court held that the equal-protection clause of the Fourteenth Amendment prohibited the segregation of schoolchildren by race. With no court order of any kind, with nothing but this statement of principle by the Court, more than five hundred school districts in states involved in the case, and in states not involved, "abandoned policies of segregation."[41] In 1955, the Court ordered that integration take place "with all deliberate speed,"[42] and officials throughout the South, except Mississippi and Alabama, indicated their intention to obey the law. In March 1956 the southern delegation to Congress issued its "Manifesto," which claimed constitutional legitimacy for the position opposed to the Court's ruling. Only then did the South first mobilize in firm resolve against integration.[43]

With the 1964 Civil Rights Act, the battle for legitimacy was won. *The New York Times* reported a typical southern restaurant owner's response:

Last year we fought them because they were breaking the law. This year, I'd be breaking the law if I refused to serve them. I'm a law-abiding citizen. If the law says feed them, I feed them. While I don't like it, I'm not going to break the law.[44]

A 1964 study reported in *Scientific American*, analyzing survey data from 1942 to that year, concluded that *Brown* v. *Board of Education* had indeed significantly hastened public acceptance of desegregation.[45] Dr. Kenneth Clark, in 1976, pointed to the psychological impact on American Blacks of the *Brown* v. *Board of Education* decision delegitimizing segregation. Within three years of the decision, he noted, "blacks who seemed to have accepted compliantly racial segregation since the latter part of the nineteenth century now openly defied institutionalized racism."[46]

For all the well-publicized resistance to integration in the North in recent years, attitudes have changed. Only 12 percent of White Americans polled in 1976 supported segregation, along with 4 percent of Blacks.[47] The Reagan administration, seen as the least sensitive to racial minorities of presidential administrations in many years, nonetheless consistently expressed opposition to racial discrimination—"at the point of a bayonet, if necessary," according to a spokesperson.[48] It may still be practiced, but it is no longer legitimate, because the Court said it was unconstitutional:

> In such a heterogeneous country as the United States, where the Constitution is one of the great unifiers of sentiment, the influence of law on opinion may be considered particularly significant. Throughout the long campaign for civil rights legislation, one of the most cogent arguments was precisely that the law could and would exert progressive influence on opinion, and no one can reasonably doubt that, in the long run, *Brown* v. *Board of Education* and related cases did have that effect.[49]

Dissent and Freedom of Speech

The Supreme Court bestows the legitimacy of the Constitution on statutes or policies it upholds on constitutional grounds. Looking at the Court as a sort of wire conducting the electricity of the Constitution to particular statutes or policies, it carries the most legitimacy "voltage" when it applies the First Amendment. In his Supreme Court opinions on the subject, Justice Hugo Black wrote, among other things, "Freedom to speak and write about public questions is as important to our government as is the heart to the human body."[50] Similarly, Professor Alexander Meiklejohn placed freedom of speech at the heart of our constitutional democracy, since it ensures the free exchange of ideas and opinions which constitute the thinking process of the community, vital to the "basic American agreement that public issues shall be decided by universal suffrage."[51]

Not every provision of the Constitution is central to its tradition. While the Court and the nation have varied in the degree of actual protection they have chosen to give free speech, free speech stands at the very top of the constitutional tradition, the constitutional myth. The constitutional tradition of free speech in American social myth,[52] on one hand, and the constitutional law of free speech, in actual constitutional content and court interpretation of it, on the other, relate to each other in complex, confusing ways. These realms intertwine, in ways that are sensed better than they are described. Freedom of speech in the United States has a strange history: In the years of greatest danger, 1812[53] and the Civil War,[54] the nation tolerated dissent far better than during a war separated from most Americans by an ocean, World War I, when our nation was in far less serious danger.[55]

The role of the American constitutional tradition in protecting speech and dissent becomes much clearer in comparison with what happens elsewhere. First, note that constitutional limitations on government do not generally exist at all outside Western Europe, several former and present British Commonwealth nations, the United States, and other scattered examples.[56] Examine some of these favored few.

One scholar remarked in 1891 that ". . . the great political powers in England are in no way the creatures of a constitution, for their existence is anterior to any fundamental law whatever."[57] Thus, there is no "fundamental law" guaranteeing individual rights: Freedom of speech, from a legal point of view, has no "greater sanctity than that enjoyed by, for example, a Lotteries and Gaming Act."[58] Another wrote that "[f]reedom of discussion is, then, in England, little else than the right to write or say anything which a jury, consisting of twelve shopkeepers, think it expedient should be said or written. . . ."[59] He also took pains to note that "the denial of the truth of Christianity [by one raised as a Christian] is by statute a criminal offence entailing very severe penalties," and promoting "feelings of ill-will and hostility between different classes" was a misdemeanor.[60] While some of this no doubt derived from sources comparable to those which motivate our more negative American critics, freedom of speech in England remains subject to "a long train of restrictions including, *inter alia*, the laws relating to treason, the Official Secrets Act, sedition, defamation, incitement to mutiny or to disaffection, obscene publication or blasphemy; and to those also that relate to incitement to a criminal offence, or to provoking public discord or incitement to racial hatred."[61]

A few years ago coverage of a spy incident made plain the degree to which British restrictions go beyond those in the United States. Early revelations about Geoffrey Prime, the Cheltenham spy for the Russians, appeared in *The New York Times* and not in the British press, which at first felt constrained not to publish them. As a result, British importers would not bring over The *New York Times* for certain days of the week of November 1, 1982, since under Section Two of the British Official Secrets Act, importers, as well as publishers, can be liable for heavy fines for providing news coverage of proscribed items.[62]

In October 1988 the British government issued an administrative order prohibiting radio and television broadcasts of interviews of persons expressing support for the Irish Republican Army. The same month, the highest British court, the Law Lords, finally lifted a ban on newspaper articles discussing the book *Spycatcher*, the memoirs of Peter Wright, a retired British intelligence operative, published in Australia in 1987.[63]

Thus, while the English and the American traditions in this area closely resemble each other,[64] more closely perhaps than any others except the Canadian (under both English and United States' influence), there remain nonetheless appreciable differences between the two.[65] Indeed, even in Canada, a serious prosecution for "promoting hatred" was brought as recently as 1984.[66] In Great Britain, the Race Relations Act of 1965 makes it a prosecutable offense to use "threatening, abusive, or insulting" language "with intent to stir up hatred" against any racial or ethnic group.[67] Denmark has similar "group libel" laws.[68]

In France, the State was expected to "direct or control the expression of opinion" through the press.[69] In 1958, after the outbreak of the Algerian revolt, French "newspapers were constantly appearing with blank spaces in the columns, so that signs of censorship were patently obvious to the public."[70]

In Germany in 1976, a lawyer was fined for "instigating race hatred,"[71] understandably a rather touchy subject in Germany but still at some variance with our notions of constitutionally protected dissent. The West German (Bonn) Constitution of 1949 states, in its Article 18, "Whoever abuses the freedom of opinion . . . to combat the fundamental free democratic order, forfeits this freedom. . . ."[72]

Israel utilizes newspaper censorship far more readily than would be tolerated here,[73] and recently excluded the press from the West Bank territories where it had been covering Palestinian riots and demonstrations.[74] Obviously, Israel has faced unusual problems of national security since it became a modern nation in 1948.

India's former Prime Minister Indira Gandhi suspended constitutional rights, jailed her opposition, and censored the press, essentially in response to nothing more than provocative opposition rhetoric.[75]

Rights, the adversary process, and dissent are "unsettling" alien Western traditions to East Asians to whom duties, harmony, and obedience are more familiar. Thus, in the 1970s, "in South Korea, the Philippines, and South Vietnam, authoritarian regimes [had replaced or did replace] representative governments," with rulers claiming that economic difficulties, foreign threats, corruption, subversion or Communist influence could not be overcome while maintaining liberty and democracy.[76] In Japan in 1974, the precarious condition of the Liberal Democratic party facing similar problems raised very serious questions as to the continued viability of Western-style democracy there.[77]

Thirty-eight years earlier, the Japanese government opposed any *discussion* of "democracy, constitutionalism, the emperor, socialism, and a host of other subjects" considered *kikenshiso*, ("dangerous thoughts").[78] Louis Wirth, who made that observation, also noted that inquiry into the nature of communism in England or the United States similarly invited labeling of even the disinterested inquirer as a Communist. But the book in which Wirth's comments appeared was published in New York.

American National Character

Scholars consider the historic American tendency toward "legalism" in our foreign policy appealing but detrimental.[79] Similarly, a review of our foreign policy from 1900 to 1950 illustrates our peculiar faith in the ability of written documents to secure for us—and for the world—beneficial international relations.[80] Woodrow Wilson, speaking of the Treaty of Versailles in 1919, said, ". . . this treaty . . . sets at liberty people all over Europe and Asia. . . . The heart of humanity beats in this document."[81] The source of such faith in the power of written documents to produce internationally the blessings of liberty must be our own American Constitution; no alternative explanation presents itself.

The United States attempted to eliminate hard liquor from its society by writing an appropriate provision into its highest law with the Eighteenth Amendment to the Constitution.[82]

This country had come to accept the idea that a society would function according to a legal blueprint written out for it.

A cross-national study of American, German, and English adolescents illustrates a different aspect of the constitutional tradition: Americans were found, typically, "the least authoritarian of the national samples. . . . Our American subjects value such individualistic ideas as autonomy, initiative, and achievement," but at the same time "there is little felt distance between the citizen and collective authority";[83] we see the impact of civil liberties, representative government, and government legitimacy.

A leading student of constitutionalism wrote, "Finally, Constitutions are influenced by what people think of them. . . . There can, indeed, be no other people anywhere in the world who regard their Constitution with greater respect than do the Americans,"[84] "and violate it more frequently," Professor Henry Abraham added, half jokingly.[85]

But the addendum doesn't affect the thesis very much. Did the Constitution generate the American faith in government and societal blueprinting by written document? Does the American citizen retain a basic, deep-seated faith in the Constitution? If the answers to these questions are yes, as I think they are, then key attributes of American society and personality derive from the constitutional tradition and at the same time are part of it. This falls short of logical proof, but it reflects common sense.

Isaac Asimov's second science-fiction novel, The Stars, Like Dust,[86] ends with a passage pressed on him by his editors over his own objection that it was corny.[87] From the book's commercial success, it appears that it must have rung a responsive chord in its American readers, just as his editors knew it would. The story told of dissatisfaction in an intergalactic empire, rumblings of desire for independence among some of the planets, and the efforts of the dissidents to find a blueprint for a secret weapon. The blueprint was said to be in the possession of a sage who believed that it could be the instrument with which a viable independence might eventually be achieved. At the climactic ending, the sage is in a position to reveal the blue-print to the revolutionaries. He tells them that there is no need to show them the document, older than all the planetary governments in the universe save one; he knows it by heart: "We the people of the United States, in order to form a more perfect union, establish justice, insure domestic tranquility, provide for the common defense, promote the general welfare, and secure the blessings of liberty to ourselves and our posterity, do ordain and establish this Constitution for the United States of America. . . ."

PART FIVE

Conclusion

XII

Reflections of the Theoretical Framework

If on occasion I fall into a mood both grandiose and pessimistic, I fear that my theory—and thus my country—may share the fate of absolute monarchy in England in the era of James I, or the royal court in the era of Castiglione's *Book of the Courtier*.[1] The most eloquent defense of an institution sometimes also serves as its death-knell.

So, perhaps, with the constitutional tradition in the United States. Prosperity and isolation shielded the blossoming of our constitutional values against the usual constraints of efficiency and security. With the decline of American prosperity much talked about,[2] if not yet quite acknowledged, and with modern

216 Daniel L. Feldman

technology, including nuclear weapons, rendering isolation impossible, the future of American constitutional values is unclear.[3]

That future will determine the success or failure of the American experiment. The Framers will have succeeded whether or not the United States remains prosperous, but they—and we—will have succeeded only if we keep before us as ideals to be sought the perfect realization of American constitutional values.

If the approach taken here were merely tautological, I would have constructed a decisionmaking framework out of five values and then proclaimed results reflecting those values. However, the five values are embedded in the American tradition. The constitutional values have nevertheless disappeared from time to time. Explicitly recognizing their role and presenting a model for their implementation may preserve and extend their force.

A five-value utilitarian framework such as mine could, slightly altered, justify Oliver North's role in the Iran-Contra affair. An "Oliver North utilitarian" would simply give more weight to efficiency and less to representativeness (assuming the two were really in conflict in the covert-operations field, an assumption subject to serious question, as I pointed out earlier in this book),[4] and would read the *Curtiss Wright* decision the way Justice Sutherland read it, not the way Justice Jackson read it.[5]

Similarly, a utilitarian giving somewhat more weight to fairness and somewhat less to representativeness might therefore countenance a more "creative" judiciary. Such a utilitarian could then treat the Douglas "privacy right" with more respect.[6]

Since my reading of history tells me that liberty, as manifested in the free flow of information, may actually enhance security, my preferred balance, as illustrated in Chapter V, weights free expression and dissent more heavily than would those whose reading of history more conventionally regards openness as pitted against security. Similarly, my discussion of criminal procedure in Chapter VII, especially at the end, reflects a view that, in that particular context, fairness and efficiency need not be locked in mortal combat and that the former may, indeed, live quite comfortably with the latter.

When discussing the role of courts in questions of distributional equality in Chapters III and VIII, I do not see so fortuitous a fit between fairness and efficiency. Those who disagree, and some do, think courts can perform relatively efficiently in dealing with such questions. Therefore, they can and do weight fairness more heavily in this context.

Nonutilitarian approaches harbor more profound flaws when applied to public policy. Rawls attempted to avoid the potential of utilitarianism for producing intuitively objectionable results, like exploiting a vulnerable minority for the sake of the greater community, but ended up producing results that offend other intuitive standards of justice. For example, his rejection of a system of rewards and punishments based on approval or disapproval of individuals' action, in favor of systems determined solely by their behavioral impact, offends my intuition that justice requires punishment for crime.[7] If his system offends intuitive notions of justice too, by what logic does it offer any improvement over utilitarianism, which at least has some other advantages? I may disagree with other utilitarians over how to weight specific values, but I cannot claim that their fundamental logic is inferior to mine. Those, like Rawls, who attempt nonutilitarian schemes of social ethics simply fail to provide useful guides for policymakers, although their moral insights may occasionally illuminate a dark corner here and there.

Various political philosophers reject utilitarianism as too flexible to provide reassuring safeguards against injustice.[8] Our five-value model, for example, might leave room for speculation and interpretation. Some analyst might decide that exploitation, or censorship, would not have bad long-term consequences. James Fishkin argues, therefore, that liberty should be guaranteed regardless of other values or consequences. He suggests as preeminent that a state be "significantly self-undermining as a result of unmanipulated debate."[9]

By this he means that a nation should arrange its social institutions to guarantee vigorous criticism and debate, and effect changes in policy if the criticism is persuasive.

However, one may as well incorporate this entire position into the five-value model, along the lines of our third and fourth rules, thus making that model just as secure, or insecure, as Fishkin's argument itself. Liberty is one of the values by which to judge policies: Policies tending to promote freedom of thought have immense social utility for that reason alone. If effective dissent is important enough to be the sine qua non of a good society, then it certainly has consequences important enough to justify its adoption as a rule.

The latter consequentialist, instrumental, or utilitarian argument has deep roots in the American tradition. With antecedents in James Madison's writings,[10] Alexander Meiklejohn taught a generation of First Amendment scholars that the meaning of its free-speech provisions should be understood in the context of American democracy as a whole, as outlined in the main text of the Constitution. For democratic majorities to operate as American constitutional theory presumes, they must have access to the full range of alternative public policies from which to make their selections.[11] Ideas like Social Security and most of our labor laws were at first unpopular and were opposed by the administration then in power. If the government is empowered to suppress such ideas, it can forestall policies that might otherwise prove superior to its own. This argument justifies free speech on the basis of all five values, not only liberty. As a utilitarian defense, i.e., that the State's protection of dissent will in the long run produce net social benefits, Meiklejohn's approach respects all the values associated with the American constitutional tradition, and therefore can work as part of a general public-administration theory, while Fishkin's approach is much more limited.

Martin Edelman worries that "[t]he pluralism which accompanied industrialization destroyed the town meeting" and thus the context in which Meiklejohn's theories operate.[12] Participatory democracy may need reinvigoration; Mortimer Adler does well to remind us that "citizenship is the primary political office under a constitutional government";[13] but the marketplace of ideas still performs its functions best if unregulated, and Meiklejohn's assessment of the role of public debate remains valid.

Like Fishkin, Ronald Dworkin selects only one of our five values for special emphasis: in Dworkin's case, equality. We noted earlier Dworkin's tendency to disregard the fact that his notion of equality requires some people to pay for the "rights" he assigns to others. When a strong tilt toward material equality requires that some people be forced to produce for other people, liberty is in jeopardy. A state with unlimited obligations to guarantee equality of material benefits must also have unlimited power to impose duties to produce those benefits.

Equality, then, despite Dworkin's protestations,[14] is not equivalent to liberty. Dworkin fails to answer persuasively H.L.A. Hart's question: What if *all* religious worship or sexual activity were to be prohibited, as opposed to one sect's worship, or homosexuality? Would the evil or harm done then be less? "The evil is the denial of liberty or respect, not *equal* liberty or *equal* respect."[15]

Dworkin explicitly rejects the kind of balance among liberty, equality, and other values suggested here.[16] His tilt toward equality derives much from John Rawls.[17] He and Rawls try to transcend utilitarian calculations to protect the dignity and self-respect of individuals, but this is not an achievable goal. Redistribution for equality must at best cause some unfair pain to individuals, and the reality seems much worse than Rawls imagines. He wrote, "Those who have been favored by nature, whoever they are, may gain from their good fortune only on terms that improve the situation of those who have lost out" in what he considers to be a just society.[18] But some future Einstein or Gandhi might have difficulty obtaining permission to further his education rather than work in a coal mine to support a few vicious, mentally deficient drug addicts—particularly if the local commissar is one of the latter.

Allan Bloom argued that utilitarianism is merely a gloss on

Hobbes and Locke anyway,[19] and therefore might question the identification of my portrayal as utilitarian. If, indeed, there are Lockean shades to my five-value rule utilitarianism, it is no wonder, given the tradition it mirrors. The distinctions we see among utilitarianism, rights-based approaches, and contractarianism were not evident to Locke and his contemporaries, and therefore the roots of those approaches co-exist, however contradictorily, within their writings.[20] Here, I have attempted to reconstruct one version of the American constitutional tradition in terms of rule-utilitarian theory for use as a guide to decisionmakers and as a map of the territory in public administration.

A recent essay on interpreting the Constitution suggests that acting unconstitutionally is sometimes necessary, but it is better to acknowledge that such action is unconstitutional, that the situation is regrettable, and that every effort will be made to avoid recurrence, than to stretch the Constitution out of shape attempting to cover such acts with it: "The Constitution is ill-served by a myth of complete constitutional flexibility."[21] The present theory of American public administration permits a balancing of the constitutional values of liberty, equality, and property on one side against security and efficiency on the other, as long as the former are protected as carefully, say, as Lincoln protected them when faced with a real crisis of national survival.[22] Unlike more rigid, "determinate" systems, which rely less on common sense and a measure of trust in fellow citizens, this one works: not always, not perfectly, but well enough.

I can apply my utilitarianism to the ordinary daily problems of political life. I help a constituent straighten out some difficulty with a government agency: The Workers' Compensation Board, say, has misplaced the constituent's file, and I bring to its attention the checks due my constituent, who consequently receives them. Shortly thereafter, the constituent sends a contribution to my campaign fund.

This is legal, but it poses a problem. If the constituent mentions to his or her neighbors that I accepted a campaign contribution after providing help, word could spread that the "right" thing to do is to reward the assemblyman's efforts with such contributions. Those who find presenting such rewards distasteful, or who cannot afford them, will refrain from seeking my intervention. My ability to do an important part of my job, i.e., performing the ombudsman function, will be reduced. While more campaign funds can strengthen me politically and in the long run can further my pursuit of the various values I hold, the price is an immediate, nonspeculative, likely reduction in representativeness. Therefore, I must return that campaign contribution.

Now consider the campaign contribution from a nonconstituent. This may be a person who has succeeded in persuading me, or who hopes in the future to persuade me, on the basis of the public interest, that I should support some policy that is also in his or her interest. If I accept this contribution, I will probably be somewhat more conscious of that contributor the next time he or she writes or calls, and I may pay more attention than I would have otherwise. This may somewhat diminish the fairness with which I try to respond to all communications on their merits.

Here, however, the cost is nebulous, speculative, and unclear (assuming there is nothing bad about the contributor). The help enables me to pursue the political agenda that I feel advances my values. That would not be enough of an argument to warrant incurring clear and definite cost. But it is enough to warrant incurring the unclear and indefinite cost of accepting legitimate campaign contributions from nonconstituents. As Mayor Koch once said, I am not a schmuck. (This entire discussion, however, should point to the immense benefits of public financing of campaigns, which, if widely utilized, would minimize many problems of this nature.)

Did I search my soul, determine my fundamental values, calibrate their appropriate weightings, structure them in a utilitarian framework, and then derive all my policy positions from that framework? Of course not. My policy positions and my personal and public value structure evolved simultaneously. No doubt, when attempting to formalize my own values into the utilitarian frame presented here, my policy positions helped me realize what my values were. A skeptic might suppose that my policy positions helped *determine* what my values were.

So I can't very well expect you to follow a route I did not take myself. More realistically, I am asking you to reconcile your policy positions with your values, and to identify the decisionmaking model, and the values that inform it, to clarify your present and future policymaking. I suspect that you will find that some form of utilitarianism, perhaps similar to the form I presented here, is in fact most comfortable for you to use for this purpose.

Identifying key values is tricky. Fairness seems like a relatively easy one for most Americans. Representativeness is likely to occur to those who work in the political system. Dissent, I believe, appeals to people in direct relation to the degree to which they are sensitive to history. I have identified these as American constitutional values. Sometimes, alternatively, I designate as American constitutional values the more elemental values—liberty, equality, property—which provide the ingredients for the former, "compound" values. Against either the elemental set or the compound set I offer the "universal" values of security and efficiency. Either of the sets of three, plus the final two, make up the five values that should guide American public policymaking.

Why exclude, say "piety," which is clearly an important value to many Americans?[23] There are many pious Americans. Certainly the colonists who planted the seeds of American civilization were generally pious. But Thomas Paine completely rejected Christianity, Jefferson denied the divinity of Christ, and Washington does not appear to have been "a pious Christian in an orthodox sense."[24] Freedom of religion in the United States meant and means freedom not to be pious, as well as freedom to be pious in the manner of your choosing.[25] The establishment clause of the First Amendment prohibits Congress from providing aid to religion, even "nondiscriminatory" aid to all religions.[26] Therefore piety, no matter how "American," cannot be an American *constitutional* value useful in guiding policy decisions. Liberty implies respect for human life and human dignity, so those aspects of piety fall under the constitutional umbrella. But that's as far as it goes.

In *The Caine Mutiny*, Herman Wouk said that "the Navy is a master plan designed by geniuses for execution by idiots." If that was ever true of the navy, it is not true of today's navy. And it was never true of the Constitution. Therefore, we must cultivate intelligence in those who will execute the Constitution's master plan. Since we don't know which of our citizenry will perform that function, and since in some measure all citizens *should* perform that function, the citizenry as a whole should be made intellectually capable of appreciating our constitutional values. Once citizens understand those values, they will appreciate them and defend them. This educational task demands our urgent attention in order to cure the current disease afflicting the American polity, whose symptoms are intensely devoted extremists and apathetic centrists.

I return to the worrisome question with which I began these reflections. Will our constitutional values survive this era? The answer depends on the depth of our commitment and the energy with which we pursue it.

Notes

Introduction

1. This acknowledges a present, but very uncomfortable, reality, which I hope is only temporary. One scholar describes it as a *"two-tier* political society, one tier, by far the smallest [*sic*] in terms of numbers, which retains its political mind (the 'professional citizenry') and a much larger tier whose political mind has either been voluntarily closed or has been stolen from it, a society in which individuals, while enjoying (for a spell) a rich though increasingly uniform social and cultural life, slowly relinquish their basic political rights to those who still have the mind to understand and use them" (Roy Speckhard, Empire State College, "For Better or for Worse: Some Observations and a Brief Commentary on the Shifting Paradigm of American Political Life," unpublished paper, presented at the Annual Meeting of the New York State Political Science Association, 4/29/88).
2. David Stockman, *The Triumph of Politics* (New York: Harper & Row, 1986), as discussed in Donald Maletz, "The Place of Constitutionalism in the Education of Public Administrators," American Political Science Association panel paper, Chicago, September 3–6, 1987. [From time to time my footnotes will refer to such APSA papers, which are presented in panel discussions at the annual meeting of APSA. These papers are available from University Microfilms International in Ann Arbor, Michigan. "ASPA" is the American Society for Public Administration, and I cite a few of their panel papers in these footnotes, too.]
3. See Chapter V.
4. "It is getting harder to *run* a constitution than to frame one," Woodrow Wilson, "The Study of Administration," 2 *Pol. Sci. O.* 197, 198. 1887.

5. Robert Pirsig, *Zen and the Art of Motorcycle Maintenance* (New York: William Morrow and Co., Inc., 1974), pp. 87–88.

6. See, e.g., Larry Baas, "The Constitution as Symbol: Change or Stability After Ten Years," APSA panel paper, Chicago, 9/3/87.

7. See, e.g., Michael Kammen, *A Machine That Would Go of Itself* (New York: Random House, 1986).

8. *Time* magazine, 7/6/87, p. 23, quoted in Baas, op. cit., p. 1.

9. *The People, Press, and Politics* (The Times-Mirror Company, September 1987), p. 128.

10. Ibid.

11. John Stuart Mill, *On Liberty* (Harmondsworth, Middlesex, England: Penguin Books, 1982 [1859]), pp. 102–104.

12. In a recent book, Sanford Levinson expressed similar hope, and suggested that a ceremonial signing of the Constitution could revive citizen commitment to constitutional aspirations: "For me, signing the Constitution—and agreeing therefore to profess at least a limited constitutional faith—commits me not to closure but only to a process of becoming and to taking responsibility for constructing the political vision toward which I strive, joined, I hope, with others" (*Constitutional Faith*, Princeton, N.J.: Princeton University Press, 1988, p. 193).

13. Herbert Storing, "Slavery and the Moral Foundations of the Republic," in Robert Horwitz, ed., *The Moral Foundations of the American Republic*, 3d ed. (Charlottesville: University Press of Virginia, 1986), p. 316.

14. *Ibid*, p. 320, citing Douglass's "Address for the Promotion of Colored Enlistments," July 6, 1863, in Philip S. Foner, ed., *The Life and Writings of Frederick Douglass* (New York: International Publishers, 1950), 3:365.

Chapter I:
A Constitutional Framework for Public Decisionmaking

1. Richard Stillman, "The Changing Patterns of Public Administration Theory in America," in Stillman, ed., *Public Administration Concepts and Cases*, 3d ed. (Boston: Houghton Mifflin Co., 1984), pp. 5–24; and see Chapter IX.

2. John Burke, *Bureaucratic Responsibility* (Baltimore: Johns Hopkins University Press, 1986), p. 39.

3. Chester Newland, "The Reagan Presidency," in Stillman, ed., op. cit., pp. 324–325.

4. David Rosenbloom, "Public Administration and the Separation of Powers," 43 *Public Administration Review* 219, May/June 1983.

5. Walter Karp, "Liberty Under Siege," *Harper's Magazine*, November 1985, pp. 53–67.

6. Jerry Mashaw, *Due Process in the Administrative State* (New Haven: Yale University Press, 1985), p. 184.

7. David Richards, *Toleration and the Constitution* (New York: Oxford University Press, 1986), p. 59.

8. See, e.g., Richards, op. cit.; Ronald Dworkin, *Taking Rights Seriously* (Cambridge, Mass.: Harvard University Press, 1978). In this chapter, we will consider modern natural-rights theories to include what Stanley Brubaker calls "moral rights" theories (see Chapter VIII, note 42), and thus Kantian theories such as that of Rawls.

9. John Rohr, *Ethics for Bureaucrats* (New York and Basel: Marcel Dekker Inc., 1978), pp. 59–76; compare Edgar Bodenheimer, "Philosophical Anthropology and the Law," 59 *Cal. L. Rev.* 653, May 1971, who considers "security, liberty, and equality" to be universal values (*Ibid*, at page 662). There is no reason to believe that Bodenheimer would reject the suggestion that liberty and equality have unusually strong support in the United States.

10. Ruth Benedict, *Patterns of Culture*, 2d ed. (Boston: Houghton Mifflin Co., 1959), p. 178ff.

11. Alexander Hamilton, John Jay, James Madison, *The Federalist Papers* (New York and Ontario: New American Library, 1961 [1787–88]), *No. 1* at 35 (Hamilton).

12. *Ibid, No. 70* at 426–427 (Hamilton).

13. *Ibid, No. 3* at 42, *No. 4* at 49 (Jay); *No. 8* at 67 (Hamilton); *No. 41* at 256 (Madison).

14. David Potter, *People of Plenty* (Chicago: University of Chicago Press, 1954).

15. Hans Morgenthau, *In Defense of the National Interest* (New York: Knopf, 1951), p. 129.

16. Andrew McLaughlin, *Foundations of American Constitutionalism* (New York: Fawcett Publications, 1961 [1932]); and see Chapter X.

17. Walter Berns, "Religion and the Founding Principle," in Robert Horwitz, ed., *The Moral Foundations of the American Republic*, 3d ed. (Charlottesville, Va.: University Press of Virginia, 1986), pp. 204–229.
18. Edward Corwin, *The "Higher Law" Background of American Constitutional Law* (Ithaca, N.Y.: Cornell University Press, 1955 [42 *Harvard Law Review* 149, 365 n. 119 (1928)].
19. *Rex* v. *University of Cambridge*, Str. 557, 567, K.B. 1723, quoted in Bernard Schwartz, "Fashioning an Administrative Law System," 40 *Administrative Law Review* 415, 425 (1988).
20. McLaughlin, op. cit., p. 107; Edward Corwin, op. cit.
21. Herbert J. Storing, "Slavery and the Moral Foundations of the American Republic," in Robert Horwitz, ed., *The Moral Foundations of the American Republic*, 3d. ed. (Charlottesville: University Press of Virginia, 1986), p. 320.
22. See Chapter X.
23. Ronald Dworkin, *A Matter of Principle* (Cambridge, Mass.: Harvard University Press, 1985), p. 370.
24. Richards, op. cit., p. 14.
25. I am indebted to Professor Tom Konda for this observation.
26. Professor John Rohr gave me the benefit of this observation.
27. See, e.g., Franklyn S. Haiman, "Nazis in Skokie: Anatomy of the Heckler's Veto," in Thomas Tedford, ed., *Perspectives on Freedom of Speech* (Carbondale and Edwardsville: Southern Illinois University Press, 1987, pp. 216–225; James Gibson and Richard Bingham, *Civil Liberties and Nazis* (New York: Praeger, 1985), esp. pp. 2, 27, 81; and Chapter VII.
28. Daniel Feldman, brief for *amicus curiae, Boreali* v. *Axelrod*, 130 A.D. 2d 107 (3d Dept. 1987, No. 54593).
29. 325 F. Supp. 781 (M.D. Ala., 1971); 334 F. Supp. 1341 (M.D. Ala. 1971); 344 F. Supp. 373 (M.D. Ala. 1972); 344 F. Supp. 387 (M.D. Ala. 1972).
30. E.g., Iredell Jenkins, *Social Order and the Limits of Law* (Princeton, N.J.: Princeton University Press, 1980), pp. 135–150.
31. For a comparison of the intuitionist, utilitarian, and contractarian schools of ethical analysis, and a discussion of the criticisms that each has directed at the others, see Daniel Feldman, "Ethical Analysis in Public Policymaking," 15 *Policy Studies Journal* 441 (1987).
32. 304 U.S. 144, 152 n. 4 (1938).

33. See, e.g., John Hart Ely, *Democracy and Distrust* (Cambridge, Mass.: Harvard University Press, 1980), p. 75.
34. Rosenbloom, op. cit.
35. See Chapter IX.
36. Rosenbloom, op. cit., p. 225.
37. Herbert Kaufman, "Emerging Conflicts in the Doctrines of Public Administration," 50 *Am. Pol. Sci. Rev.* 1057–1073 (1956).
38. *Ibid*, at 1063.

Chapter II:
Representativeness vs. Efficiency

1. Woodrow Wilson, "The Study of Administration," 2 *Pol. Sci. Q.* 197 (1887).
2. See Frederick Mosher, *Democracy and the Public Service*, 2d ed. (New York: Oxford University Press, 1982), pp. 102–109; Lief Carter, *Administrative Law and Politics* (Boston: Little, Brown & Co., 1983), p. 75.
3. E. S. Savas, *Privatizing the Public Sector* (Chatham, N.J.: Chatham House Publications, 1982), pp. 1–2.
4. James Pfiffner, "The Reagan Budget Juggernaut," in Stillman, ed., *Public Administration Concepts and Cases* (Boston: Houghton Mifflin Co., 1984), p. 391; Aaron Wildavsky, *The Politics of the Budgetary Process*, 4th ed. (Boston: Little, Brown & Co., 1984), Preface.
5. *The Federalist No. 52* at 327 (Madison).
6. *Ibid, No. 69* at 414 (Hamilton).
7. Kenneth Davis, *Administrative Law Text*, 3d ed., (St. Paul, Minn.: West Publishing Co., 1972), p. 6; and see Chapter V.
8. Mosher, op. cit., pp. 64–73.
9. Mosher, op. cit., pp. 102–109; Carter, op. cit., p. 75.
10. Congress enacted 664 bills in the 1985–86 session (Norman Ornstein et al., *Vital Statistics on Congress 1987–88* Washington, D.C.: Congressional Quarterly Inc., 1987, p. 170); agencies published 4,483 final rules and regulations in the *Federal Register* in 1985 and 4,589 in 1986 (Richard Craypool, director of the Executive Agencies Division for the Office of the *Federal Register*,

telephone conversation with Mindy Bockstein, legislative assistant to author, 9/6/88).

11. Comments by National Labor Relations Board Administrative Law Judge Leonard Wagman to author, 8/16/88.

12. *Atkins* v. *United States*, 556 F.2d 1028 (Ct. Claims 1977), cert. den. 434 U.S. 1009 (1978).

13. 462 U.S. 919 (1983).

14. U.S. Constitution Article I, Section 7.

15. 462 U.S. at 952.

16. See Chapter IX.

17. Louis Fisher, "Judicial Misjudgments About the Lawmaking Process: The Legislative Veto Case," 45 *Pub. Admin. Rev.* 705 (1985).

18. 478 U.S. 714 (1986).

19. 478 U.S. at 736.

20. See Chapter IX; Louis Fisher, "The Administrative World of *Chadha* and *Bowsher*," 47 *Pub. Admin. Rev.*, 213–14 (1987); Leonard W. Levy, *Original Intent and the Framers' Constitution* (New York and London: Macmillan Publishing Company, 1988), pp. 31, 391.

21. 478 U.S. at 722.

22. Fisher, 1987, op. cit.

23. Louis Fisher, *Constitutional Dialogues* (Princeton, N.J.: Princeton University Press, 1988), p. 225.

24. *Ibid*, pp. 225–228.

25. 108 S. Ct. 2597 (1988).

26. "Excerpts from Ruling Upholding Independent Counsel Law," The *New York Times*, 6/30/88, A18:4, From Dissenting Opinion by Justice Scalia.

27. Ibid. at columns 1–3, From the Opinion by Justice Rehnquist.

28. Anthony Lewis, "No to King George," *N.Y. Times*, 6/30/88, A23:1.

29. *Boreali* v. *Axelrod*, No. 47-304-87 at 6 (Sup. Ct. Schoharie County, 1987).

30. 66 N.Y.2d 185, 486 N.E.2d 794, 495 N.Y.S.2d 936 (1985).

31. 24 N.Y.2d 427, 248 N.E.2d 871, 301 N.Y.S.2d 23 (1969).

32. *Boreali* v. *Axelrod*, 130 A.D.2d 107, 111, 518 N.Y.S.2d 440, 442 (1987).

33. 130 A.D.2d at 118, 518 N.Y.S.2d at 444.

34. E.g., *Clark* v. *Cuomo* 66 N.Y.2d 185, 190.

35. A.2926b.

36. *Boreali* v. *Axelrod*, Sup. Ct. Schoharie County, op. cit., Plaintiff's Memorandum, Exhibit I, 80, Transcript of 1/28/87 Testimony before the Legislative Administrative Regulations Review Committee.

37. Brief for *amicus curiae, Boreali* v. *Axelrod*, op. cit., 3–4.

38. *Boreali* v. *Axelrod*, 71 N.Y.2d 1, 11, 517 N.E.2d 1350, 1355, 523 N.Y.S.2d 464, 469 (1987).

39. *Ibid*, at 13, 517 N.E.2d at 1356, 523 N.Y.2d at 471.

40. Bernard Rosen, *Holding Government Bureaucracies Accountable* (New York: Praeger Publishers, 1982), p. 120.

41. See, e.g., Daniel Feldman, *Reforming Government* (New York: William Morrow and Co., Inc., 1981).

42. See, e.g., David Rosenbaum, "Panel's Chairman Says Poindexter Lacks Credibility," *N.Y. Times*, 7/18/87, 1:6; and Chapter III.

43. Steven Elliott, "The Tension Between Member Goals and Staff Goals in Congress," unpublished, Rockefeller College, State University of New York at Albany, 1986; Christine DeGregorio, "Partners in the Policymaking Process: Subcommittee Chairs and Senior Aides," APSA panel paper, Washington, D.C., September 1–4, 1988.

44. *Boreali* v. *Axelrod*, No.47-304-87 at 5 (Sup. Ct. Schoharie County 1987).

Chapter III:
Fairness vs. Efficiency

1. Lief Carter, *Administrative Law and Politics* (Boston: Little, Brown & Co., 1983), p. 14.

2. See sources cited in Daniel Feldman, "Administrative Agencies and the Rites of Due Process," 7 *Fordham Urban Law Journal* 229, n.1–4 (1978).

3. Jeffrey Hockett, "Justices Jackson, Frankfurter, and Black: A Contrast of Constitutional Faiths," APSA panel paper, Washington, D.C., September 1–4, 1988, p. 9.

4. Lon Fuller, *The Morality of Law*, rev. ed. (New Haven: Yale University Press, 1969), p. 172.

5. *N.Y. Times*, 5/9/60, 31:8; 5/15/60, 77:1.

6. Lon Fuller, "Collective Bargaining and the Arbitrator," 1963 *Wisconsin Law Review* 3, 32–33, citing M. Polanyi, *The Logic of Liberty* (London: Routledge and K. Paul, 1951), pp. 170–84.
7. 419 U.S. 565 (1975).
8. 419 U.S. at 574.
9. *Chance* v. *Board of Examiners*, 561 F.2d 1079, 1081 (2d Cir. 1977).
10. 446 F. Supp. 716 (W.D. La. 1978).
11. Bernard Schwartz, *Administrative Law* (Boston: Little, Brown & Co., 1976), p. 28, Section 125 and cases cited therein.
12. 435 U.S. 78 (1978).
13. Rehnquist's majority opinion: 435 U.S. at 80–81; Powell's concurrence: 435 U.S. at 93; Marshall's partial concurrence: 435 U.S. at 98; 102–104 *N.Y. Times*, 3/2/78, A9:1.
14. 435 U.S. at 85–90.
15. N.Y.C. Income Maintenance Procedure 78-76.
16. 42 U.S.C. Sections 601–610 (1976).
17. *Ibid*, Section 602(a).
18. N.Y.C. Income Maintenance Procedure, op. cit.
19. 427 F. Supp. 576 (S.D.N.Y. 1977).
20. 427 F. Supp. at 579.
21. *Rush* v. *Smith*, 573 F.2d 110, 118 (2d Cir. 1978).
22. N.Y. Comp. Codes R. and Regs. tit 18, Section 352.1 (1986).
23. See Chapter IX, text at notes 83 to 86; also Jack Tweedie, "The Dilemma of Clients' Rights in Social Programs: Individuals and Collective Concerns in Administration," APSA panel paper, 1988, p. 6.
24. Bernard Schwartz, op. cit., p. 30.
25. See, e.g., Feldman, 1978, op. cit., 244–252; J. S. Fuerst and Roy Petty, "Due Process—How Much Is Enough?," *The Public Interest*, Spring 1985, p. 96.
26. 325 F. Supp. 781 (M.D. Ala. 1971); 344 F. Supp. 1341 (M.D. Ala. 1971); 344 F. Supp. 373 (M.D. Ala. 1972); 344 F. Supp. 387 (M.D. Ala. 1972).
27. Judges may take "judicial notice" of other matters, bearing on the case before them, but this is a very limited exception, since "a judicially noticed fact must be one not subject to reasonable dispute. . . ." (Federal Rules of Evidence 201[b]). The specific standards Johnson set in his decisions were in fact largely based on agreements between the parties (Philip J. Cooper, *Hard Judi-*

cial Choices, New York: Oxford University Press, 1988, p. 182), but Alabama officials were forced to reach those agreements if they were to avoid other, probably more drastic outcomes. The point is that Johnson had no way of replicating the institutional resource-allocating role of the legislature, and yet by entering so deeply into this matter, he had to try to do just that.

28. *Wyatt* v. *Aderholt*, 503 F.2d 1305, 1317 (5th Cir. 1974).
29. *Wyatt* v. *Stickney*, 344 F. Supp. at 377.
30. See text preceding note 6, *supra*.
31. 344 F. Supp. at 374 (citing *Wyatt* v. *Stickney*, 325 F. Supp. 781 (M.D. Ala. 1971).
32. 325 F. Supp. at 784.
33. See Chapter IX.
34. William Van Alstyne, "Cracks in 'The New Property': Adjudicative Due Process in the Administrative State," 62 *Cornell L. Rev.* 445 (1977).
35. 416 U.S. 134 (1974).
36. See e.g., *Board of Regents* v. *Roth*, 408 U.S. 564 (1972).
37. Van Alstyne, op. cit., 487.
38. *Wyatt* v. *Aderholt*, 503 F.2d 1305, 1318.
39. Cooper, op. cit., p. 199.
40. Archibald Cox, "The New Dimensions of Constitutional Adjudication," 57 *Wash. L. Rev.* 791, 827 (1976). See also Tinsley E. Yarbrough, "The Political World of Federal Judges as Managers," 45 *Pub. Admin. Rev.* 660, 663 (1985).
41. Some patients should not have been confined at Bryce in the first place (Cooper, op. cit., p. 196), and they, at least, may have benefited from release.
42. 397 U.S. 471 (1970).
43. William Banks and Jeffrey Straussman, *"Bowsher* v. *Synar:* The Emerging Judicialization of the Fisc," Center for Interdisciplinary Legal Studies, Syracuse University College of Law Working Paper Series, Syracuse, New York, APSA panel paper, Chicago, 9/3/87, p. 10.
44. Ralph Cavanaugh and Austin Scott, "Thinking About Courts: Toward and Beyond a Jurisprudence of Judicial Competence," 14 *Law and Society Review* 371, 410 (1980).
45. *Ibid*, at 410, citing "State Prisons on Trial," 5 *State Legislatures* 6, 1979.
46. *Ibid*, at 411, quoting Ronald Dworkin, *Taking Rights Seriously* (Cambridge, Mass.: Harvard University Press, 1978), p. 146.

47. Linda Harriman and Jeffrey Straussman, "Do Judges Determine Budget Decisions? Federal Court Decisions in Prison Reform and State Spending for Corrections," 43 *Pub. Admin. Rev.* 343, 350 (1983).
48. Fuller, 1969, op. cit.
49. Dworkin, 1978, op. cit., p. 22.
50. *Ibid*, p. 84.
51. *Ibid*, p. 82.
52. *Ibid*, p. 94, n. 1.
53. 198 U.S. 45 (1905).
54. 198 U.S. at 75.
55. Stanley Brubaker, "Reconsidering Dworkin's Case for Judicial Activism," 46 *Journal of Politics* 503, 512, n.11 (1984).
56. See Iredell Jenkins, (Cambridge, Mass.: 1980), pp. 59–60, 151–152; Louis Lusky, *By What Right?*(Charlottesville, Va.: The Michie Company, 1975), p.107; John Hart Ely, *Democracy and Distrust, Special Order and the Limits of Law* (Princeton, N.J.: Princeton University Press, Harvard University Press, 1980), p. 15; William F. Harris, "Bonding Word and Polity," 76 *Am. Pol. Sci. Rev.* 34, 1982. William Julius Wilson, in *The Truly Disadvantaged* (Chicago: University of Chicago Press, 1987), makes the interesting argument that race-specific policies, including affirmative action, do not effectively address the problems of the ghetto underclass because their benefits are usurped by those nonunderclass minority group members best equipped to take advantage of them. Of course, Wilson was not addressing the question of courts versus legislatures, but his analysis, if correct, suggests at least that legislatures, who may in a more principled way change and adjust their policies, undertake these problems of resource redistribution; courts, if they redistribute resources among groups in society, must at least claim to do so on the basis of principle, not policy, and thus cannot very easily reverse themselves if and when their decisions prove unworkable or counterproductive.
57. 347 U.S. 483 (1954).

Chapter IV:
Dissent vs. Security

1. Walter Karp, "Liberty Under Siege," *Harper's Magazine*, November 1985, pp. 53–67.

2. See e.g., David Rosenbaum, "Panel's Chairman Says Poindexter Lacks Credibility," *N.Y. Times*, 7/18/87, 1:6.
3. See Chapter V.
4. Charles and Mary Beard, *A Basic History of the United States* (New York: Doubleday, Doran and Co., 1944), pp. 168–169.
5. Leonard Levy, "Liberty and the First Amendment," 68 *Am. Hist. Rev.* 22, 29 (1962).
6. Harold Hyman, "War Powers in 19th Century America," 9 *This Constitution/Project '87* 4, 6 (1985).
7. James G. Randall, *Constitutional Problems Under Lincoln* (New York: D. Appleton & Co., 1926).
8. *Ibid*, p. 477, n. 1.
9. 68 U.S. (1 Wall.) 243 (1864).
10. U.S. Constitution Article I, Section 9.
11. Abraham Lincoln, Letter to Erastus Corning and Others, June 12, 1863, in John G. Nicolay and John Hay, eds., *Complete Works of Abraham Lincoln* (New York: The Century Company, 1894), Vol. II, pp. 345–352, 298 at 308. I am greatly indebted to Judge Joseph Bellacosa of the New York State Court of Appeals for bringing this material to my attention.
12. John W. Burgess, *Political Science and Constitutional Law* (Boston: Ginn and Company, 1891), Vol. I, pp. 250–252.
13. Randall, op. cit., p. 477, n. 1.
14. 323 U.S. 214 (1944).
15. Eugene V. Rostow, "The Japanese-American Cases—A Disaster," 54 *Yale Law Journal* 489 (1945); Charles Reich, "Mr. Justice Black and the Living Constitution," 76 *Harv. L. Rev.* 673 (1963).
16. Paul L. Murphy, *World War I and the Origin of Civil Liberties* (New York: W. W. Norton & Co., 1979).
17. Robert J. Steamer, review of Paul Murphy, op. cit., 74 *Am. Pol. Sci. Rev.* 1094, 1095 (1980).
18. *New York Times* v. *United States*, 403 U.S. 713 (1971).
19. *Dellums* v. *Powell*, 566 F.2d 167 (D.C. Cir. 1977), cert. den. 438 U.S. 916 (1978).
20. Telephone conversation with Arthur B. Spitzer, legal director, American Civil Liberties Union Fund, Washington, D.C., 1/11/83. The amount of damages for most protesters was finally settled by an order directing entry of a partial final judgment in the case (D.C. Federal District Court, #2271-71, 5/1/81). It

would almost certainly have been closer to $10,000 per protester had the protest demonstration been significantly thwarted by the police, instead of having been "virtually complete before any substantial number of arrests had been made" (566 F.2d at 196).

21. James Reston, "The End of the Tunnel," *N.Y. Times*, 4/30/75, 41:1.
22. Associated Press, "Measure to Pay War Detainees Goes to Reagan," *N.Y. Times*, 8/5/88, A10:1; Linda Greenhouse, "Supreme Court Roundup," *N.Y. Times*, 11/1/88, A23:1–4.
23. *United States* v. *Schwimmer*, 279 U.S. 644, 653 (1928).
24. Karp, op. cit., p. 65.
25. United States v. Morison, 57 U.S.L.W. 3239 (1988).
26. Karp, op. cit., pp. 55–56.
27. *Ibid*, pp. 55–56.
28. *Ibid*, p. 62.
29. *Ibid*, p. 63.
30. *Ibid*, p. 54.
31. See, e.g., James Gibson and Richard Bingham, *Civil Liberties and Nazis* (New York: Praeger, 1985).
32. A. Stephen Boyan, Jr., "Presidents and National Security Powers: A Judicial Perspective," APSA panel paper, D.C., Sept. 1–4, 1988.
33. Morton Halperin and Daniel Hoffman, *Top Secret: National Security and the Right to Know* (Washington, D.C.: New Republic Books, 1977), p. 73.

Part Two:
Applications

1. Charles Lindblom, "The Science of 'Muddling Through,'" 19 *Public Administration Review* 79, 82, Spring 1959.

Chapter V:
The Iran-Contra Affair

1. See, e.g., Seymour Hersh, "Who's in Charge Here?," *The New York Times Magazine*, 34, 71, 11/22/87; see also Lance Liebman,

"Legislative Morality in the Proposed CIA Charter," in Joel Fleishman et al., eds., *Public Duties: The Moral Obligations of Public Officials* (Cambridge, Mass.: Harvard University Press, 1981), pp. 248–265.

2. See, e.g., Hans Morgenthau, *In Defense of the National Interest* (New York: Alfred A. Knopf, 1951), p. 101; George Kennan, *American Diplomacy 1900–1950* (New York: New American Library, 1951).

3. Ray Stannard Baker and William E. Dodd, eds., *The Public Papers of Woodrow Wilson: War and Peace* (New York: Harper & Bros., 1927), Vol. II, pp. 277–292.

4. Liebman, op. cit.; see also Stansfield Turner, *Secrecy and Democracy* (Boston: Houghton Mifflin Company, 1985), p. 145.

5. See, e.g., Turner, op. cit.

6. 22 United States Code Sec. 2422 (1979).

7. Liebman, op. cit.

8. This includes only those wars fought under congressional declarations or under the War Powers Act of 1973, which authorizes the use of the armed forces for sixty to ninety days under the direction of the president prior to a congressional declaration of war in a dangerous hostile situation.

9. Liebman, op. cit., p. 263; but see Morton Halperin, "Prohibiting Covert Operations," *The Nation*, 3/21/87.

10. See Turner, op. cit., pp. 171, 177.

11. Quoted in Liebman, op. cit., p. 255; see also Turner, op. cit., pp. 220, 269–271.

12. United States Constitution Article I, Section 8.

13. United States Constitution Article II, Section 2.

14. Louis Henkin, *Foreign Affairs and the Constitution* (Mineola, N.Y.: The Foundation Press, Inc., 1972), p. 43, and see also notes 10, 11, and 12 to discussion on page 43 at pages 297–298; see also Louis Henkin, "Foreign Affairs and the Constitution," 66 *Foreign Affairs* 284, 292 (Winter 1987–88).

15. Leonard Levy, *Original Intent and the Framers' Constitution* (New York: Macmillan, 1988), p. 47, citing *The Federalist Nos. 69* and *75*.

16. *Ibid*, p. 30: ". . . the Framers intended Congress to control the making and conduct of war, the Senate to control foreign policy, and the President to [31] control the ceremonial functions of representing the nation in its foreign policy, personally or through diplomats."

17. Paul Kennedy, *The Rise and Fall of the Great Powers* (New York: Random House, 1987), p. 85: The upkeep of armed forces could consume "80 or even 90 percent" of a country's expenditures; "[a]fter each bout of fighting (and especially after 1714 and 1763), most countries desperately needed to draw breath, to recover from their economic exhaustion, and to grapple with the internal discontents which war and higher taxation had all too often provoked. . . ."

18. Henkin, 1987–88, op. cit., p. 289.

19. Henkin, 1972, p. 333, n. 61.

20. *Myers* v. *United States*, 272 U.S. 52, 293 (1926), Brandeis, J., dissenting.

21. Louis Fisher, comments to author 8/12/88, and Louis Fisher, "The Efficiency Side of Separated Powers," 5 *Journal of Am. Stud.* 113 (August 1971).

22. *The Chinese Exclusion Case*, 130 U.S. 581, 591 (1889), quoted in Louis Fisher, "The Legitimacy of the Congressional National Security Role" Washington, D.C.: Congressional Research Service, 11/19/87, p. 4.

23. Louis Fisher, 8/12/88.

24. See Henkin, op. cit., p. 107, note.

25. See, e.g., Henkin, 1972, op. cit., p. 333 n. 61.

26. Fisher, op. cit., 8/12/88, p. 4

27. Henkin, 1987–88, op. cit., pp. 300–301.

28. 50 U.S.C.A.Sec. 413 (West Supp. 1989).

29. See Turner, op. cit., pp. 145–146.

30. 50 U.S.C.A.Sec. 413 (a), (West Supp. 1989).

31. See Turner, op. cit.

32. 50 U.S.C.A. Sec. 413 (b), (c), (West Supp. 1989).

33. 46 Fed. Reg. 59,941 (1981).

34. H.R. Rep. No. 433, 100th Cong., Sess. (1987); S. Rep. No. 216, 100th Cong., Sess. (1987). Reports of the Congressional Committees Investigating the Iran-Contra Affair, hereafter cited as "Report."

35. Report, p. 27.

36. *Ibid*, pp. 27, 31.

37. The Harris Survey, 9/29/83, p. 3, cited in Report, p. 52, n. 31.

38. Richard Meislin, "Majority in Poll Still Think Reagan Lied on Iran-Contra Issue," *N.Y. Times*, 7/18/87, 1:4; Marjorie Connelly, New York Times/CBS Poll, telephone conversation, 1/20/88.

39. Report, p. 37, citing testimony of former Assistant for National

Affairs Robert McFarlane (Hearings 100-2, 5/11/87, at pp. 5, 20–21) and of Oliver North (Hearings, 100-7, Part I, 7/7/87, at p. 74.)

40. *Ibid*, pp. 37–245.
41. *Ibid*, pp. 262–263.
42. *Ibid*, p. 285.
43. North successfully concealed the existence of Secord's "Enterprise," however, until the congressional Iran-Contra hearings (*Ibid*, p. 286).
44. *Ibid*, p. 298.
45. David Rosenbaum, "Panel's Chairman Says Poindexter Lacks Credibility," *N.Y. Times*, 7/18/87, A1:6–A6:6.
46. Maureen Dowd, "Low Key Mood, and Some Regrets," *N.Y. Times*, 7/18/87, A6:2.
47. *Ibid*, A6:1.
48. Ibid.
49. Report, p. 387.
50. Justice John Marshall's statement in the House of Representatives, 1800, quoted in Henkin, 1972, op. cit., p. 45, and 1987–88, op. cit., p. 292.
51. See Henkin, 1987–88, op. cit., p. 294.
52. Marshall, op. cit., quoted in Report, pp. 389–390.
53. 299 U.S. 304 (1936).
54. *Youngstown Sheet & Tube Co.* v. *Sawyer*, 343 U.S. 579 (1952); see Louis Fisher, "Executive-Legislative Relations in Foreign Policy," presented at the United States-Mexico Comparative Constitutional Law Conference, Mexico City, 6/17/88, rev. 6/24/88, pp. 8–14.
55. *Ibid*, p. 150.
56. *N.Y. Times*, 7/1/85, A10, quoted in Report, p. 161.
57. Report, pp. 378–381.
58. See, e.g., Anthony Cave Brown, *Bodyguard of Lies* (New York: Harper & Row, Publishers, Inc., 1975).
59. Hearings, Testimony, 8/6/87, pp. 173–175, quoted in Fisher, op. cit., p. 17, and in Report, p. 382.
60. Report, p. 391.
61. See Turner, op. cit., pp. 150–151.
62. See, e.g., Minority Report, Report, pp. 489–496.
63. *The Federalist No. 75* at 451 (Hamilton), quoted in Report, p. 406.

64. Report, pp. 423–427.
65. *Ibid*, p. 423.
66. Ibid.
67. Graham Allison, *Essence of Decision* (Boston: Little, Brown & Co., 1971), pp. 188, 192.
68. See *Ibid*, pp. 131–132.
69. See Chapter IV, note 24.
70. B. H. Liddell Hart, *Strategy*, 2d rev. ed. (New York: New American Library, 1974 [1954]), p. 220. See also Paul Kennedy, op. cit., e.g. p. 76ff., for a discussion of the relationship between military strategy and overall national strategy. Kennedy was a student of Hart's at Oxford.
71. *Top Secret: National Security and the Right to Know* (Washington, D.C.: New Republic Books, 1977), p. 57.
72. See *Ibid*, pp. 58–65.
73. *Ibid*, pp. 66–67; see also Turner, op. cit., pp. 147, 277; see Robert M. Gates, "The CIA and American Foreign Policy," 66 *Foreign Affairs* 215, 228–229 (Winter 1987–88).

Chapter VI:
First Amendment Issues

1. See Donald Alexander Downs, *Nazis in Skokie* (Notre Dame, Ind.: University of Notre Dame Press, 1985), pp. 65–66, but see p. 77.
2. *Ibid*, pp. 102–103.
3. Aryeh Neier, *Defending My Enemy* (New York: E. P. Dutton, 1979), p. 165.
4. *Ibid*, p. 164.
5. *Ibid*, p. 167.
6. *Ibid*, p. 164; see, similarly, Franklyn S. Haiman, *Speech and Law in a Free Society* (Chicago: University of Chicago Press, 1981), pp. 154–155.
7. See Downs, op. cit., *passim*.
8. *Ibid*, p. 93.
9. 1985 N.Y. Laws 231; N.Y. Penal Law Section 245.11 (McKinney Supp. 1989).
10. Both Louis Fisher and Professor Thomas Stoddard wonder

whether the decision in *Erznoznik* v. *City of Jacksonville*, 422 U.S. 205 (1975) might protect a purveyor of sexually explicit photographs accosting citizens on a public thoroughfare. That decision invalidated as unconstitutional a Jacksonville city ordinance prohibiting the showing of movies with nudity when the picture would be visible from a public street, outside the viewing area controlled by the management. The Court held that the "limited privacy interest of persons on the public streets cannot justify this censorship of otherwise protected speech on the basis of its content" (Ibid. at 212).

However, in a preceding footnote, the Court distinguished the facts in *Erznoznik* from those when the speaker sought to "force confrontation with the potentially offensive aspects of the work," where suppression was upheld, *Ginzburg* v. *United States*, 383 U.S. 463, 470 (1966), quoted in *Erznoznik* (Ibid.) at 210, n. 6. In *Erznoznik*, the footnote continued, "appellant is not trying to reach, much less shock, unwilling viewers" (Ibid. at 211, n. 6). In our example, the purveyor would have to be quite unreasonable to think that no one would be shocked.

Nevertheless, Justice Powell, in his opinion for the Court, does not appear to be following the Meiklejohn approach, which provides a higher degree of protection for political speech. Meiklejohn's distinction between political and nonpolitical speech appears on its face to be a substantive, "contents" distinction, but actually serves a process value: the provision of the widest possible range of policy alternatives to the decisionmaking public. Of course, discrimination on the basis of *political* content would be unacceptable to Meiiklejohn, and to me.

11. Downs, op. cit., p. 21.
12. *Ibid*, p. 87; see also Haiman, op. cit., pp. 153–154, quoting Dr. William Niederland, clinical professor emeritus of psychiatry.
13. Downs, op. cit.
14. 315 U.S. 568 (1942).
15. 315 U.S. at 572.
16. *Feiner* v. *New York*, 340 U.S. 315, 320–321 (1951).
17. See, e.g., *Terminiello* v. *Chicago*, 337 U.S. 1 (1949).
18. 403 U.S. 15, 25 (1971).
19. 405 U.S. 578 (1972).
20. Downs, op. cit., p. 2, citing *Brandenburg* v. *Ohio*, 395 U.S. 444 (1969).

21. *Ibid*, p. 4.
22. *Ibid*, p. 13.
23. See *Hustler Magazine Inc.* v. *Falwell*, 108 S. Ct. 876 (1988).
24. Downs, op. cit., p. 171, n. 8.
25. *Ibid*, pp. 14, 30, citing Skokie, Ill., Ordinances 994–996 (date ?) and quoting Skokie, Ill., Ordinance 995 (date ?)
26. *Collin* v. *Smith*, 447 F. Supp. 676, aff'd, 578 F.2d 1197 (7th Cir. 1978).
27. 447 F. Supp. at 692–693.
28. 447 F. Supp. at 702.
29. 447 F. Supp. at 687.
30. Downs, op. cit., p. 15.
31. *Ibid*, p. 11, citations omitted.
32. *Ibid*, p. 163.
33. *Ibid*, pp. 5–6, citing Walter Berns, *Freedom, Virtue, and the First Amendment* (Chicago: Gateway, 1965).
34. Ibid.
35. *Ibid*, p. 126.
36. *Ibid*, pp. 126–127.
37. *Ibid*, pp. 151–152.
38. *Ibid*, pp. 152–153.
39. *Ibid*, p. 153.
40. 315 U.S. 568, 572 *Chaplinsky* v. *New Hampshire*, (1942).
41. Haiman, op. cit., p. 134.
42. *Ibid*, p. 152.
43. Downs, op. cit., pp. 159–160.
44. Haiman, op. cit., p. 259.
45. Anthony Dickey, "English Law and Race Defamation," *New York Law Forum*, 14, 24 (1968), quoted in Haiman, op. cit., p. 98.
46. Haiman, op. cit., p. 94.
47. *Ibid*, p. 99.
48. Downs, op. cit., pp. 94–120.
49. *Ibid*, p. 120.
50. Ibid.
51. *Shad Alliance* v. *Smith Haven Mall*, 66 N.Y.2d 496, 513, 488 N.E.2d 1211, 1212, 498 N.Y.S.2d 99, 110 (1985).
52. 326 U.S. 501 (1946).
53. 326 U.S. at 506–507.
54. *Amalgamated Food Employees* v. *Logan Valley Plaza*, 391 U.S. 308 (1968).

55. *Lloyd Corp.* v. *Tanner*, 407 U.S. 551 (1972); *Hudgens* v. *NLRB*, 424 U.S. 507 (1976).
56. *PruneYard Shopping Center* v. *Robbins*, 447 U.S. 74, 83 (1980).
57. 66 N.Y. 2d 496, 488 N.E.2d 1211, 498 N.Y.S.2d 99 (1985).
58. 66 N.Y.2d at 506, 488 N.E.2d at 1217, 498 N.Y.S. 2d at 105 n. 7.
59. Ibid.
60. *Ibid*, at 502, 488 N.E.2d at 1215, 498 N.Y.S.2d at 103.
61. N.Y. Constitution Article I, Section 8.
62. 66 N.Y.2d at 506, 488 N.E.2d at 1217, 498 N.Y.S.2d at 105 (citation omitted).
63. Ibid.
64. Ibid. at 112–114, 488 N.E.2d at 1221–1223, 498 N.Y.S.2d at 109–111.
65. Ibid. at 500, 488 N.E.2d at 1213, 498 N.Y.S.2d at 101 n. 3.
66. The same bill, A.748 of the 1987–88 session, passed the Assembly on March 14, 1988. See *N.Y. Times*, 5/1/88, Section I, 40:3. A. 10512 of the 1985–86 session, introduced by then-Speaker Stanley Fink and co-introduced by the author, along with other members of the Legislature, was also the same bill. It passed the Assembly on June 18, 1986. The Critical Choices Convention, a statewide commemoration of the bicentennial of New York ratification of the U.S. Constitution, held in Poughkeepsie, New York, on July 25 and 26, 1988, adopted as one of its resolutions a similar statement, also introduced by the present author.

Chapter VII:
Organized Crime Control Act

1. Organized Crime Control Act, Ch. 516 of the Laws of 1986, hereinafter cited as OCCA. The Act created Article 460 of the New York Penal Law and added amendments to the Criminal Procedure Law and the Civil Practice Laws and Rules.
2. 18 U.S.C., Sections 1961–1968 (1970), hereinafter cited as RICO.
3. Transcript, Public Hearings on Organized Crime Control Act, Office of the New York State Attorney General, 2 World Trade Center, New York, N.Y., February 24, 1983, and at Legislative Office Building, Albany, N.Y., March 10, 1983; and see, e.g., Ariz. Rev. Stat. Ann. Sections 13-2301 to 13-2316; Cal. Penal

Code Sections 186–186.8; Colo. Rev. Stat. Sections 18-17-101 to 18-17-109; Ga. Code Sections 16-14-1 to 16-14-15; Hawaii Rev. Stat. Sections 842-2 to 842-12.

4. Letter from Robert Abrams, New York State Attorney General, and Patrick Henry, District Attorney for Suffolk County and President of the New York District Attorneys Association on behalf of the New York State Law Enforcement Council, to Warren Anderson, State Senate Majority Leader, June 26, 1986, and see *infra*.

5. For a discussion of the New York law's relative merits in this regard, see Ethan Brett Gerber, "'A RICO You Can't Refuse': New York's Organized Crime Control Act," 53 *Brooklyn L. Rev.* 979, 1988. For criticism of the older statutes, see, e.g., *United States* v. *Anderson*, 626 F.2d 1358, 1364, n. 8 (8th Cir. 1980); *United States* v. *Ivic*, 700 F.2d 51, 64–65 (2d Cir. 1983); *U.S.* v. *Grywacz*, 603 F.2d 682, 692 (7th Cir. 1979) (Swygert, J., dissenting), cert. denied, 446 U.S. 935 (1980); *United States* v. *Rone*, 598 F.2d 564, 573–574 (9th Cir. 1979) (Ely, J., dissenting), cert. denied, 445 U.S. 946 (1980); *United States* v. *Altese*, 542 F.2d 104, 107–111 (2d Cir. 1976) (Van Graafeiland, J., dissenting), cert. denied, 429 U.S. 1039 (1977); Barry Tarlow, "RICO: The New Darling of the Prosecutor's Nursery," 49 *Fordham L. Rev.* 165, 169 n. 11, 192, n. 139 (1980); John F. Driscoll, "*U.S.* v. *Sutton:* Reining In on Runaway RICO," 42 *U. Pitt. L. Rev.* 131 (1980).

6. e.g., Wayne Barrett, "The GOP Goes Soft on Crime," *The Village Voice*, 7/8/86, 12; "Perfidious Albany," Editorial, *New York Daily News*, 7/4/86; "Organized Crime Bill Passes," Associated Press, 7/3/86; "Effort to Get Organized Crime Bill Moves Forward," Associated Press, 6/27/86.

7. See John Rohr, *Ethics for Bureaucrats* (Basel and New York: Marcel Dekker, Inc., 1978), p. 67.

8. Memorandum from Assemblyman Daniel Feldman discussing A.6315, 4/18/83.

9. 18 U.S.C. Sections 1961–1962 (1982).

10. Even our first draft was somewhat more restrictive than RICO, based on some American Bar Association recommendations (1982 A.B.A. Sec. of Criminal Justice, *Report to the House of Delegates*). See also Transcript, Public Hearings, *supra* note 3, 2/24/83, Testimony of Ronald Goldstock, pp. 35–36.

11. One issue, at least, deserves to be excepted from this summary: Both parties to the negotiations agreed relatively early that there would be no private right of action in OCCA. This was partly because we felt that private litigants generally had an adequate forum in the federal courts under RICO, and partly because we knew that the controversy surrounding this issue was and is so severe that it might have made it impossible to reach agreement on other provisions of the bill. The equities of our decision to forgo a private right of action would have been different had there been no such right at the federal level.

12. *United States* v. *Kotteakos*, 328 U.S. 750, 772–775 (1946).

13. *Krulewitch* v. *United States*, 336 U.S. 440, 454 (1949), (Jackson, J., concurring).

14. *Golliher* v. *United States*, 362 F.2d 594, 603 (8th Cir. 1966); see also *Parker* v. *United States*, 404 F.2d 1193, 1196 (9th Cir. 1969): "Joint trials of persons charged together with committing the same offense or with being an accessory to its commission are the rule rather than the exception." Prior to enactment of OCCA, N.Y. Crim. Proc. Law Section 200.40, allowed joinder if: a) defendants are all charged with every offense; or b) all offenses charged are based on a common scheme or plan; or c) all offenses charged are based on the same "criminal transaction."

15. *Braverman* v. *United States*, 317 U.S. 49, 53 (1942).

16. *United States* v. *Elliott*, 571 F.2d 880, 902 (8th Cir. 1978), cert. denied, 439 U.S. 953 (1978).

17. G. Robert Blakey and Ronald Goldstock, "RICO and Labor Racketeering," 17 *Am. Crim. L. Rev.* 341, 347 n. 51, (1980).

18. See, e.g., Permanent Subcommittee on Investigations of Senate Committee on Government Operations, S. Rep. No. 72, 89th Cong., 1st Sess. 117 (1967), cited in John McClellan, "The Organized Crime Act (S.30) or Its Critics: Which Threatens Civil Liberties?" 46 *Notre Dame L. Rev.* 55, 60 n. 8 (1970).

19. Blakey and Goldstock, op. cit., 347–348, n.53.

20. "The President's Commission on Law Enforcement and Administration of Justice in 1967 estimated that organized crime annually earned six to seven billion dollars, an amount equal to the combined annual incomes of the ten largest legitimate corporations in the nation" (R. Clark, *Crime in America*, pp. 55–56, 1970, quoted in Driscoll, op. cit.).

21. Blakey and Goldstock, op. cit., 348, n. 53.

22. *United States* v. *Turkette*, 452 U.S. 576 (1981); see also *Ianelli* v. *United States*, 420 U.S. 770, 787 n. 19 (1975).
23. *Braverman* v. *United States*, 317 U.S. 49 (1942).
24. Driscoll, op. cit., pp. 136–137, describing *Sutton*, where the Court reversed convictions for predicate acts once RICO charge was dropped on appeal, stating that the "government no longer had a sufficiently direct connective link between the defendants to allow them to be tried together."
25. *United States* v. *Elliott*, 571 F.2d 880, 900–903 (8th Cir.), cert. denied 439 U.S. 953 (1978).
26. See Tarlow, op. cit.; see also Note, "Elliott v. U.S.: Conspiracy Law and the Judicial Pursuit of Organized Crime Through RICO," 65 *Va. L. Rev.* 109 (1979); A.B.A. report, op. cit., n. 157.
27. See, e.g., Nancy Ickler, "Conspiracy to Violate RICO: Expanding Traditional Conspiracy Law," 58 *Notre Dame L. Rev.* 587, 596 (1983): "the focus on interdependence, central to both the chain and wheel metaphors."
28. See, e.g., *United States* v. *Anderson*, 626 F.2d 1358 (8th Cir. 1980); *United States* v. *Weisman*, 624 F.2d 1118 (2d Cir. 1980); *United States* v. *Rone*, 598 F.2d 564, 571 (9th Cir. 1979); *United States* v. *Elliott*, 571 F.2d 880, 899 n. 23 (8th Cir.), cert. denied 439 U.S. 953 (1978).
29. See, e.g., *United States* v. *Elliott*, ibid.
30. *Ibid*, at 898; see also *United States* v. *Anderson*, op. cit., n. 175, at 1368.
31. Tarlow, op. cit., p. 193, citing *United States* v. *Turkette*, 452 U.S. 576, 584 (1980); Congressional Statement of Findings and Purpose, S. Rep. No. 617, 91st Cong., 2d Sess. 56–57, 1970, *U.S. Code, Cong. & Admin. News* 4007, 4032-4, Organized Crime Control: Hearings on S.30 and Related Proposals Before Subcomm. No. 5 of the House Comm. on the Judiciary, 91st Cong., 2d Sess. 170, 1970, Statement of John Mitchell, Attorney General.
32. See *United States* v. *Capetto*, 502 F.2d 1351 (7th Cir. 1974), cert. denied 420 U.S. 925 (1975); *United States* v. *Altese*, 542 F.2d 104 (2d Cir. 1976), cert. denied 429 U.S. 1039 (1977); *United States* v. *Elliott*, op. cit.; *United States* v. *Aleman*, 609 F.2d 298 (7th Cir. 1979), cert. denied 445 U.S. 946 (1980); *United States* v. *Rone*, op. cit. See also *United States* v. *Swiderski*, 593 F.2d 1246, 1248-9 (D.C. Cir. 1978), cert denied, 441 U.S. 933 (1979). Cf.

United States v. Anderson, op. cit.; United States v. Sutton, 605
F.2d 260 (6th Cir. 1979).

33. United States v. Elliott, 571 F.2d at 897.

34. See Tarlow, op. cit., at 192 n. 139, 198, 209, and 213.

35. See Gerber, op. cit., at 987–989.

36. Professor James Jacobs points out that conspiracy charges can be
used to join defendants to similar effect (letter to author,
1/24/88). However, Blakey and Goldstock (op. cit.) note that the
great difficulty in inferring conspiracy agreements in many organized-crime areas, such as labor racketeering, has rendered conspiracy law "of limited utility" in this area.

37. Likewise, Professor Jacobs notes that much of this criticism of
RICO can be directed at conspiracy joinder as well (ibid.). But
such criticism could only be as extensive as conspiracy joinder's
reach, and as noted directly above, note 36, it does not reach as
far as RICO.

38. Model Penal Code and Commentaries Section 5.03 (Official Draft
and Revised Comments 1962). For pre-OCCA New York State
joinder provisions, see note 14 above.

39. Not the Eighth Circuit. The Eighth Circuit had taken a step
toward resolving this problem by requiring that the enterprise,
whether legal or illegal, must have an "ascertainable structure
which exists for the purpose of maintaining operations directed
toward an economic goal that has an existence that can be defined apart from the commission of the predicate acts constituting
the 'pattern of racketeering activity,'" United States v.
Anderson, 626 F.2d 1358, 1372 (8th Cir. 1980). The court noted
that the use of "a separate and distinct" enterprise creates a focal
point for RICO violations to ensure that the predicate acts
(which must relate to the enterprise—for example, an enterprise
conducted through a pattern of racketeering activity) have some
degree of interrelatedness (ibid.). The final version of OCCA reflects, in part, the Eighth Circuit's view of the criminal enterprise in its definition: "[C]riminal enterprise means a group of
persons sharing a common purpose of engaging in criminal conduct, associated in an ascertainable structure distinct from a pattern of criminal activity, and with a continuity of existence,
structure and criminal purpose beyond the scope of individual
criminal incidents" (N.Y. Penal Law Section 460.10 (3)). It goes
even further by requiring the existence of a distinct criminal en-

terprise even where a legitimate enterprise exists as a target. See Section 460.20 (1) (a) and (b); 460.20 (3); and 460.00, Legislative Findings.

One should note, though, that the earlier Eighth Circuit position as set forth in *United States* v. *Elliott*, 571 F.2d 880 (1978), which appears to remain the position of most jurisdictions (see, e.g., sources cited in note 28, and which is frequently cited for the broad sweep it imputes to RICO, and is so cited here (see notes 26 and 27), actually does set some limits on its reach. Elliott himself, the named defendant, was held by that court to have been so distant from, and so peripheral to, any organized crime activity that the court severed him from the indictment. Nonetheless, the court's famous dictum in *Elliott*, that "the RICO net is woven tightly to trap even the smallest fish," is generally reflective of the thrust of the opinion and of the prevailing opinion now *outside* the Eighth Circuit.

40. See note 10, above.
41. See, e.g., note 11, above.
42. A.229, Sess (1985), proposed OCCA language for Section 460.00(3)(a).
43. Letter of 2/13/85 from Martin Marcus, first assistant director, New York State Organized Crime Task Force, to author, discussing amendments to A.229 "designed to reach those situations—like those involving criminal conduct engaged in by different 'crews' in an organized crime family—where the relationship is more between the actors than the acts, that is, where those carrying out separate criminal ventures share membership in or association with a single criminal group."
44. See note 17, above, and accompanying text.
45. N.Y. Crim. Proc. Law Section 200.40(1) discussed at note 14, above.
46. OCCA, note 1, above. This added Section 200.40(1)(d) to New York's Criminal Procedure Law.
47. See note 4, above.
48. Jesus Rangel, "All 20 Acquitted in Jersey Mob Case," *N.Y. Times*, 8/27/88, 1:1.
49. "Absurd Lengths for a Mob Trial," Editorial, *N.Y. Times*, 9/1/88, A24:1.
50. See Chapter V, text at note 60.

Chapter VIII:
Constitutional Theory

1. 198 U.S. 45 (1904).
2. But see Ronald Kahn, "Ely, Perry, Tribe, and Modern Constitutional Theory/Practice," APSA panel paper, Washington, D.C., September 1–4, 1988. Kahn argues that both *Lochner* and post-*Lochner* jurisprudence must be understood in terms of a combination of process values and "rights" (substantive due process) values, e.g. at p. 10.
3. 304 U.S. 144 (1938).
4. 304 U.S. at 152, n.4, citations omitted.
5. Herbert Wechsler, "Toward Neutral Principles of Constitutional Law," 73 *Harv. L. Rev.* 1 (1959).
6. I borrowed the above categories of contemporary American constitutional theory, with minor alterations, from Professor Martin Edelman, *Democratic Theories and the Constitution* (Albany, N.Y.: SUNY Press, 1984).
7. Leonard W. Levy, *Original Intent and the Framers' Constitution*, (New York and London: Macmillan Publishing Company, 1988), p. 372, citing Brennan's speech at Georgetown University, 10/12/85, pp. 23–24.
8. *Ibid*, p. 97.
9. *Dennis* v. *United States*, 341 U.S. 494 (1951); *Barenblatt* v. *United States*, 360 U.S. 109 (1959); *Communist Party* v. *Subversive Activities Control Board*, 367 U.S. 1 (1961); *Scales* v. *United States*, 367 U.S. 203 (1961).
10. *Shelton* v. *Tucker*, 364 U.S. 479 (1960); *NAACP* v. *Button*, 371 U.S. 415 (1963); *Gibson* v. *Florida Legislative Investigation Comm.*, 372 U.S. 539 (1963).
11. *Colegrove* v. *Green*, 328 U.S. 549, 556 (1946), and dissents in *Baker* v. *Carr*, 369 U.S. 186, 266 and 330 (1962) (Frankfurter and Harlan, J.J., dissenting); see Rogers Smith, *Liberalism and American Constitutional Law* (Cambridge, Mass.: Harvard University Press, 1985), pp. 123–124.
12. See Levy, op. cit., *passim*, but especially at p. 1: "Madison, the quintessential Founder, discredited original intent. . . ," and at p. 377: "Both [Rehnquist and Bork] are conservative judicial activists who clad themselves in the sheep's garb of judicial self-

restraintsmanship. . . . Each prefers business over government, government over the individual, and the states over the nation."

13. Robert Bork, "Neutral Principles and Some First Amendment Problems," 47 *Ind. L. J.* 1, 20–23 (1971).

14. *Ibid*, at 31, and see 32–33.

15. Linda Greenhouse, "The Bork Battle: Visions of the Constitution," *N.Y. Times*, 10/4/87, IV1:1 at c.2.

16. Robert Bork, *Tradition and Morality in Constitutional Law*, (Washington, D.C.: American Enterprise Institute for Policy Research, 1984), p. 5.

17. Bork, 1971, op. cit., 19. Former Chief Justice Burger, and Chief Justice Rehnquist and Justice O'Connor continue to apply the realist model to reapportionment cases. O'Connor, in her concurring opinion in *Davis* v. *Bandemer*, 487 U.S. 109, 144 (1986), rejected the plurality holding by Justice White that nonracial but partisan gerrymandering presents a justiciable issue: ". . . the cases on which the Court relies do not require that we take this next and most far-reaching step into the 'political thicket,'" citing *Colegrove* v. *Green*, op. cit. Burger and Rehnquist joined in O'Connor's concurrence. Also, Burger, in a separate concurrence, 478 U.S. at 143, quoted Frankfurter's dissent in *Baker* v. *Carr*, 369 U.S. 186, 270 (1962), including the stark comment that "appeal for relief does not belong here."

18. 347 U.S. 483 (1954). See Bork, 1971, op. cit., 14–15.

19. Bork, 1971, op. cit.

20. 381 U.S. 479 (1965).

21. 410 U.S. 113 (1973).

22. 381 U.S. at 484.

23. Bork, 1971, op. cit., 7.

24. 381 U.S. at 507, 571–572.

25. Greenhouse, op. cit., at column 3.

26. Bork, 1971, op. cit., 11.

27. Edelman, 1984, op. cit., p. 138.

28. 389 U.S. 258 (1967).

29. See *Elfbrandt* v. *Russell*, 384 U.S. 11 (1966); *Keyishian* v. *Board of Regents*, 385 U.S. 589 (1967).

30. John Hart Ely, *Democracy and Distrust*, (Cambridge, Mass.: Harvard University Press, 1980).

31. *Ibid*, p. 258, n. 52.

32. *Ibid*, p. 13.

33. *Ibid*, p. 12.
34. *Ibid*, p. 75.
35. *Ibid*, p. 240, n. 76.
36. *Ibid*, p. 63.
37. *Ibid*, pp. 230, n. 5, and 106.
38. *Ibid*, p. 73.
39. 395 U.S. 444 (1969).
40. Ely, op. cit., pp. 115 and 232–233, n. 24.
41. Bork, 1971, op. cit., 23. Critics have raised a number of issues with respect to Ely's approach. Some argue that Ely sets impossible goals. Either he must inject some substantive values into his model of due process, or else he cannot justify the level of judicial activism he supports: Perhaps he could justify court intervention on the basis of the second paragraph of the *Carolene Products* footnote, where groups would otherwise be excluded from the political process, but he cannot justify intervention on the basis of the third paragraph, where legislation, after the rough-and-tumble of the political process, then appears to work a prejudice against "discrete and insular minorities." Rogers Smith says, ". . . Ely cannot resist injecting a more demanding egalitarian restraint on majoritarian actions drawn from Dworkin's 'fundamental values' theory . . ." (*Liberalism and American Constitutional Law*, Cambridge, Mass.: Harvard University Press, 1985, pp. 90–91, and see p. 174).

    But Smith may be wrong. Ely justified third-paragraph interventions only where such prejudice in some significant, even if indirect, way excludes the group in question from the political process, and where Smith alleges that Ely smuggles in Dworkin's concepts, Ely actually quotes Dworkin only in the context of giving minorities representative participation, a process-related value. Ely explicitly rejects the proposition, at that point, that minority groups are immune from treatment, at the hands of majorities, less favorable than the majority gives itself (op. cit., p. 82).

    Indeed, Gary Jacobsohn complains that Ely does not incorporate substantive values into his jurisprudence, disapproving Ely's statement that "preserving fundamental values is not an appropriate constitutional task" (*The Supreme Court and the Decline of Constitutional Aspiration*, Totowa, N.J.: Rowman & Littlefield, Publishers, 1986, p. 101, citing Ely, op. cit., p. 88). But

Jacobsohn takes Ely too much at his word: the "process" values Ely would have the Constitution preserve may well be sufficiently "fundamental" to achieve many of the goals even Jacobsohn seeks.

If so, a third critic, Stanley Brubaker, concludes that Ely's values must "smuggle in" substantive content, but even if one takes Ely at his word and considers his values "procedural," they still "stand in need of justification" ("Fear of Judging: A Commentary on Ely's Theory of Judicial Review," 12 *The Political Science Reviewer*, 207, at, e.g., 236 [1982]). Thus, the critics appear to urge Ely either to move back toward Frankfurter or ahead toward Dworkin. We will reject either option but for the moment will examine the "substantive due process" approaches of Dworkin and other liberal natural and moral rights theorists.

42. Edelman refers to "natural rights," not "moral rights." Professor Stanley Brubaker argues convincingly that it would be more accurate to call intellectual descendants of Kant, like Rawls and Dworkin, "moral-rights" theorists, while reserving the "natural-rights" label for theorists more clearly in the Lockean tradition (Brubaker, op. cit., p. 236, n. 82). I am much indebted to Professor Brubaker for this observation. At the risk of creating confusion by contravening conventional current usage, which is to call all of them "natural-rights" theorists, I adopt Brubaker's distinction. Both natural-rights and moral-rights theorists impose substantive values emerging from intuitionist philosophical approaches. But natural-rights theorists, following Locke, tend to be more minimalist. Later, I will discuss the approach of Hugo Black, who explicitly attacked natural-law theory in his dissent in *Adamson* v. *California*, 332 U.S. 46, 68–92, especially at 75, in 1946, but who built his contractarian theory on natural-law foundations. Black was at least somewhat "interpretivist," reading relatively little into the Constitution but certainly finding liberty and property values there. By contrast, David Richards, who builds his theory on moral-rights foundations, reads far more into the Constitution.

Richards claims to premise his jurisprudence on an "individualistic contract" of sorts (*Toleration and the Constitution*, New York: Oxford University Press, 1986). He says that the social contract, from Locke to Rawls, "elaborat[es] the underlying moral concept of free, rational, and equal persons, for the free

and rational consent of each person to regulative political principles expresses this moral concept" (*Ibid*, p. 101). For Richards,
as for Black, the Constitution provides liberty primarily for the
individual, and only secondarily for purposes of self-government:
The "moral sovereignty of the person" remains paramount (*Ibid*,
p. 168, and see pp. 177–178).

Richards cites Rawls and Dworkin throughout the book, and
even uses a version of Dworkin's troublesome "equal concern and
respect" formulation, which Richards calls "equal respect." However, he does distance himself from Rawls a little, explicitly noting that he emphasizes the relationship between free speech and
conscience more than Rawls does (*Ibid*, p. 169, n. 13).

Richards claims Lockean natural-rights antecedents for his
contract, but as with Rawls and Dworkin, his clearer antecedents
are in Kantian moral rights: Richards calls his central concept
"the moral sovereignty of the person" (*Ibid*, p. 168). For Richards, as for Black, then, free-expression issues do not hinge on
questions of the role of the expression in providing policy alternatives, or in performing any other function for the polity. Although Richards lays claim to satisfying that Meiklejohnian
function too, his own jurisprudence, like Black's, truly rests free-
expression rights on individual moral autonomy (*Ibid*, p. 147).

But Black's jurisprudence, with its natural-rights bent, strives
to remain within some objectively ascertainable bounds, which
for Black were defined as interpretivism, meaning not stretching
the Constitution beyond reasonable interpretations of what the
Framers seem to have meant. The contrast between Black and
Richards on privacy issues points up the essentially unbounded
character of Richards' moral-rights-based jurisprudence.

In implicitly rejecting Black's dissent in *Griswold* v.
Connecticut, 381 U.S. 479, 507 (1965), Richards at least takes a
plausible position. In accepting the holding of *Roe* v. *Wade*, 410
U.S. 113 (1973), as constitutional, where the principles of Black's
Griswold dissent would have applied far more powerfully, Richards weaves together a rich, ingenious, and outrageously wrong
argument (op. cit., pp. 231–269). Richards subtly attacks the religious qualities of many of the anti-abortion arguments to undermine their legitimacy, describes the historical basis for locating
privacy among the abstract "background rights" of the person,
and then utilizes his own "moral sovereignty of the person" prin-

ciple to present the woman's desire for an abortion as a right invoking constitutional protection.

Michael Perry, in contrast, would have overturned the Texas anti-abortion statute in *Roe* v. *Wade* on the basis of liberty, not "privacy" or "moral sovereignty." Perry's approach would have forced legislatures to assure that anti-abortion statutes at least contained exceptions to save the life and health of the mother, to exclude cases of rape and incest, and to cover other situations clearly placing liberty value at stake (*Morality, Politics, and Law*, New York: Oxford University Press, 1988, pp. 6– 142, cited in Kahn, op. cit., p. 43). Chief Justice Rehnquist's plurality opinion in *Webster* v. *Reproductive Health Services*, 1989 W.L. 70950 (#88-605, decided 7/3/89), did not add to the clarity of legal reasoning on this issue. Rehnquist stated his preference for the "liberty interest" approach, but saw no reason to "elaborate" the merits of that "liberty interest" approach over other approaches in constitutionally assessing the Missouri anti-abortion statute in question, at 16.

Perry's argument, overturning at least some anti-abortion legislation, and arguments for pro-choice legislation generally, win the field, at least in my opinion. But Richards makes no such argument; rather, he defends the Court's assumed power to overturn contrary legislation. His defense is not plausible. Nothing he says answers the objection that no meaningful or neutral principle distinguishes this "discovered right" from a wide range of other, thus far undiscovered, "rights" that a court, permitted to "discover" what "abstract background rights" it will, might pull out of the sky.

Richards acknowledges that his differences with Ely here rest on different political theories: Ely's democratic pluralism versus Richards's Rawlsian contractarianism (op. cit., p. 17). If so, the respects levels of integrity of the jurisprudence they produce speak well for the former, Richards's rather conclusory description of Ely's work as a "striking failure" (*Ibid*, p. 14), notwithstanding.

Richards tries to appear to criticize Ely from the left, i.e., that Ely's pluralist democracy reflects an acceptance of interest-group dominance, rather than true democracy through "public argument and debate" (*Ibid*, p. 17). But this misleads: Richards must and does reject "popular sovereignty" (*Ibid*, pp. 5–6, 11) in his own political theory. He dislikes "state imposition of judgments" on matters of religious belief (*Ibid*, p. 169). So he declares a state law prohibiting abortion (which may not have been based on religious beliefs) to have been an imposition of religious belief. Then he has the Court overrule the legislature, when the legislature is the closest approximation of popular sovereignty that we have, by invalidating the law.

43. See, e.g., Ronald Dworkin, *Taking Rights Seriously* (Cambridge, Mass.: Harvard University Press, 1978), pp. 18, 79, 32.
44. *Ibid*, pp. 267, 149, 133.
45. 410 U.S. 113.
46. Dworkin, 1978, op. cit., 129.
47. *Ibid*, 180, 105, 93.
48. Jacobsohn, op. cit., p. 42.
49. Dworkin, 1978, op. cit., p. 278.
50. See Chapter X.
51. Dworkin, 1978, op. cit., 22, and Dworkin's comments to the author at the Oxford University Law Library, 11/9/82.
52. Jacobsohn, op. cit., pp. 6, 55, 11.
53. *Ibid*, pp. 78–80.
54. Edelman, 1984, op. cit., p. 173. Jacobsohn, op. cit., p. 66, notes that Douglas concurred in Black's dissent in *Adamson* v. *California*, 332 U.S. 46, 68–92 (1946), attacking natural-law theory, especially at 75. It is very unlikely that Black and Douglas were at that time or at any time distinguishing between natural-law theory and moral-law theory; they surely would have included the latter in their attack as well had they made such distinctions. But that attack was decades before the developments in Douglas's thinking noted here, and the developments in Black's thinking noted below.
55. *Harper* v. *Virginia Board of Elections*, 383 U.S. 663 (1966).
56. 376 U.S. 52, 67 (1964) (Douglas, J., dissenting).
57. 403 U.S. 124, 171 (1971) (Douglas, J., dissenting).
58. Edelman, 1984, op. cit., pp. 180–188.
59. *Ibid*, p. 191.
60. *Ibid*, p. 176.
61. *Ibid*, p. 198.
62. 385 U.S. 374, 401 (1967) (Douglas, J., concurring).
63. 418 U.S. 323, 356 (1974) (Douglas, J., dissenting).
64. Edelman, 1984, op. cit., p. 201.

65. See, e.g., Mortimer Adler, *We Hold These Truths* (New York: Macmillan, 1987).
66. *The Federalist No. 63*, (Madison).
67. Edelman, 1984, op. cit., p. 216.
68. Ibid.
69. 478 U.S. 109 (1986).
70. Edelman, 1984, op. cit., 226.
71. Edelman, 1988, op. cit.
72. See, e.g., *Elfbrandt* v. *Russell*, 384 U.S. 11 (1966); *Keyishian* v. *Board of Regents*, 385 U.S. 589 (1967).
73. Edelman, 1984, op. cit., pp. 228–229.
74. 354 U.S. 476 (1957).
75. See Chapter VI, text at notes 51 to 66.
76. Edelman, 1984, op. cit., pp. 235–238.
77. See Adler, op. cit.
78. Edelman, 1984, op. cit., pp. 216, 243.
79. *New York Times* v. *United States*, 403 U.S. 713 (1971).
80. 403 U.S. at 726–727.
81. Edelman, 1984, op. cit., p. 307.
82. *Ibid*, pp. 283–286.
83. *Ibid*, p. 286.
84. *Ibid*, pp. 246–253.
85. *Scales* v. *United States*, 367 U.S. 203, 259 (1961) (Black, J., dissenting); *Noto* v. *United States*, 367 U.S. 290, 300 (1961) (Black, J., concurring).
86. Edelman, 1984, op. cit., p. 270.
87. Henry Abraham, notes to author, 2/2/88.
88. Edelman, 1984, op. cit., 278–279.
89. The late Iredell Jenkins provided an interesting approximation of Black's value system. Jenkins was a Virginian who adopted Black's home state of Alabama and taught at the State University in Tuscaloosa for many decades.

    Like Black, Jenkins distrusted new "rights" (*Social Order and the Limits of Law*, Princeton, N.J.: Princeton University Press, 1980, p. 380). Black refused to accept Douglas's creation of the new right of privacy in *Griswold*, for example, out of more than mere "interpretivism." Black's interpretivism had its place, but like Ely, and unlike Frankfurter and Harlan, he approved of Court intervention in the "political thicket" of reapportionment, for example. Edelman, in giving Black a special category to de-

scribe his "individualistic contract," seems more accurate than
Ely, who tends to categorize him more strictly as an interpretivist. Of course, Jenkins follows Black in his interpretivism
too, believing that "substantive justice" is for legislatures, "procedural justice" for courts (*Ibid*, p. 325).

For Jenkins, "law is a necessary but not sufficient cause—or instrument—of order," and should not be overtaxed (*Ibid*, pp. 337,
344). Black relies on law to do less than Douglas thinks it can do;
and his "contract" calls for less than the Brennan/Meiklejohn contract calls for. Black will not find a constitutional right of privacy,
despite his love for privacy; but he also will not find a constitutional right to demonstrate in noisy and obnoxious ways. The individual must be left to his own devices, to some extent: If he
cannot persuade his fellow citizens to vote for a legislature that
will permit contraceptives, he must take the consequences; but
he will not be subjected to undue noise and disturbance from
demonstrators when seeking peace and quiet in his home.

Jenkins warned that too much legal intervention can "weaken
the sense of individual responsibility and self-reliance," but society does need law, especially as it becomes more complex:
"[P]rovision must be made for establishing norms of behavior: for
prescribing and prohibiting certain modes of conduct, for defining
personal and property rights . . . for allocating social duties,
functions, and privileges" (*Ibid*, p. 337).

Jenkins saw "the tasks of law and the goals of justice" as including "the cultivation of human potentialities, the establishment of control over authority, the inculcation and acceptance of
responsibility, and the assurance of continuity within the social
whole." But schools, churches, neighborhoods, class structure,
even heredity and environment, work along with law on these
tasks (*Ibid*, pp. 327, 339–343). For Jenkins,

> . . .the just society is one that secures to man such famil-
> iar but elusive values as freedom, equality, security, and
> opportunity. It gives them the public support and protection
> that they need to make good their inadequacies, and it al-
> lows them the room to exercise initiative and direct their
> private lives [*Ibid*, p. 324].

The sense one gets from Black's decisions is that he saw the
same vision.

Chapter IX:
Administrative Theory

1. See, e.g., *Budget of the United States Government, Fiscal Year 1983*, pp. 38–39.
2. Richard Stillman, "The Changing Patterns of Public Administration Theory in America," in Stillman, ed., *Public Administration Concepts and Cases*, 3d ed. (Boston: Houghton Mifflin Co., 1984).
3. Stillman, *Ibid*, p. 6.
4. John Rohr, *To Run a Constitution* (Lawrence, Kan.: University Press of Kansas, 1986), pp. 131–134.
5. *Ibid*, p. 78.
6. *Ibid*, p. 30.
7. Frederick Mosher, *Democracy and the Public Service*, 2d ed. (New York: Oxford University Press, 1982), p. 58.
8. See J. Q. Wilson, "The Rise of the Bureaucratic State," in Francis Rourke, ed., *Bureaucratic Power in National Policy Making*, 4th ed. (Boston: Little, Brown & Co., 1986), pp. 125, 129.
9. Rohr, op. cit., p. 91.
10. Stillman, op. cit., p. 15.
11. Philip Cooper, "Public Law and Public Administration," ASPA panel paper, Anaheim, California, April 1986, p. 6.
12. Mosher, op. cit., p. 66.
13. Henry Sumner Maine, *Ancient Law*, 10th ed. (Boston: Beacon Press, 1963 [1861]), p. 165.
14. Frederick Taylor, "Scientific Management," 1912, in Jay Schaffritz and Albert Hyde, eds., *Classics of Public Administration* (Oak Park, Ill.: Moore Publishing Co., 1978), p. 17.
15. Max Weber, "Bureaucracy," 1922, in Schaffritz and Hyde, eds., *Ibid*, p. 23.
16. Cooper, op. cit., noting the contribution of Carl Schurz.
17. Mosher, op. cit., p. 73.
18. Stillman, op. cit., p. 14.
19. David H. Rosenbloom, "Public Administration Theory and the Separation of Powers," 43 *Pub. Admin. Rev.* 219, 220 (1983).
20. Stillman, op. cit., p. 16; Rosenbloom, op. cit., p. 220; Cooper, op. cit., p. 7; but see Hindy Lauer Schachter, "Efficiency in the Municipal Reform Literature: A New View," APSA panel pa-

per, Washington, D.C., Sept. 1–4, 1988, arguing that even the reformers and scholars of that period regarded efficiency as a vehicle toward other values, not as an ultimate goal itself.

21. In Wilson's *Congressional Government*, 1885, cited in Rohr, op. cit., pp. 4, 61. Louis Fisher says of Woodrow Wilson's comment here, "There is no evidence that he knew what he was talking about" (comments to author, 8/12/88).
22. Rohr, op. cit., p. 84.
23. *Ibid*, p. 85.
24. *Ibid*, p. 61.
25. *Ibid*, p. 67.
26. *Ibid*, p. 74.
27. *Ibid*, p. 87.
28. Rosenbloom, op. cit., p. 220.
29. Stillman, op. cit., p. 17.
30. Mosher, op. cit., p. 83.
31. Rohr, op. cit., p. 136.
32. Mosher, op. cit., pp. 83–102.
33. *Kendall* v. *United States ex rel. Stokes*, 37 U.S. (12 Pet.) 522, 610 (1838), quoted in Rohr, op. cit., pp. 135, 141.
34. Rohr, *Ibid*, pp. 137–139.
35. "Report of the President's Committee on Administrative Management," 74th Cong., 2d Sess. (Washington, D.C.: Government Printing Office, 1937), p. 2, quoted in Rohr, *Ibid*, p. 145.
36. *Ibid*, pp. 152–153.
37. *Ibid*, pp. 147–149.
38. Stillman, op. cit., p. 23.
39. Cooper, op. cit., p. 18.
40. "Public law litigation is alive and well," David Rosenbloom, comments to this writer, 2/2/88.
41. Stillman, op. cit., pp. 7–8.
42. Mosher, op. cit., p. 64.
43. The tradition is rooted in the Roman law barring the *procurator* from creating "another *procurator*," except subject to certain restrictions (Horst Emke, "'Delegata Potestas Non Potest Delegari,' A Maxim of American Constitutional Law," 47 *Cornell L. Q.* 50, 51 (1961). Bracton, in the thirteenth century, in the course of helping to engender the new separation of executive, legislative, and judicial power in England, argued that the king does not own his powers, but is "entrusted" with them, trusted

personally by God and by his people, and his powers therefore "were not to be conveyed" by him to another. Bracton cited the old Roman maxim *Delegata potestas non potest delegari*, "a delegated power cannot be further delegated" (*Ibid*, pp. 53–56).

In the fourteenth century, a similar principle appeared in Talmudic law in Spain, i.e., that in the public sector, "authority cannot be delegated by a body required to exercise its own discretion" (Menachem Elon, ed., *The Principles of Jewish Law*, Jerusalem, Israel: Keter Publishing House Ltd., 1975, p. 648). Elon cites the *Responsa Ribash* # 228 of Rabbi Isaac ben Sheshet Perfet for this principle of Jewish Law. Ben Sheshet Perfet, also known as ben Sheshet Barfat, was born in Valencia, Spain, in 1326 and died in Algiers in 1408 (Rabbi Joseph I. Singer, Manhattan Beach Jewish Center, Brooklyn, letter to author, 4/13/88).

In the sixteenth century, Richard Hooker, studying Bracton's earlier work, noted the principle, and Locke took it from Hooker (Emke, op. cit., pp. 53–56). Locke applied it to the legislature, whose lawmaking power, he said, is "sacred and unalterable in the hands where the Community have once placed it" (John Locke, *Two Treatises of Government*, Peter Laslett, ed., New York and Ontario: New American Library, 1963, Second Treatise, Section 143, at p. 401). Locke quotes Hooker in support of this section of his treatise, as saying that "any Prince or Potentate of what kind soever" may impose laws justly upon society only "by express Commission immediately and personally received from God, or else by Authority derived at the first from their [society's] consent. . . ." (Richard Hooker, *Ecclesiastical Polity*, I.1.Sec.10, quoted by John Locke, op. cit.). Further, Locke said straightforwardly, "The Legislative cannot transfer the Power of Making Laws to any other hands. For it being but a delegated Power from the People, they, who have it, cannot pass it over to others" (Locke, op. cit., Section 141, at p. 408).

44. Emke, op. cit.
45. *Shankland* v. *Washington*, 30 U.S. (5 Pet.) 390, 395 (1831), cited in Bernard Schwartz, *Administrative Law* (Boston: Little, Brown & Co., 1976), p. 33, n. 8.
46. Kenneth C. Davis, *Administrative Law Text*, 3d ed. (St. Paul, Minn.: West Publishing Co., 1972), p. 6.

47. *United States* v. *Shreveport Grain Elevator Co.*, 287 U.S. 77, 85.
48. Stillman, op. cit., pp. 7–12.
49. *United States* v. *Chicago, M. St. P. & P. R.R. Co.*, 282 U.S. 311, 324, 1931.
50. *Panama Refining Co.* v. *Ryan*, 293 U.S. 388 (1935); and *Schechter Poultry Corp.* v. *United States*, 295 U.S. 495 (1935).
51. Davis, *op. cit.*, p. 28.
52. James Fesler, "Policymaking at the Top of Bureaucracy," in Francis Rourke, ed., *Bureaucratic Power in National Politics*, 4th ed. (Boston: Little, Brown & Co., 1986), p. 324.
53. See Rosenbloom, op. cit., p. 221; John C. Donovan, *The Politics of Poverty* (New York: Pegasus, 1967).
54. Stillman, op. cit., p. 21.
55. Cooper, op. cit., pp. 15–16.
56. Rosenbloom, op. cit., p. 221.
57. Rohr, op. cit., pp. 149–150; Mosher, op. cit., pp. 102–109.
58. Public Law 95-454, Section 3 and Section 2301(b)(1), quoted in Rosenbloom, op. cit., p. 221.
59. Professor David Rosenbloom, comments to author, 2/2/88.
60. Stillman, op. cit., p. 10.
61. Rohr, op. cit., p. 132. Louis Fisher notes that Madison was very inconsistent in this regard, elsewhere arguing strongly for implied powers (comments to the author, 8/12/88). See Fisher, *Constitutional Conflicts Between Congress and the President* (Princeton, N.J.: Princeton University Press, 1985), pp. 19–22; Federalist 44.
62. Elton Mayo, "Hawthorne and the Western Electric Company" [1945], in Stillman, ed., op. cit., pp. 171–180; F. J. Roethlisberger, "The Hawthorne Experiments" [1941], in Schaffritz and Hyde, eds., op. cit., p. 67.
63. Stillman, op. cit., p. 18, citing, for example, Chester Barnard, probably the master theorist of informal groups.
64. Rosenbloom, op. cit., p. 222.
65. 272 U.S. 52, 293 (1926) (Brandeis, J., dissenting). Fisher thinks Brandeis was wrong, i.e., separation of powers may well promote efficiency (comments to the author, 8/12/88).
66. Rosenbloom, op. cit.
67. Rohr, op. cit., p. x.
68. Rosenbloom, op. cit., p. 224.
69. Rohr, op. cit., pp. 154–170.

70. Jerry Mashaw, *Due Process in the Administrative State* (New Haven: Yale University Press, 1985), p. 28.
71. Cooper, op. cit., p. 14.
72. But cf. Mashaw, op. cit., pp. 40–41.
73. Davis, op. cit., p. 90. For another interesting discussion of police officer discretion, see H. Richard Uviller, "Cops and Robbers," 13 *Columbia* 16, 1988, describing some of a Columbia law professor's experiences on sabbatical spent on patrol with police officers on the Lower East Side of New York City.
74. Davis, op. cit., p. 88.
75. Daniel Feldman, "Administrative Agencies and the Rites of Due Process," 7 *Fordham Urb. L. J.* 229, 241 (1978).
76. Davis, op. cit., p. 102.
77. *Cady* v. *Roberts & Co.*, 40 S.E.C. 907 (1961).
78. *SEC* v. *Chenery Corp.*, 332 U.S. 194 (1947).
79. *NLRB* v. *American Can Company*, 658 F.2d 746, 758 (10th Cir. 1981).
80. 261 A.D. 373, 375 25 N.Y.S.2d 617, 620 (4th Dept. 1941).
81. 397 U.S. 254, 262 (1970).
82. Feldman, 1978, op. cit., p. 232.
83. See, e.g., *Rush* v. *Smith*, 427 F. Supp. 576 (S.D.N.Y. 1977), and my discussion of that case in Feldman, 1978, op. cit., pp. 235–236.
84. *Ibid*, pp. 240–241.
85. *Ibid*, p. 242, citing the following: "There are 'fewer than 200 full-time lawyers for the estimated two million residents who qualify for free legal aid in noncriminal matters' in New York" (*N.Y. Times*, 10/14/77, B2:1). "More than 15.7 million poor do not have effective access to legal assistance" (Legal Services Corporation, *Annual Report for Fiscal Year 1976*, p. 8).
86. See, e.g., Richard Lacayo, "The Sad Fate of Legal Aid," *Time*, 6/20/88, p. 59.
87. *Bell* v. *Burson*, 402 U.S. 535 (1971).
88. *Gray Panthers* v. *Harris*, 629 F.2d 180 (D.C. Cir. 1980).
89. Robert Martin and Fred Geldon, "Planning for the Negotiated Settlement of Claims," Bureau of National Affairs, Washington, D.C., 1982.
90. 326 U.S. 327 (1945).
91. Lon L. Fuller, *The Morality of Law*, rev. ed., (New Haven and London: Yale University Press, 1969), p. 172.

92. Rohr, op. cit., pp. 89, 182.
93. John Rohr, *Ethics for Bureaucrats* (New York and Basel: Marcel Dekker Inc., 1978).
94. Rohr, 1986, op. cit., pp. 84, 192–194.
95. John Burke, *Bureaucratic Responsibility* (Baltimore: Johns Hopkins University Press, 1986), p. 112, citing *The New York Times*, 2/13/81, 2/14/81, 3/15/81.
96. Burke, op. cit.
97. *Ibid.*
98. *Ibid*, p. 39.
99. *Ibid*, p. 58.
100. *Ibid*, p. 167.
101. *Ibid*, p. 41.
102. *Ibid*, p. 141.
103. *Ibid*, p. 135, citing Ronald Dworkin, *Taking Rights Seriously*, (Cambridge, Mass.: Harvard University Press, 1978), p. 227.
104. Stillman, op. cit., p. 21.
105. Mashaw, op. cit., p. 218.

Chapter X:
Components of the Tradition

1. Andrew McLaughlin, *Foundations of American Constitutionalism* (New York: Fawcett Publications Inc., 1961 [1932]), p. 14.
2. *Ibid*, p. 34; see also William Marty, "Religion, the Constitution, and Modern Rivals: Our Founders and Theirs," APSA panel paper, Chicago, September 3–6, 1987, p. 3.
3. Genesis 9:9–17.
4. Genesis 22:16–18.
5. Exodus 34:10–27.
6. McLaughlin, op. cit., p. 16.
7. *Ibid*, pp. 18–23.
8. A. J. Beitzman, *A History of American Political Thought* (New York: Dodd, Mead & Co., 1972), p. 35, and A. P. Grimes, *American Political Thought* rev. ed. (New York: Holt, Rinehart & Winston, 1960), p. 15, quoted in Marty, op. cit., p. 3. Also quoted in David Wootton, Introduction, *Divine Right*

and Democracy, Wootton, ed. (Harmondsworth, Middlesex, England: Penguin Books, 1986), p. 63.

9. McLaughlin, op. cit., pp. 26–28.

10. *Ibid*, p. 35.

11. See Marty, op. cit., p. 4.

12. McLaughlin, op. cit., pp. 39–40.

13. *Ibid*, pp. 46–50.

14. See, e.g., Thomas Pangle, "The Constitution's Human Vision," 86 *The Public Interest* 77, 79 (1987).

15. See McLaughlin, op. cit., p. 58.

16. Bernard Schwartz, "Fashioning an Administrative Law System," 40 *Admin. L. Rev.* 415, 420 (Summer 1988). See text at Chapter V, note 43.

17. Schwartz, op. cit., p. 423.

18. *Ibid*, p. 52.

19. *Ibid*, p. 76.

20. *The Works of the Right Honorable Edmund Burke* (London: C. and J. Rivington, 1926), Vol. III, pp. 23–132, quoted in James Stoner, "Behind the 'facts submitted to a Candid World': Constitutional Arguments for Independence," APSA panel paper, Chicago, September 3–6, 1987, pp. 9–10.

21. James I (of England), "The Trew Law of Free Monarchies," in David Wootton, ed., op. cit., p. 104.

22. Edward Corwin, *The "Higher Law" Background of American Constitutional Law* (Ithaca, New York: Cornell University Press, 1955 [42 Harv. L. Rev., 149 (1928)]).

23. Bernard Schwartz, *The Roots of Freedom*, (New York: Hill and Wang, 1967), p. 116.

24. *Ibid*, pp. 121–122.

25. *Ibid*, p. 179.

26. McLaughlin, op. cit., pp. 100–101.

27. Schwartz, 1967, op. cit., p. 177.

28. J. R. Pole, *The Gift of Government* (Athens, Ga.: University of Georgia Press, 1983), p. 66.

29. Stoner, op. cit., pp. 11–12.

30. J. R. Pole, conversation with author, New York University, February 10, 1988.

31. McLaughlin, op. cit., pp. 112–121; see also Louis Fisher, *Constitutional Dialogues* (Princeton, N.J.: Princeton University Press, 1988), pp. 46–47.

32. McLaughlin, op. cit., p. 137; Forrest McDonald, *Novus Ordo Seclorum* (Lawrence, Kan.: University Press of Kansas, 1985) p. 28.
33. McLaughlin, op. cit., pp. 136–138.
34. McDonald, op. cit., p. 278, citing *Papers of Alexander Hamilton*, ed. Harold C. Syrett, Vol. 8 (New York: Columbia University Press, 1965), p. 98.
35. *The Federalist No. 9* at 72 (Hamilton).
36. See Thomas Pangle, "The Federalists," 8 *Humanities* #2 (March/April 1987), pp. 14, 16; McDonald, op. cit., p. 188; Gordon Wood, "Democracy and the Constitution," in Robert Goldwin and William Schiambra, eds., *How Democratic Is the Constitution?* (Washington and London: American Enterprise Institute for Public Policy Research, 1980), p. 11.
37. Wood, op. cit., p. 10.
38. *The Federalist No. 10* (Madison); Wood, op. cit., p. 11.
39. *The Federalist No. 51* (Madison).
40. McDonald, op. cit., pp. 13–36.
41. *Ibid*, p. 13.
42. Paul Kennedy, *The Rise and Fall of the Great Powers* (New York: Random House, 1987), pp. 19–20.
43. Adda Bozeman, *Politics and Culture in International History* (Princeton, N.J.: Princeton University Press, 1960), pp. 348–349.
44. McDonald, op. cit., p. 36.
45. Leonard Levy, *The Emergence of a Free Press* (New York: Oxford University Press, 1985), p. 91; Maurice Ashley, "Constitutionalism and the Sovereign State in the Seventeenth Century," in *Chapters in Western Civilization*, ed. Staff of Columbia College, Vol. I, 3d ed. (New York: Columbia University Press, 1961), pp. 450–451.
46. Levy, op. cit., p. 6; McDonald, op. cit., p. 47.
47. F. W. Maitland, *The Constitutional History of England*, ed. H.L.A. Fisher (Cambridge, England: Cambridge University Press, 1965 [1908]), pp. 241–242.
48. McDonald, op. cit., p. 46; see also Levy, op. cit., p. 3.
49. Levy, op. cit., p. 184.
50. *Ibid*, p. 297.
51. *Ibid*, Preface, p. xi.
52. *Ibid*, pp. 120–121; McDonald, op. cit., p. 47.

53. Levy, op. cit., Preface, p. x.
54. *Ibid*, pp. xi, xix.
55. Charles and Mary Beard, *Basic History of the United States* (New York: Doubleday, Doran & Company, 1944), p. 170.
56. Levy, op. cit., Preface, p. xii.
57. *Ibid*, pp. x–xi; see also Leonard Levy, *Original Intent and the Framers' Constitution* (New York and London: Macmillan Publishing Company, 1988), pp. 195–220, especially pp. 211–212.
58. Levy, 1985, p. xvii.
59. *Ibid*, p. 349.
60. *Ibid*, pp. 348–349.
61. J. R. Pole, *The Pursuit of Equality in American History* (Berkeley, Los Angeles and London: University of California Press, 1978), p. 9.
62. *Ibid*, pp. 16–22.
63. Lawrence M. Friedman and Harry N. Scheiber, eds., *American Law and the Constitutional Order* (Cambridge, Mass.: Harvard University Press, 1978), Preface, p. viii.
64. Pole, 1978, op. cit., pp. 37–43.
65. Herbert J. Storing, "Slavery and the Moral Foundations of the American Republic," in Robert H. Horwitz, ed., *The Moral Foundations of the American Republic*, 3d ed. (Charlottesville: University Press of Virginia, 1986), pp. 316, 324, 327.
66. *Ibid*, p. 316; Kenneth Stampp, "Chattles Personal," in Friedman and Scheiber, op. cit., p. 212.
67. Storing, op. cit., p. 330.
68. Pole, 1978, op. cit., pp. 68–69, n. 18; 90; see also Rhys Isaac, *The Transformation of Virginia 1740–1790* (Chapel Hill, N.C.: University of North Carolina Press, 1982), e.g., p. 321.
69. Richard Hofstadter, "The Founding Fathers: An Age of Realism," in Horwitz, ed., op. cit., pp. 64, 69, 72. Note that by 1800, even the wage earner in the United States was better off than counterparts in Western Europe: Wages in the United States were one-third higher (Kennedy, op. cit., p. 178).
70. Gordon Wood, "The Democratization of Mind in the American Revolution," in Horwitz, ed., op. cit., p. 123.
71. Willard Hurst, "The Release of Energy," in Friedman and Scheiber, op. cit., p. 119.
72. Martin Edelman, *Democratic Theories and the Constitution* (Albany, N.Y.: SUNY Press, 1984), p. 27.

73. *Ibid*, p. 25.
74. *Ibid*, p. 27.
75. In his 1988 book, *Constitutional Faith*, Sanford Levinson wrote, ". . . The vital challenge facing the American faith community is the possibility of expanding the relevant 'we' in 'We the People,' who must ultimately endorse the faith if it is to live as anything other than an ideological charade" (Princeton, N.J.: Princeton University Press, p. 193).
76. Robert A. Goldwin, "Of Men and Angels: A Search for Morality in the Constitution," in Horwitz, ed., op. cit., p. 28.
77. Pole, 1983, op. cit., p. 5.
78. See, e.g., Roger Hilsman, *To Move A Nation* (New York: Doubleday & Co., 1967), pp. 279–280.
79. Benjamin Barber, "The Compromised Republic: Public Purposelessness in America," in Horwitz, ed., op. cit., p. 47.
80. Martin Diamond, "Ethics and Politics: The American Way," in Horwitz, ed., op. cit., pp. 92–94.
81. John Locke, *Two Treatises of Government*, ed. Peter Laslett (New York: Cambridge University Press, 1963), pp. 376–377.
82. Robert Horwitz, "John Locke and the Preservation of Liberty," in Horwitz, ed., op. cit., p. 137.
83. Diamond, op. cit., p. 84.
84. Alexis de Toqueville, *Democracy in America* (New York: Alfred A. Knopf, 1945), Vol. II, p. 112.
85. Diamond, op. cit., p. 108. But see William Galston, "Liberal Virtues," 82 *Am. Pol. Sci. Rev.* 1277 (1988), for a more complex view, a view that argues that some classical aspects of virtue remained central to the visions of the state held by Locke and by the Framers.
86. Pole, 1978, op. cit., p. 52.
87. *The Federalist No. 10* at 78 (Madison).
88. Professor Graham Walker of the University of Pennsylvania notes that a sizable minority and maybe as much as half of the American people were still shocked when they discovered—in the 1970s—that America was a secular state. He thinks that "piety" might still rank among the key American values, and would therefore add it to my list of liberty, equality, property, security, and efficiency.
89. Walter Berns, "Religion and the Founding Principle," in Horwitz, ed., op. cit., pp. 224–229. Louis Fisher notes that in revo-

lutionary America, "property included your ideas and religious beliefs." "To Locke, it was more than land and possessions. It was life, liberty and estate" (comments to author, 8/5/88). But his stress was on property. It would have been different if, say, "liberty" were the operative word, including life, property, and, say, "freedom." Human nature being what it is, I would have to think that "land and possessions" were what most Americans thought of when they thought of property, even if Madison, as Fisher points out, (*ibid.*) "regarded *conscience* as the most important property."

90. See, e.g., David Potter, *People of Plenty* (Chicago: University of Chicago Press, 1954).

91. Lawrence M. Friedman, "Notes Toward a History of American Justice," in Friedman and Scheiber, op. cit., p. 16; see also David Flaherty, "Law and the Enforcement of Morals in Early America," and William E. Nelson, "Emerging Notions of Modern Criminal Law in the Revolutionary Era," in Friedman and Scheiber, op. cit.

92. Pole, 1978, op. cit., p. 90.

93. *Ibid*, pp. 117, 147, 156.

94. Willard Hurst, "The Release of Energy," in Friedman and Scheiber, op. cit., pp. 120, 145–146.

95. See Edelman, op. cit., p. 24.

96. Hurst, op. cit., p. 112.

97. Paul Gates, "An Overview of American Land Policy," in Friedman and Scheiber, op. cit., p. 125.

98. Harry Scheiber, "Property Law, Expropriation, and Resource Allocation by Government, 1789–1910," in Friedman and Scheiber, op. cit., p. 133.

99. Hurst, op. cit., p. 113.

100. *Ibid*, pp. 110, 115–116, 117.

101. Edelman, op. cit., pp. 34. 36.

102. *Truax* v. *Corrigan*, 257 U.S. 312 (1921), quoted *Ibid*, p. 36.

103. Edelman, op. cit., p. 36.

104. See *Ibid*, p. 41.

105. Pole, 1978, op. cit., p. 217.

106. Charles Reich, "The New Property," in Friedman and Scheiber, op. cit., p. 379.

107. E.g., *Wilkie* v. *O'Connor*, 261 A.D. 373, 25 N.Y.S.2d 617 (4th Dept. 1941).

108. 397 U.S. 254 (1970).
109. Reich, op. cit., pp. 390, 392.
110. Pole, 1978, op. cit., citing study by Robert E. Lane, pp. 333–334; 351.

Chapter XI:
Evidence of the Tradition

1. *The Federalist No. 1* at 33 (Hamilton).
2. Arthur S. Miller, *Democratic Dictatorship* (Westport, Conn.: Greenwood Press, 1981), pp. xi–xii.
3. David Kairys, *The Politics of Law* (New York: Pantheon Books, 1982), pp. 1–2.
4. David Potter, *The Americans: The National Experience* (New York and Toronto: Random House, 1965), pp. 427–430.
5. Potter, op. cit.
6. See Charles Beard, *An Economic Interpretation of the Constitution* (New York: The Macmillan Company, 1913).
7. Frederick Jackson Turner, *The Frontier in American History* (New York: Holt, Rinehart & Winston, 1962 [1920; original paper, 1893]).
8. Allan Nevins and Henry Steele Commager, *A Pocket History of the United States* (New York: Washington Square Press, 1956), pp. 143–144.
9. *Ibid*, p. 220.
10. Phillip S. Paludan, "The American Civil War Considered as a Crisis in Law and Order," 7 *Am. Hist. Rev.* 1013 (1972).
11. Frederick P. Lewis, book review of Arthur S. Miller, op. cit., 76 *Am. Pol. Sci. Rev.* 417 (1982).
12. 384 U.S. 436 (1966).
13. Kairys, op. cit., p. 15.
14. *Juillard* v. *Greenman*, 110 U.S. 421, 1884.
15. Alexis de Toqueville, *Democracy in America* (New York: Alfred A. Knopf, 1945), Vol. I, pp. 198–199.
16. New York: Pyramid Publications, 1967 [1876].
17. *Engel* v. *Vitale*, 370 U.S. 421, 1962; Abington Township v. Schempp, 374 U.S. 203, 1963.
18. Kenneth Dolbeare, "The Supreme Court and the States," in T.

Becker and M. Feeley, eds., *The Impact of Supreme Court Decisions* (New York: Oxford University Press, 1969), p. 202.

19. Ibid.
20. John Kessel, "Public Perceptions of the Supreme Court," 10 *Midwest Journal of Political Science* 167 (1966).
21. Toqueville, op. cit., Vol. I, p. 290.
22. According to Louis Fisher, not even the Supreme Court, which applies judicial review, exercises constitutional supremacy. If Congress or the president disagrees with the Court, Fisher has argued, history will vindicate one or another (Louis Fisher, *Constitutional Dialogues* (Princeton, N.J.: Princeton University Press, 1988). In any case, the Constitution, not the institutions, retains supremacy.
23. Emile Boutmy, *Studies in Constitutional Law: France-England-United States*, transl. E. M. Dicey (London and New York: Macmillan and Co., 1891), p. 152.
24. Daniel Feldman, "Administrative Agencies and the Rites of Due Process," 7 *Fordham Urban Law Journal* 229 (1978).
25. Louis Lusky, *By What Right?* (Charlottesville, Va.: The Michie Company, 1975), p. 35.
26. *Youngstown Sheet & Tube Co.* v. *Sawyer*, 343 U.S. 579 (1952).
27. James Reston, "Impeachment Politics," *N.Y. Times*, 4/10/74, 41:5.
28. *United States* v. *Nixon*, 418 U.S. 683 (1974).
29. Anthony Lewis, "Sounding Loud and Clear," *N.Y. Times*, 3/7/74, 39:1.
30. Walter Bagehot, *The English Constitution* (London and Glasgow: Collins/Fontana, 1963).
31. "The Constitution Is Alive and Well," *N.Y. Times*, 8/11/74, IV:17:2.
32. *Youngstown Sheet & Tube Co.*, 343 U.S. at 579.
33. Miller, op. cit., p. 72.
34. Robert Dahl, *Democracy in the United States* (Chicago: Rand McNally & Co., 1972), pp. 200–210.
35. *Panama Refining Co.* v. *Ryan*, 293 U.S. 388 (1935); *Schechter Poultry Corp.* v. *U.S.*, 295 U.S. 495 (1935).
36. Ibid.
37. E.g., *NLRB* v. *Jones & Laughlin Steel Corp.*, 301 U.S. 1 (1937).
38. Charles Black, *The People and the Court* (New York: Macmillan, 1960), p. 38.
39. June L. Tapp and Fred Krinsky, eds., *Ambivalent America*,

(Beverly Hills, Calif.: Macmillan Company, 1971), p. 6, quoting Dwight D. Eisenhower, *Vital Speeches*, Vol. 18, 9/1/52.

40. 347 U.S. 483 (1954).
41. Alexander Bickel, *The Least Dangerous Branch* (Indianapolis and New York: Bobbs-Merrill Company, 1962), p. 246.
42. *Brown* v. *Board of Education (II)*, 349 U.S. 294 (1955).
43. Bickel, op. cit., p. 256.
44. C. Peter Magrath, *Constitutionalism and Politics* (Glenview, Ill.: Scott, Foresman and Co., 1968), p. 155, quoting *The New York Times*, 7/4/64, 1 and 4. Louis Fisher notes that the restaurant owner was referring to the 1964 statute, not the 1954 Court decision in *Brown* v. *Board of Education*. However, it is difficult to deny the impact of *Brown* v. *Board of Education*. See text at notes 41 and 42 above, and 45 and 46 below.
45. H. Hyman and P. Sheatsley, "Attitudes Toward Desegregation," 211 *Scientific American* 16 (1964).
46. Quoted in Nat Hentoff, "The Integrationist," *The New Yorker*, 8/23/82, 37.
47. Louis Harris, "Poll: Most Are Still Anti-Busing, But...," *New York Post*, 7/3/76, 7:3.
48. "Reagan and States' Rights: Meeting Two Goals," *N.Y. Times*, 3/4/81, A24:1, continued from A1.
49. J. R. Pole, "Sunset Over the Statute Book," review of Guido Calabresi, *A Common Law for the Age of Statutes*, in *Times Literary Supplement*, 9/24/82, 1029.
50. *Milk Wagon Drivers Union* v. *Meadowmoor Dairies*, 312 U.S. 287, 301 (1941).
51. Alexander Meiklejohn, *Free Speech and Its Relation to Self-Government* (New York: Harper and Row, 1948), p. 27.
52. Asher Bob Lans, "A Study in the Tradition of the Constitution in the United States," 1939, unpublished master's thesis in sociology, available at Butler Library, Columbia University.
53. Leonard Levy, "Liberty and the First Amendment," 68 *Am. Hist. Rev.* 22, 29.
54. James Randall, *Constitutional Problems Under Lincoln* (New York: D. Appleton and Co., 1926), p. 481.
55. Grover O'Connor, "Free Speech," 1942, p. 15 (privately published). Available in Langdell Library of Harvard Law School.
56. K. C. Wheare, *Modern Constitutions* (London: Oxford University Press, 1966 [1951]), pp. 5–6.

57. Boutmy, op. cit., p. 148.
58. Samuel E. Finer, *Five Constitutions* (Harmondsworth, England: Penguin Books, 1979), p. 84.
59. A. V. Dicey, *Introduction to the Study of the Law of the Constitution*, (London: Macmillan and Co., 1961 [1908]), p. 246.
60. *Ibid*, pp. 244–245.
61. Finer, op. cit., p. 84; see also Eric Barendt, *Freedom of Speech* (Oxford, England: Oxford University Press, 1987), pp. 317–321, for a discussion of the British Public Order Act of 1986, which strongly reaffirms British restrictions on certain forms of disruptive speech.
62. Noted by Mr. Geoffrey Marshall at a seminar under his direction, "Confidentiality and Secrecy," Nuffield College, Oxford University, 10/10/82. See also discussion of Official Secrets Act in Barendt, op. cit., pp. 167–172.
63. Craig R. Whitney, "Civil Liberties in Britain: Are They Under Siege?" *N.Y. Times*, 11/1/88, A18:1-4.
64. Bernard Schwartz, *The Roots of Freedom: A Constitutional History of England* (New York: Hill and Wang, 1967), pp. 214–215.
65. The late Mr. Philip Williams, of Nuffield College, Oxford University, helped me arrive at the conclusion that the McCarthy-era Smith Act prosecutions in the United States, so much more repressive than English government policy of that period, derived from the American tendency toward tyranny of the majority overwhelming the American civil-liberties tradition. Williams concurred in my conclusion that the latter is stronger in the United States than in England, but the former is vastly stronger in the United States, during conversations at Nuffield, 10/15/82.
66. Harold Troper, "James Keegstra, Teacher of Hate," 53 *Congress Monthly* 2, 7, February 1986.
67. Franklyn Haiman, *Speech and Law in a Free Society* (Chicago: University of Chicago Press, 1981), p. 90.
68. *Ibid*, p. 89.
69. A. V. Dicey, op. cit., p. 259.
70. Frede Castberg, *Freedom of Speech in the West* (Oslo: Oslo University Press, 1960), p. 33.
71. Associated Press, "Guilty Verdict in Holocaust 'Lie,'" *New York Post*, 2/24/76, 14. This was a violation of Section 130 of the German Penal Code. See Barendt, op. cit., p. 165.
72. Castberg, op. cit., p. 379; see also Finer, op. cit., p. 204; Charles Lamm Markmann, "Civil Liberties? Was Ist Das? A Report from

the German Federal Republic," 1 *Civil Liberties Review* 42, 43 (1974).

73. Jay Bushinsky, "Rabin Yields in Flap on Censorship," *New York Post*, 1/22/76, 13.

74. See, e.g., John Kifner, "Israeli Soldiers Begin Sealing Off Arab Territories," *N.Y. Times*, 3/29/88, A1:3, A6:5.

75. Tom Wicker, "Could It Happen Here?," *The New York Times*, 6/29/75, 15:1.

76. Richard Hallaron, "Japanese Wonder If Their Democracy Can Survive," *N.Y. Times*, 12/22/74, IV:2:3.

77. Ibid.

78. Louis Wirth, Preface to Karl Mannheim, *Ideology and Utopia*, trans. Wirth and Edward Shils (New York: Harcourt Brace & World, Inc., 1938), p. xiv.

79. Hans Morgenthau, *In Defense of the National Interest* (New York: Alfred A. Knopf, 1951), p. 101.

80. George F. Kennan, *American Diplomacy 1900–1950* (New York: New American Library, 1951).

81. Ray Stannard Baker and William E. Dodd, eds., *The Public Papers of Woodrow Wilson: War and Peace* (New York: Harper & Bros., 1927), Vol. II, pp. 277–292.

82. William J. Glasgow, "Prohibition and Alcoholic Beverage Control: An Inevitable Confrontation Between Law and Social Custom," 1972, unpublished, available at Langdell Library of Harvard Law School.

83. Joseph Adelson and Lynette Beall, "Adolescent Perspectives on Law and Government," 4 *Law and Society* 495, 501–502 (1970).

84. Wheare, op. cit., pp. 112–113.

85. Comment to author at American Political Science Association convention, New York City, 1971.

86. New York: Lancer Paperbacks, 1950.

87. Isaac Asimov, *In Memory Yet Green* (New York: Avon Books, 1979), p. 600.

Chapter XII:
Reflections on the
Theoretical Framework

1. See Chapter X, note 21, regarding James I. See Baldassare Castiglione, *Book of the Courtier* (excerpts), trans. L. E. Opdyke,

1903 [1507], in *Introduction to Contemporary Civilization in the West*, ed. Staff of Columbia College, 3d ed. (New York: Columbia University Press, 1960), Vol. I, p. 610.

2. E.g., Paul Kennedy, *The Rise and Fall of the Great Powers* (New York: Random House, 1987).

3. "The fact that the public rhetoric of American political culture remains organized, in substantial ways, as a faith community centered on the Constitution, may mislead us as to the health of that culture. . . . [A] once-strong, indeed culturally dominant, mode of thought can collapse almost literally overnight" (Sanford Levinson, *Constitutional Faith*, Princeton, N.J.: Princeton University Press, 1988, p. 52). "The 'death of constitutionalism' may be the central event of our time, just as the 'death of God' was that of the past century. . . ." (*Ibid*, p. 172).

4. Chapter V.

5. See Chapter V at note 52.

6. See Chapter VIII, text at notes 20 to 23.

7. For an excellent discussion of this problem, see Stanley Brubaker, "Can Liberals Punish?," 82 *Am. Pol. Sci. Rev.* 821, 830 (1988).

8. See, e.g., James Fishkin, "Justifying Liberty: The Self-Reflective Argument," APSA panel paper, New Orleans, August 1985; David Richards, *Toleration and the Constitution* (New York: Oxford University Press, 1986), p. 175.

9. Fishkin, op. cit., p. 12.

10. Leonard Levy, "Liberty and the First Amendment," 68 *Amer. Hist. Rev.* 22, 32–37 (1962).

11. Alexander Meiklejohn, *Free Speech and Its Relation to Self-Government* (New York: Harper & Row, 1948).

12. Martin Edelman, *Democratic Theories and the Constitution* (Albany, N.Y.: SUNY Press, 1984), p. 223.

13. Mortimer Adler, *We Hold These Truths* (New York: Macmillan, 1987), p. 18.

14. See, e.g., Ronald Dworkin, *A Matter of Principle* (Cambridge, Mass.: Harvard University Press, 1985), p. 366.

15. H.L.A. Hart, "Between Utility and Rights," 79 *Colum. L. Rev.* 828, 845 (1979).

16. Dworkin, 1985, op. cit., p. 188. By deriving some logical inconsistencies from utilitarian premises, Dworkin, if he is correct, demonstrates no more than the applicability of Gödel's Theorem to political theory. Gödel's Theorem states that a set of axioms de-

scribing number theory cannot be both complete and consistent: If one wishes to describe the field completely, one must accept some degree of inconsistency. Douglas Hofstadter found that Gödel's Theorem has broad applicability to various mathematical and nonmathematical fields (*Gödel, Escher, Bach: An Eternal Golden Braid*, New York: Basic Books, Inc., 1979). With respect to government one might say, "No consistent set of rules to govern public affairs will ever be complete." Indeed, one scholar said something similar about rules of social justice (Tom Beauchamp, "Distributive Justice and the Difference Principle," in H. Gene Blocker and Elizabeth H. Smith, eds., *John Rawls' Theory of Social Justice*, Athens, Ohio: Ohio University Press, 1980, p. 159). The logical inconsistencies that may be inherent in utilitarianism do not, however, prevent it from being a useful theory to guide public decisionmaking.

Another scholar, Donald Regan, uses different definitions of act utilitarianism and rule utilitarianism than we have, implicit in his description of "co-operative utilitarianism," ("CU"), which he claims solves the problems he identifies in each: "The follower of CU neither ignores other co-operators' behaviour [like Regan's act utilitarians] nor treats it as merely part of the circumstances in which he acts [like Regan's rule utilitarians]." Regan's act utilitarians calculate the results of the actions they are considering to determine whether or not they will be just, without reference to what others will do in response. Regan's rule utilitarians calculate the results of the actions they are considering with reference to what others will do in response.

"Instead, he [the co-operative utilitarian] identifies fellow co-operators and then self-consciously joins in a shared effort to produce the best possible consequences" (*Utilitarianism and Co-operation*, New York: Oxford University Press, 1980, p. 211). This is not far from our formulation, with fellow citizens as co-operators and commitment to the American constitutional tradition and our rules as the shared effort. Any resemblance between this portrayal and John Rawls's "original position" (Rawls, op. cit., pp. 17–22 and *infra*), is misleading, since ours is based on a wide range of values—the five we identified at the outset, and on a real historical tradition, not an imaginary one.

17. John Rawls, *A Theory of Justice* (Cambridge, Mass.: Harvard University Press, 1971).

18. *Ibid*, p. 101.
19. Allan Bloom, "Justice: John Rawls vs. the Tradition of Political Philosophy," 69 *Am. Pol. Sci. Rev.* 648, 657 (1975).
20. See e.g., Jerry Mashaw, *Due Process in the Administrative State* (New Haven: Yale University Press, 1985), p. 184; and Richards, op. cit., p. 59.
21. Sotirios Barber, *On What the Constitution Means* (Baltimore: Johns Hopkins University Press, 1984), p. 191.
22. See *Ibid*, pp. 186–190.
23. See Chapter X, note 88.
24. Walter Berns, "Religion and the Founding Principle," in Robert Horwitz, ed., *The Moral Foundations of the American Republic*, 3d ed. (Charlottesville: University Press of Virginia, 1986), respectively at pp. 222, 221, and 212–213.
25. An extensive and eloquent statement of this principle can be found in "The Williamsburg Charter: A National Celebration and Reaffirmation of the First Amendment Religious Liberty Clauses," June 25, 1988, available from The Williamsburg Charter Foundation, Washington, D.C. The Charter includes among its signers an extraordinarily broad range of American political and religious leadership, from former Presidents Gerald Ford and Jimmy Carter to the present writer.
26. Rehnquist wrote an opinion to the contrary in *Wallace* v. *Jaffree*, 105 S. Ct. 2479, 2516, 2520, 1985. But "Rehnquist was flat wrong" (Leonard Levy, *Original Intent and the Framers' Constitution*, New York and London: Macmillan Publishing Company, 1988), p. 320.

Sources

Abrams, Robert, N.Y. State Attorney General, and Patrick Henry, District Attorney for Suffolk County. Letter on behalf of New York State Law Enforcement Council to Warren Anderson, New York State Senate Majority Leader, 6/26/86.

Adelson, Joseph, and Lynette Beall. "Adolescent Perspectives on Law and Government." 4 *Law and Society* 495, 1970.

Adler, Mortimer. *We Hold These Truths*. New York: Macmillan, 1987.

Allison, Graham. *Essence of Decision*. Boston: Little, Brown & Co., 1971.

American Bar Association, Section of Criminal Justice. *Report to the House of Delegates*. 1982.

American Law Institute. *Model Penal Code and Commentaries*. Philadelphia, Pa., 1985.

Asimov, Isaac. *In Memory Yet Green*. N.Y.: Avon Books, 1979.

Asimov, Isaac. *The Stars, Like Dust*. N.Y.: Lancer Paperbacks, 1950.

Associated Press. "Effort to Get Organized Crime Bill Moves Forward." 6/27/86.

Associated Press. "Guilty Verdict in Holocaust 'Lie.'" *New York Post*, 2/24/76, 14.

Associated Press. "Measure to Pay War Detainees Goes to Reagan." *The New York Times*, 8/5/88, A10:1.

Associated Press. "Organized Crime Bill Passes." 7/3/86.

Baas, Larry. "The Constitution as Symbol: Change or Stability After Ten Years." APSA panel paper, Chicago, 9/3/87.

Bagehot, Walter. *The English Constitution*. London and Glasgow: Collins/Fontana, 1963.

Banks, William, and Jeffrey Straussman. "*Bowsher* v. *Synar:* The Emerging Judicialization of the Fisc." APSA panel paper, Chicago, 9/3/87.

Barber, Sotirios. *On What the Constitution Means*. Baltimore: Johns Hopkins University Press, 1984.

Barendt, Eric. *Freedom of Speech.* New York: Oxford University Press, 1987.

Barrett, Wayne. "The GOP Goes Soft on Crime." *The Village Voice,* 7/8/86, 12.

Beard, Charles. *An Economic Interpretation of the Constitution.* New York: The Macmillan Company, 1913.

Beard, Charles and Mary. *A Basic History of the United States.* New York: Doubleday, Doran and Co., 1944.

Becker, T., and M. Feeley, eds. *The Impact of Supreme Court Decisions.* New York: Oxford University Press, 1969.

Benedict, Ruth. *Patterns of Culture,* 2d ed. Boston: Houghton-Mifflin Co., 1959.

Bentham, Jeremy. *Nonsense Upon Stilts,* ed. Jeremy Waldron. New York: Methuen, Inc., 1987.

Bickel, Alexander. *The Least Dangerous Branch.* Indianapolis: The Bobbs-Merrill Company, 1962.

Black, Charles. *The People and the Court.* New York: Macmillan, 1960.

Blakey, G. Robert, and Ronald Goldstock. "RICO and Labor Racketeering." 17 *Amer. Crim. L. Rev.* 341, 1980.

Blocker, H. Gene, and Elizabeth H. Smith, eds. *John Rawls' Theory of Social Justice.* Athens, Ohio: Ohio University Press, 1980.

Bloom, Allan. "Justice: John Rawls and the Tradition of Political Philosophy." 69 *APSR* 648–62, June 1975.

Bodenheimer, Edgar. "Philosophical Anthropology and the Law." 59 *Cal. L. Rev.* 653, May 1971.

Boorstin, Daniel. *The Americans: The National Experience.* New York: Random House, 1965.

Bork, Robert. "Neutral Principles and Some First Amendment Problems." 47 *Ind. L. J.* 1, Fall 1971.

———. *Tradition and Morality in Constitutional Law.* Washington, D.C.: American Enterprise Institute for Policy Research, 1984.

Boutmy, Emil. *Studies in Constitutional Law: France-England-United States,* trans. E. M. Dicey. London and New York: Macmillan and Co., 1891.

Boyan, A. Stephen, Jr. "Presidents and National Security Powers: A Judicial Perspective." APSA panel paper, Washington, D.C., 9/1/88.

Bozeman, Adda. *Politics and Culture in International History.* Princeton, N.J.: Princeton University Press, 1960.

Brubaker, Stanley. "Can Liberals Punish?" 82 *Amer. Pol. Sci. Rev.* 821, September 1988.

————. "Fear of Judging: A Commentary on Ely's Theory of Judicial Review." 12 *The Political Science Reviewer* 207, 1982.

————. "Reconsidering Dworkin's Case for Judicial Activism." 46 *Journal of Politics* 503, 1984.

Burgess, John W. *Political Science and Constitutional Law.* Boston: Ginn and Company, 1891.

Burke, John P. *Bureaucratic Responsibility.* Baltimore: Johns Hopkins University Press, 1986.

Bushinsky, Jay. "Rabin Yields in Flap on Censorship." *New York Post*, 1/22/76, 13.

Carter, Lief. *Administrative Law and Politics.* Boston: Little, Brown and Co., 1983.

Castberg, Frede. *Freedom of Speech in the West.* Oslo: Oslo University Press, 1960.

Cavanaugh, Ralph, and Austin Scott. "Thinking About Courts: Toward and Beyond a Jurisprudence of Judicial Competence." 14 *Law and Society Review* 371, Winter 1980.

Cave Brown, Anthony. *Bodyguard of Lies.* New York: Harper & Row, 1975.

Columbia College Staff, eds. *Chapters in Western Civilization*, 3d ed., two vols. New York: Columbia University Press, 1961.

————. *Introduction to Contemporary Civilization in the West*, 3d ed., two vols. New York: Columbia University Press, 1960.

Commager, Henry Steele. "The Constitution Is Alive and Well." *The New York Times*, 8/11/74, IV, 17:2.

Connelly, Marjorie, staff, New York Times/CBS Poll, telephone conversation with author, 1/20/88.

Cooper, Philip. *Hard Judicial Choices.* New York: Oxford University Press, 1988.

————. "Public Law and Public Administration." APSA panel paper, Anaheim, California, April 1986.

Corwin, Edward S. "The 'Higher Law' Background of American Constitutional Law." 42 *Harv. L. Rev.* 149–185, 365–409, 1928–9, reissued by Cornell University Press, Ithaca, N.Y., 1955.

Cox, Archibald. "The New Dimensions of Constitutional Adjudication." 57 *Wash. L. Rev.* 791, 1976.

Craypool, Richard, Director of Executive Agencies Division, Office of the Federal Register, telephone conversation with Mindy Bockstein, legislative assistant to author, 9/6/88.

Dahl, Robert. *Democracy in the United States.* Chicago: Rand McNally & Co., 1972.

Davis, Kenneth. *Administrative Law Text,* 3d ed. St. Paul: West Publishing Co., 1972.

Dicey, A. V. *Introduction to the Study of the Law of the Constitution.* London: Macmillan and Co., [1908] 1961.

Donovan, John C. *The Politics of Poverty.* New York: Pegasus, 1967.

Dowd, Maureen. "Low Key Mood, and Some Regrets." *The New York Times,* 7/18/87, A6:2.

Downs, Donald Alexander. *Nazis in Skokie.* Notre Dame, Ind.: University of Notre Dame Press, 1985.

Driscoll, John F. *"U.S.* v. *Sutton:* Reining in on Runaway RICO." 42 *U. Pitt. L. Rev.* 131, 1980.

Dworkin, Ronald. *Law's Empire.* Cambridge, Mass.: Harvard University Press, 1986.

———. *A Matter of Principle.* Cambridge, Mass.: Harvard University Press, 1985.

———. *Taking Rights Seriously.* Cambridge, Mass.: Harvard University Press, 1978.

Edelman, Martin. *Democratic Theories and the Constitution.* Albany, N.Y.: SUNY Press, 1984.

Elliott, Steven. "The Tension Between Member Goals and Staff Goals in Congress." Unpublished, 1986, Rockefeller College, SUNY Albany.

"Elliott v. *U.S.:* Conspiracy Law and the Judicial Pursuit of Organized Crime Through RICO." Note, 65 *Va. L. Rev.* 109, 1979.

Elon, Menachem, ed. *The Principles of Jewish Law.* Jerusalem: Keter Publishing House Ltd., 1975.

Ely, John. *Democracy and Distrust.* Cambridge, Mass.: Harvard University Press, 1980.

Emke, Horst. "'Delegata Potestas Non Potest Delegari,' A Maxim of American Constitutional Law." 47 *Cornell L. Q.* 50, 1961.

Feldman, Daniel. "Administrative Agencies and the Rites of Due Process." 7 *Fordham Urban Law Journal* 229, 1978.

———. *Amicus curiae* brief, *Boreali* v. *Axelrod,* #54593, 3d Dept., N.Y. 1987.

———. "Ethical Analysis in Public Policymaking." 15 *Policy Studies Journal* 441, March 1987.

———. *Reforming Government.* New York: William Morrow and Co., 1981.

Finer, Samuel. *Five Constitutions*. Harmondsworth, England: Penguin Books, 1979.

Fisher, Louis. "The Administrative World of *Chadha* and *Bowsher*." 47 *Public Admin. Rev.* 213–4, May/June 1987.

———. *Constitutional Conflicts Between Congress and the President*. Princeton, N.J.: Princeton University Press, 1985.

———. *Constitutional Dialogues*. Princeton, N.J.: Princeton University Press, 1988.

———. "The Efficiency Side of Separated Powers." 5 *Journal of American Studies* 113, Cambridge University Press, 8/71.

———. "Executive-Legislative Relations in Foreign Policy." Paper presented at the United States-Mexico Comparative Constitutional Law Conference, Mexico City, 6/17/88, rev. 6/24/88.

———. "Judicial Misjudgments About the Lawmaking Process: The Legislative Veto Case." 45 *Public Admin. Rev.* 705, November 1985.

———. "The Legitimacy of the Congressional National Security Role." Washington, D.C.: Congressional Research Service, 11/19/87.

Fishkin, James. "Justifying Liberty: The Self-Reflective Argument," unpublished, prepared for the 1985 meeting of the American Political Science Association.

Fleishman, Joel, et al., eds. *Public Duties: The Moral Obligations of Public Officials*. Cambridge, Mass.: Harvard University Press, 1981.

Friedman, Lawrence M., and Harry N. Scheiber, eds. *American Law and the Constitutional Order*. Cambridge, Mass.: Harvard University Press, 1978.

Fuerst, J. S., and Roy Petty. "Due Process—How much is enough?" *The Public Interest*, Spring 1985, 96.

Fuller, Lon. "Collective Bargaining and the Arbitrator." 1963 *Wis. L. Rev.* 3, 32–33.

———. *The Morality of Law*, rev. ed. New Haven: Yale University Press, 1969.

Galston, William. "Liberal Virtues." 82 *Amer. Pol. Sci. Rev.* 1277, December 1988.

Gates, Robert M. "The CIA and American Foreign Policy." 66 *Foreign Affairs* 215, Winter 1987–88.

Gerber, Ethan Brett. "'A RICO You Can't Refuse': New York's Organized Crime Control Act," 53 *Brooklyn L. Rev.* 979, 1988.

Gibson, James, and Richard Bingham. *Civil Liberties and Nazis.* New York: Praeger, 1985.

Glasgow, William J. "Prohibition and Alcoholic Beverage Control: An Inevitable Confrontation Between Law and Social Custom." Unpublished, 1972. Available at Langdell Library of Harvard Law School.

Goldwin, Robert, and William Schiambra, eds. *How Democratic Is the Constitution?* Washington, D.C.: American Enterprise Institute for Public Policy Research, 1980.

Greenhouse, Linda. "The Bork Battle: Visions of the Constitution." *The New York Times,* 10/4/87, IV 1:1.

————. "Supreme Court Roundup." *The New York Times,* 11/1/88, A23:1–4.

Haiman, Franklyn S. *Speech and Law in a Free Society.* Chicago: University of Chicago Press, 1981.

Halloran, Richard. "Japanese Wonder If Their Democracy Can Survive." *The New York Times,* 12/22/74, IV, 2:3.

Halperin, Morton. "Prohibiting Covert Operations." *The Nation,* 3/21/87.

Halperin, Morton, and Daniel Hoffman. *Top Secret: National Security and the Right to Know.* Washington, D.C.: New Republic Books, 1977.

Hamilton, Alexander, James Madison, and John Jay. *The Federalist Papers.* New York: The New American Library, 1961.

Harriman, Linda, and Jeffrey Straussman. "Do Judges Determine Budget Decisions?" 43 *Pub. Adm. Rev.* 343, July/August 1983.

Harris, Louis. "Poll: Most Are Still Anti-Busing, But. . . ." *New York Post,* 7/3/76.

Harris, William F. New York: "Bonding Word and Polity." 76 *APSR* 34, 1982.

Hart, H.L.A. "Between Utility and Rights." 79 *Col. L. Rev.* 828, 1979.

Henkin, Louis. *Foreign Affairs and the Constitution.* Mineola, N.Y.: The Foundation Press, Inc., 1972.

Henkin, Louis. "Foreign Affairs and the Constitution." 66 *Foreign Affairs* 284, Winter 1987–88.

Hentoff, Nat. "The Integrationist." *The New Yorker,* 8/23/82.

Hersh, Seymour. "Who's in Charge Here?" *The New York Times Magazine,* 34, 11/22/87.

Hilsman, Roger. *To Move a Nation.* N.Y.: Doubleday & Co., 1967.

Hockett, Jeffrey. "Justices Jackson, Frankfurter, and Black: A Contrast of Constitutional Faiths." APSA panel paper, Washington, D.C., 1988.

Hofstadter, Douglas R. *Gödel, Escher, Bach: An Eternal Golden Braid.* N.Y.: Basic Books, Inc., 1979.

Horwitz, Robert, ed. *The Moral Foundations of the American Republic*, 3d ed. Charlottesville: University Press of Virginia, 1986.

Hyman, H., and P. Sheatsley. "Attitudes Toward Desegregation." 211 *Scientific American* 16, 1964.

Hyman, Harold. "War Powers in Nineteenth Century America: Abraham Lincoln and His Heir." in *this Constitution*, Project '87, Washington, D.C., Winter 1985.

Ickler, Nancy. "Conspiracy to Violate RICO: Expanding Traditional Conspiracy Law." 58 *Notre Dame L. Rev.* 587, 1983.

Isaac, Rhys. *The Transformation of Virginia 1740–1790.* Chapel Hill, N.C.: University of North Carolina Press, 1982.

Jacobsohn, Gary. *The Supreme Court and the Decline of Constitutional Aspiration.* Totowa, N.J.: Rowman & Littlefield, 1986.

Jenkins, Iredell. *Social Order and the Limits of Law.* Princeton, N.J.: Princeton University Press, 1980.

Kahn, Ronald. "Ely, Perry, Tribe, and Modern Constitutional Theory/Practice." APSA panel paper, Washington, D.C., 9/1/88.

Kairys, David. *The Politics of Law.* New York: Pantheon Books, 1982.

Kammen, Michael. *A Machine That Would Go of Itself.* New York: Random House, 1986.

Karp, Walter. "Liberty Under Siege." *Harper's Magazine*, November 1985, 53–67.

———. *Liberty Under Siege.* N.Y.: Henry Holt and Co., 1988.

Kaufman, Herbert. "Emerging Conflicts in the Doctrines of Public Administration." 50 *APSR* 1057–73, December 1956.

Kennan, George. *American Diplomacy 1900–1950.* New York: New American Library, 1951.

Kennedy, Paul. *The Rise and Fall of the Great Powers.* New York: Random House, 1987.

Kessel, John. "Public Perceptions of the Supreme Court." 10 *Midwest J. of Pol. Sci.* 167, 1966.

Kifner, John. "Israeli Soldiers Begin Sealing Off Arab Territories." *The New York Times*, 3/29/88, A1:3.

Lacayo, Richard. "The Sad Fate of Legal Aid." *Time*, 6/20/88, 59.

Lans, Asher Bob. "A Study in the Tradition of the Constitution in the United States." Unpublished master's thesis in sociology, 1939. Available at Butler Library, Columbia University.

Levinson, Sanford. *Constitutional Faith.* Princeton, N.J.: Princeton University Press, 1988.

Levy, Leonard. *The Emergence of a Free Press.* New York: Oxford University Press, 1985.

———. "Liberty and the First Amendment." 68 *Amer. Hist. Rev.* 22, 1962.

———. *Original Intent and the Framers' Constitution.* New York: Macmillan Publishing Company, 1988.

Lewis, Anthony. "No to King George." *The New York Times,* 6/30/88, A23.

———. "Sounding Loud and Clear." *The New York Times,* 3/7/74, 39:1.

Lewis, Frederick. Review of Arthur Miller, *Democratic Dictatorship.* 76 *Amer. Pol. Sci. Rev.* 417, 1982.

Liddell Hart, B. H. *Strategy,* 2d rev. ed. New York: New American Library, 1974 [1954].

Lincoln, Abraham. Letter to Erastus Corning and Others, June 11, 1863. John G. Nicolay and John Hay, eds. *Complete Works of Abraham Lincoln.* New York: The Century Company, 1894, Vol. II, 345. Judge Joseph Bellacosa, New York State Court of Appeals, brought this material to the author's attention.

Lindblom, Charles. "The Science of 'Muddling Through.'" 19 *Public Admin. Rev.* 79, Spring 1959.

Locke, John. *A Letter Concerning Toleration,* 2d ed., trans. (from Latin) William Popple. Indianapolis: The Bobbs-Merrill Company, Inc., 1955.

———. *Two Treatises of Government,* ed. Peter Laslett. New York: New American Library, 1963.

Lusky, Louis. *By What Right?* Charlottesville, Va.: The Michie Company, 1975.

McClellan, John. "The Organized Crime Act (S.30) or Its Critics: Which Threatens Civil Liberties?" 46 *Notre Dame L. Rev.* 55, 1980.

McDonald, Forrest. *Novus Ordo Seclorum.* Lawrence, Kan.: University Press of Kansas, 1985.

McLaughlin, Andrew. *Foundations of American Constitutionalism.* New York: NYU Press, 1932; Fawcett Publications, Inc., 1961.

Magrath, C. Peter. *Constitutionalism and Politics*. Glenview, Ill.: Scott, Foresman & Co., 1968.

Maine, Henry Sumner. *Ancient Law*, 10th ed. Boston: Beacon Press, [1861] 1963.

Maitland, F. W. *The Constitutional History of England*, ed. H.L.A. Fisher. Cambridge, England: Cambridge University Press, 1965 [1908].

Marcus, Martin, First Assistant Director, New York State Organized Crime Task Force, letter to author, 2/13/85.

Markmann, Charles Lamm. "Civil Liberties? Was Ist Das? A Report from the German Federal Republic." 1 *Civil Liberties Review* 42, 1974.

Marshall, Geoffry. "Confidentiality and Secrecy." Seminar, Nuffield College, Oxford University, 10/10/82.

Martin, Robert, and Fred Geldon. "Planning for the Negotiated Settlement of Claims." Washington, D.C.: Bureau of National Affairs, 1982.

Marty, William. "Religion, the Constitution, and Modern Rivals: Our Founders and Theirs." APSA panel paper, Chicago, 9/3/87.

Mashaw, Jerry. *Due Process in the Administrative State*. New Haven: Yale University Press, 1985.

Meiklejohn, Alexander. *Free Speech and Its Relation to Self-Government*. New York: Harper & Row, 1948.

Meislin, Richard. "Majority in Poll Still Think Reagan Lied on Iran-Contra Measure." *The New York Times*, 7/18/87, 1:4.

Mill, John Stuart. *On Liberty*. Harmondsworth, England: Penguin Books, [1859] 1982.

Mill, John Stuart, and Jeremy Bentham. *Utilitarianism and Other Essays*, ed. Alan Ryan. Harmondsworth, England: Penguin Books, 1987.

Miller, Arthur. *Democratic Dictatorship*. Westport, Conn.: Greenwood Press, 1981.

Morgenthau, Hans. *In Defense of the National Interest*. New York: Knopf, 1951.

Morrison v. *Olson*, "Excerpts from Ruling Upholding Independent Counsel Law." *The New York Times*, 6/30/88, A18, A23.

Mosher, Frederick C. *Democracy and the Public Service*, 2d ed. New York: Oxford University Press, 1982.

Murphy, Paul. *World War I and the Origins of Civil Liberties*. New York: W. W. Norton & Co., 1979.

Neier, Aryeh. *Defending My Enemy*. New York: E. P. Dutton, 1979.

Nevins, Allan, and Henry Steele Commager. *A Pocket History of the United States*. New York: Washington Square Press, 1956.

New York *Daily News*, Editorial, "Perfidious Albany," 7/4/86.

The New York Times, 5/9/60, 31:8; 5/15/60, 77:1; 10/14/77, B2; "Reagan and States' Rights: Meeting Two Goals," 3/4/81, A24:1; 5/1/88, I, 40:3; Editorial, "Absurd Lengths for Mob Trial," 9/1/88.

O'Connor, Grover. "Free Speech." Privately published, 1942. Available in Langdell Library of Harvard Law School.

Ornstein, Norman, et al. *Vital Statistics on Congress 1987–88*. Washington, D.C.: Congressional Quarterly Inc., 1987.

Paludan, Phillip S. "The American Civil War Considered as a Crisis in Law and Order." 7 *Amer. Hist. Rev.* 1013, 1972.

Pangle, Thomas. "The Constitution's Human Vision." 86 *The Public Interest* 77, Winter 1987.

———. "The Federalists." 8 *Humanities* 2, March/April 1987.

The People, Press, and Politics. The Times-Mirror Company, September 1987.

Perry, Michael. *Morality, Politics, and Law*. New York: Oxford University Press, 1988.

Pirsig, Robert. *Zen and the Art of Motorcycle Maintenance*. New York: William Morrow & Co., 1974.

Pole, J. R. *The Gift of Government*. Athens, Ga.: University of Georgia Press, 1983.

———. *The Pursuit of Equality in American History*. Berkeley, Calif.: University of California Press, 1978.

———. "Sunset over the Statute Book," review of Guido Calabresi, *A Common Law for the Age of Statutes*. *Times Literary Supplement*, 9/24/82, 1029.

Potter, David. *People of Plenty*. Chicago: University of Chicago Press, 1954.

Public Hearings on Organized Crime Control Act, Office of the New York State Attorney General, 2 World Trade Center, New York, N.Y., 2/24/83, and Legislative Office Building, Albany, N.Y., 3/10/83. Transcript.

Randall, James G. *Constitutional Problems Under Lincoln*. New York: D. Appleton and Co., 1926.

Rangel, Jesus. "All 20 Acquitted in Jersey Mob Case." *The New York Times*, 8/27/88, 1:1.

Rawls, John. *A Theory of Justice*. Cambridge, Mass.: Harvard University Press, 1971.

Regan, Donald. *Utilitarianism and Co-operation*. New York: Oxford University Press, 1980.

Reich, Charles. "Mr. Justice Black and the Living Constitution." 76 *Harv. L. Rev.* 673, 1963.

Reston, James. "The End of the Tunnel." *The New York Times*, 4/30/75, 41:1.

———. "Impeachment Politics." *The New York Times*, 4/10/74, 41:5.

Richards, David. *Toleration and the Constitution*. New York: Oxford University Press, 1986.

Riley, Jonathan. "On the Possibility of Liberal Democracy." 79 *Amer. Pol. Sci. Rev.* 1135, 1985.

Rohr, John. *Ethics for Bureaucrats*. New York: Marcel Dekker, Inc., 1978.

———. *To Run a Constitution*. Lawrence, Kan.: University Press of Kansas, 1986.

Rosen, Bernard. *Holding Government Bureaucracies Accountable*. New York: Praeger Publishers, 1982.

Rosenbaum, David. "Panel's Chairman Says Poindexter Lacks Credibility." *The New York Times*, 7/18/87.

Rosenbloom, David H. "Public Administration Theory and the Separation of Powers." *Public Administration Review* 219, May/June 1983.

Rostow, Eugene V. "The Japanese-American Cases—A Disaster." 54 *Yale Law Journal* 489, 1945.

Rourke, Francis, ed. *Bureaucratic Power in National Policy Making*, 4th ed. Boston: Little, Brown & Co., 1986.

Savas, E.S. *Privatizing the Public Sector*. Chatham, N.J.: Chatham House Publishers, 1982.

Schachter, Hindy Lauer. "Efficiency in the Municipal Reform Literature: A New View." APSA panel paper, Washington, D.C., 9/1/88.

Schaffritz, Jay, and Albert Hyde, eds. *Classics of Public Administration*. Oak Park, Ill.: Moore Publishing Co., 1978.

Schwartz, Bernard. *Administrative Law*, 2d ed. Boston: Little, Brown and Co., 1984.

———. "Fashioning an Administrative Law System." 40 *Administrative L. Rev.* 415, Summer 1988.

————. *The Roots of Freedom.* New York: Hill & Wang, 1967.

Shapiro, Ian. *The Evolution of Rights in Liberal Theory.* New York: Cambridge University Press, 1986.

Singer, Rabbi Joseph, Brooklyn, New York, letter to author, 4/13/88.

Smith, Rogers. *Liberalism and American Constitutional Law.* Cambridge, Mass.: Harvard University Press, 1985.

Spitzer, Arthur, Legal Director, American Civil Liberties Union Fund, Washington, D.C., telephone conversation with author, 1/11/83.

Steamer, Robert J. Review of Paul Murphy, *World War I and the Origins of Civil Liberties.* 74 *Amer. Pol. Sci. Rev.* 1094, 1980.

Stillman, Richard, ed. *Public Administration Concepts and Cases,* 3d ed. Boston: Houghton Mifflin Co., 1984.

Stoner, James. "Behind the 'facts submitted to a Candid World': Constitutional Arguments for Independence." APSA panel paper, Chicago, 9/3/87.

Tapp, June, and Fred Krinsky. *Ambivalent America.* Beverly Hills, Calif.: Glencoe Press, 1971.

Tarlow, Barry. "RICO: The New Darling of the Prosecutor's Nursery." 49 *Fordham L. Rev.* 165, 1980.

Tedford, Thomas, ed. *Perspectives on Freedom of Speech.* Carbondale, Ill.: Southern Illinois University Press, 1987.

Toqueville, Alexis de. *Democracy in America.* New York: Alfred A. Knopf, 1945 [1835].

Troper, Harold. "James Keegstra, Teacher of Hate." 53 *Congress Monthly* 2, February 1986, 6–8.

Turner, Frederick Jackson. *The Frontier in American History.* New York: Holt, Rinehart & Winston, 1962 [1920; original scholarly paper, 1893].

Turner, Stansfield. *Secrecy and Democracy.* Boston: Houghton Mifflin Company, 1985.

Tweedie, Jack. "The Dilemma of Clients' Rights in Social Programs: Individuals and Collective Concerns in Administration." APSA panel paper, Washington, D.C., 9/1/88.

U.S. Congress. Report of the Congressional Committees Investigating the Iran-Contra Affair: H. Rept. No. 100-433, S. Rept. No. 100-216, November 1987.

Uviller, H. Richard. "Cops and Robbers." 13 *Columbia* 16, 2/88.

Van Alstyne, William. "Cracks in 'The New Property': Adjudicative

Due Process in the Administrative State." 62 *Cornell L. Rev.* 445, 1977.

Wagman, Leonard, Administrative Law Judge, National Labor Relations Board, comments to author, 8/16/88.

Wechsler, Herbert. "Toward Neutral Principles of Constitutional Law." 73 *Harv. L. Rev.* 1, 1959.

Wheare, K. C. *Modern Constitutions*, 2d ed. London: Oxford University Press, 1966.

Whitney, Craig. "Civil Liberties in Britain: Are They Under Siege?" *The New York Times*, 11/1/88, A18:1.

Wicker, Tom. "Could It Happen Here?" *The New York Times*, 6/29/75, 15:1.

Wildavsky, Aaron. *The Politics of the Budgetary Process*, 4th ed. Boston: Little, Brown and Co., 1984.

Wilson, William Julius. *The Truly Disadvantaged*. Chicago: University of Chicago Press, 1987.

Wilson, Woodrow. "The Study of Administration." 2 *Political Science Quarterly*, June 1887.

Wills, Gary. *Inventing America*. New York: Random House, 1979.

Wirth, Louis. Preface to Karl Mannheim. *Ideology and Utopia*, trans. Wirth and Edward Shils. New York: Harcourt Brace & World, Inc., 1938.

Wolff, Robert Paul. *Understanding Rawls*. Princeton, N.J.: Princeton University Press, 1977.

Wootton, David, ed. *Divine Right and Democracy*. Harmondsworth, England: Penguin Books, 1986.

Yarbrough. "The Political World of Federal Judges as Managers." 45 *Pub. Adm. Rev.* 660, 1985.

Table of
Statutes and Directives

Ariz. Rev. Stat. Ann. Sections 13-2301 to 13-2316 (ch7, n3)
Cal. Penal Code Sections 186-186.8 (ch7, n3)
Colo. Rev. Stat. Sections 18-17-101 to 18-17-109 (ch7, n3)
Executive Order 12333, 46 F.R. 59941, 1981
Federal Rules of Evidence, 28 U.S.C.A., Rule 201(b)
Ga. Code Sections 16-14-1 to 16-14-15 (ch7, n3)
Hawaii Rev. Stat. Sections 842-2 to 842-12 (ch7, n3)
Immigration and Nationality Act
Intelligence Oversight Act, 1980
Internal Revenue Code
National Labor Relations Act
National Security Directive 159
National Security Act, 50 U.S.C. 413, 1947
National Security Act, Hughes-Ryan Amendment, 22 U.S.C. 2422, 1974
National Security Decision Directive 84, 1983
New York State Public Health Law, Section 225
Organized Crime Control Act, N.Y. Penal Law Art. 460, 1986
Pendleton Act of 1883 (federal)
Race Relations Act of 1965 (U.K.)
Racketeer Influenced and Corrupt Organizations Act, 18 U.S.C. 1961-8, 1970
Schmidt-Feldman Law, N.Y. Penal Law Sec. 245.11, Ch. 231, 1985
War Powers Act of 1973 (ch5, n8)

Table of Cases

INDEX